Women
&
Public Policy

Women
&
Public Policy
A Revolution
in Progress

M. Margaret Conway
David W. Ahern
Gertrude A. Steuernagel

with chapters by
Earlean McCarrick
Robert H. Jerry II

PRESS

A Division of Congressional Quarterly Inc.
Washington, D.C.

Copyright © 1995 Congressional Quarterly Inc.

Library of Congress Cataloging-in-Publication Data

Conway, M. Margaret (Mary Margaret). 1935-
    Women and public policy: a revolution in progress / M. Margaret
Conway, David W. Ahern, Gertrude A. Steuernagel; with chapters by
Earlean McCarrick, Robert H. Jerry II.
    p. cm.
    Includes bibliographical references and index.
    ISBN 0-87187-923-9
    1. Women--Government policy--United States. 2. Women's rights-
-United States. 3. Women--United States--Economic conditions.
4. Women--United States--Social conditions. I. Ahern, David W.
II. Steuernagel, Gertrude A. III. Title.
HQ1236.5.U6C66   1995
305.42'0973--dc20   95-30134
                                                                          CIP

For all the Conways
M.M.C.

For my mother, Janet Ahern
D.A.

For my husband, Scott Walker, and our son, Sky,
truly a revolutionary in progress
G.S.

Contents

Preface   *xi*

About the Authors   *xv*

1 Women and Public Policy   **1**

Defining Culture   1

A Brief History   5

Cultural Change and Public Policy   8

Notes   13

Suggestions for Further Reading   16

2 Women and Educational Policy   **18**

Educational Policy in Cultural and Historical
  Context   19

The Current Status of Women in Higher Education   21

Discrimination against Women in Higher Education   23

Women, Education, and the Policy Process   25

Title IX and the Battle over Implementation   26

Policy Adjudication: Grove City College's Challenge
  to Title IX   31

Looking Ahead   32

Notes   34

Chronology   36

Suggestions for Further Reading   37

3 Women and Health Care Policy   **38**

Women, Culture, and Public Policy on Health Care   39

Contemporary Women's Health Issues and the Policy-making
  Process   43

Policy Silences   49

Notes   51

Chronology   54

Suggestions for Further Reading   54

4 *Equal Employment Opportunity Policy*   56

Employment Discrimination: Theories of Cause and Change   57
Patterns of Employment   58
A History of Employment Policy   60
The Implementation of Equal Opportunity Policy   68
The Problem of Sexual Harassment   70
Criteria for Proof of Discrimination   71
Effects of Equal Opportunity Policy
  on Women's Employment   72
The Concept of Comparable Worth   74
The Outlook for Women   76
Notes   78
Chronology   81
Suggestions for Further Reading   82

5 *Economic Equity: Credit, Housing, and Retirement*
  Income   83

The Problem of Credit Discrimination   83
The Problem of Housing   91
The Problems of Retirement Income and the Feminization
  of Poverty   93
Notes   98
Chronology   100
Suggestions for Further Reading   101

6 *Gender and Insurance*   102

The Question Presented   103
Basics of Insurance and Rating   103
The Use of Gender as a Rating Criterion   105
Existing and Proposed Restrictions on the Use of
  Gender in Insurance Rating   107
Public Policy Implications of Gender-Based Rating   110
Notes   118
Chronology   121
Suggestions for Further Reading   122

7 *Women and Family Law: Marriage and Divorce*   124

Laws and Public Policies Governing Marriage   126
Laws and Public Policies Governing Divorce   134
Notes   144
Chronology   146
Suggestions for Further Reading   147

8 *Women and Child Care* 148

Can the Needs of Women and Children Be Separated? 150
Cultural Context of the Child Care Problem 151
The Increasing Importance of Child Care Issues 153
Historical Background of Child Care and Family
  Leave Issues 157
The Problems of Child Care and Family Leave:
  A Need for Public Awareness 164
Notes 165
Chronology 167
Suggestions for Further Reading 168

9 *Women and the Criminal Justice System* 169

The Functions of Law in American Society 170
Women as Decision Makers in the Criminal Justice System 171
Women as Criminals 175
Women as Crime Victims 179
Abortion: From Crime to Constitutional Right 184
Notes 187
Chronology 191
Suggestions for Further Reading 192

10 *A Revolution in Progress* 193

Notes 200
Suggestions for Further Reading 201

Index 203

Preface

This book is an introduction to the subject of women and public policy. The unifying theme of its ten chapters is the impact of cultural change on both women's roles in American society and patterns of public policy as they affect women and their families. While gender is not the only social characteristic of importance (class, race, and age, for instance, are also influential), we believe it warrants specific inquiry. Commonalities exist in women's lives.

It is our hope that this book will be of interest to a variety of audiences, including students of public policy and women's studies. Although each chapter contains discussions of relevant court cases, laws, and executive orders, no prior knowledge of the policy process or of women's issues is assumed on the part of the reader.

Chapter 1 presents working definitions of culture and public policy. The relationship between public policy and cultural change, particularly in regard to the increasing participation of women in the work force, receives special attention. The discussion centers on the policy-making process and the impact of policy silences on that process. Consideration is also given to three models of the policy process that are useful in stimulating systematic and critical analysis of the issues raised in subsequent chapters.

Chapter 2 is an examination of the impact of educational policy on women. An overview of the cultural and historical context of educational policy is followed by a discussion of the status of women in education, patterns of discrimination against women, and Title IX and its implementation.

Chapter 3 explores the question of why women's views have been relatively absent from public debate in the health policy area. Considerable attention is given to the context of women's lives—including marriage, childbearing, and employment—and how it affects women's access to health care. Factors affecting women's access to private health insurance and the dependence of many women and their families on Medicaid and Medicare receive special emphasis. The chapter also examines public policy concerning reproductive issues.

The subject of Chapter 4 is equal employment opportunity policy—specifically, issues of implementation and the key issues in employment policy, including occupational segregation, Title VII, sexual harassment, and comparable worth. Also examined is the central issue of the effects of federal equal employment opportunity policy on women's employment patterns.

Chapter 5 focuses on issues of economic equity in the policy areas of credit discrimination, housing, and retirement income. A brief history of the Equal Credit Opportunity Act is followed by an analysis of its impact. The "four A's" of housing—availability, adequacy, affordability, and accessibility—are discussed in the context of women's lives; the problems of single-parent households and of elderly women are highlighted. Also examined is the problem of acquiring adequate income for retirement; particular attention is given to issues concerning women's access to social security and employer-provided pensions and tax-deferred personal pension plans.

In Chapter 6, Robert Jerry considers the case for gender-neutral insurance. A discussion of technical issues and terms is followed by an examination of the use of gender as a rating criterion for life insurance, retirement annuities, and health and disability insurance. Attention is given to federal and state regulations concerning gender discrimination in insurance.

In Chapter 7 Earlean McCarrick places women and family law in a cultural context, with a focus on the areas of marriage and divorce. Among the topics covered are marital property law, a married woman's domicile and legal surname, marriage and criminal law, marriage and social security benefits, alimony, federal retirement benefits, and child custody and child support.

The subject of Chapter 8 is women and the issue of child care; special attention is given to the question of whether the needs of women and children can be separated. Also included is a detailed discussion of child care and an examination of the Family and Medical Leave Act of 1993.

In Chapter 9 McCarrick provides an overview of women and the criminal justice system. The chapter includes a discussion of women as criminals and women as victims of crime. It also represents detailed analyses of current policies on rape and spousal abuse.

Chapter 10 explores questions such as how far the government can and should go in encouraging cultural change. The three models of the policy-making process discussed in Chapter 1 are assessed in terms of their utility for the study of women and public policy.

Effort has been taken to make the material in this volume accessible to students. With the exception of the concluding chapter, each chapter begins with a vignette offering a glimpse into the life of one woman. These examples are intended to personalize the material for students and may be used by the instructor as a starting point for class discussion. At the end of each chapter is a list of suggested readings, including current books and important journal articles. The wide range of material covered includes cultural studies and works on feminist theory, as well as public policy sources. Chapters 2 through 9 include chronologies of the major events discussed in the chapter. They are intended as summaries for students' convenience.

The authors wish to acknowledge the contributions of Brenda Carter, our editor at CQ Press and an authority on the use of e-mail, who kept us on course; and of Lydia Duncan, an outstanding manuscript editor. We also thank the students in our women and politics classes. Their questions prompted this book. Finally, we would like to thank the following reviewers whose comments helped us revise and refine various drafts of this book: Rita Mae Kelly, Arizona State University; Kathleen Knight, University of Houston; Micheline Ridley Malson, Duke University; Diane E. Wall, Mississippi State University; Susan Welch, Pennsylvania State University; and Dvora Yanow, California State University-Hayward.

M. Margaret Conway
David W. Ahern
Gertrude A. Steuernagel

About the Authors

David W. Ahern is associate professor of political science and chair of the political science department at the University of Dayton. His articles on political socialization have appeared in *The Public Opinion Quarterly, Political Behavior,* and *Simulation and Games.*

M. Margaret Conway is professor of political science at the University of Florida, Gainesville. She is author of *Political Participation in the United States, second edition* (CQ Press, 1991) and coauthor of *Political Analysis: An Introduction; Parties and Politics in America;* and *The American Party System: Stability and Change.* She has published widely in academic journals.

Robert H. Jerry II is professor and Herbert Herff Chair of Excellence in Law at the University of Memphis. He is the author of *Understanding Insurance Law* and has written numerous articles in the field of insurance law.

Earlean M. McCarrick is associate professor of government and politics at the University of Maryland, College Park. She is author of *The U.S. Constitution: A Guide to Information Sources* and of such articles as "The Supreme Court and the Evolution of Women's Rights."

Gertude A. Steuernagel is professor of political science at Kent State University. She is the author of *Political Philosophy as Therapy: Marcuse Reconsidered* and coeditor of *Foundations for a Feminist Restructuring of the Academic Disciplines.* Her articles have appeared in *Women in Politics, Polity,* and the *Journal of Politics.*

1

Women and Public Policy

In 1776 Abigail Adams wrote a letter to her husband, John Adams (a leader in the American Revolution and second president of the United States), in which she made the following request:

> In the new code of laws which I suppose it will be necessary for you to make, I desire you would remember the ladies and be more generous and favorable to them than your ancestors. Do not put much unlimited power into the hands of the husbands. Remember, all men would be tyrants if they could. If particular care and attention is not paid to the ladies, we are determined to foment a rebellion, and will not hold ourselves bound by any laws in which we have no voice or representation.[1]

She hoped (in vain) that the legal status of women would be improved and that political rights would be conferred on them by the new government. In 1993 Hillary Rodham Clinton was appointed by her husband, Bill Clinton (the forty-second president) to head the administration's task force on health care reform. An established attorney and a children's rights advocate, she serves in the administration as an unpaid volunteer. It is one of the few times since their marriage that she has earned less than her husband.

DEFINING CULTURE

Cultural changes in the ways women live their lives constitute one of the major revolutions of the twentieth century. These changes have caused Americans to rethink who they are, both as individuals and as members of the community. The role of government in determining the quality of life in modern society (frequently labeled "public policy") is a controversial

1

but ubiquitous factor that has to be considered in any effort to understand women's lives.

This book addresses the impact of public policy on women's lives and the impact of changes in women's lives on public policy. Many changes in women's lives are either a direct or an indirect result of public policy, and many of the changes in how public policy is made, including which issues should be the subject of public policy, are linked to cultural changes in women's lives. Abigail Adams lived in a patriarchal society in which males had legal and economic power over women and cultural expectations regarding the proper roles for women and men were clearly defined. Consequently, women who wanted a public policy that would lead to greater equality between women and men had to rely ultimately on the good graces of men to bring about change. Hillary Rodham Clinton has more opportunities to impact public policy directly. Like her husband, she received a quality education and achieved success in her chosen career. Because she and her husband view their marriage as a partnership, they share responsibility for the care of their daughter, and thus can combine family and professional responsibilities.

Since culture is a dominant theme in this book, a discussion of its significance for women and public policy is in order. "Culture" is a complex term that is not easily defined. It can be used in contexts so broad as to render it of little use to those seeking to understand the way of life of a group of people.[2] Culture can be defined as "a core of traditional ideas, practices, and technology shared by a people."[3] When we speak of culture, we are referring to the products of human activity.[4] A focus on culture assumes that much of what matters to a woman—her identity or sense of self, her beliefs, attitudes, and values—is learned through interaction with the people and institutions she encounters throughout her life. A cultural approach to public policy emphasizes the impact of factors such as class, life-style, religion, ethnic identification, and race on women's understanding of the political significance of their gender, a perception frequently referred to as their "gender consciousness."[5] In the words of three prominent students of American politics, "culture counts."[6] This is not to say that factors such as economic influences are unimportant. But the emphasis of this book is less on the economic effects of class than on how, and to what extent, a particular set of life circumstances affects a woman's perception of who she is, how she got there, what she wants to do with her life, and what she wants for herself and her family. Women living at the time of Abigail Adams and women living at the time of Hillary Rodham Clinton have different interpretations of what it means to be a woman.

Individuals become part of their culture in a number of ways. The learning process takes place in the family, the school, the workplace, the place of worship, and the community. Many individuals learn political values indirectly—which is another way of saying that they learn politically relevant attitudes, such as that toward authority—in their home and their school. Ethnic background, race, or religion may be important in helping some individuals develop a sense of who they are. For women, development of a sense of identity that includes gender has been an important step in bringing the interests they share as women into the public policy arena.

Culture is dependent on social groups for its creation and its transmission.[7] At any given time, within the dominant culture there are frequently a number of subcultures with varying degrees of meaning for those who constitute them. Many of the people involved in the women's movement of the 1960s, for example, advanced ideas about the "proper" role of women that contrasted sharply with those of the dominant culture.

A number of contemporary trends illustrate the connection between cultural change and public policy. Clearly, the emergence of women as an electoral force and the increasing number of women who are seeking and winning election to public office reflect women's changing status in American culture—as a result of this change, they have exerted a greater impact on public policy. The emergence of women in politics was not a single cataclysmic event but rather reflected a series of changes in expectations about what women would and could do with their lives and the acceptability of certain actions, such as voting and running for and holding political office. The 1992 elections are a case in point. Women cast 54 percent of the votes in the presidential election,[8] and a record number of women sought and attained House and Senate seats. A comparison of the results of the 1990 and 1992 elections reveals that the proportion of women in state legislatures increased from 18 percent to 21 percent, and the proportion of state executive offices held by women increased from 18 percent to 22 percent.[9] The media frequently referred to 1992 as the "Year of the Woman," but this phrase is misleading. Women did not simply wake up on January 1, 1992, and collectively proclaim: "This is our time!" The groundwork for the "Year of the Woman" had been laid as a result of the changes that have taken place in women's lives in the past twenty years (including an increase in their educational and employment opportunities), along with the organizational efforts of such groups as Emily's List, the National Women's Political Caucus, and the Women's Campaign Fund.

Title IX of the Higher Education Amendments of 1972, for example, opened up a number of opportunities for women and resulted in their increased involvement in athletics and the professions. The Equal Pay Act of 1963, the Supreme Court's 1973 ruling in *Roe v. Wade*, and the Pregnancy Discrimination Act of 1978 have all redefined what it means to be a woman in American society.

Sexual harassment, domestic violence, reproductive rights, and child care have become part of the public policy agenda because of the changes in women's roles and women's increasingly strong political presence.

The twentieth century has witnessed unprecedented changes in women's lives.[10] Perhaps the most significant change, from a cultural and public policy perspective, has been the entry into the work force of married women with small children. In the middle of the twentieth century, less than 20 percent of these women worked outside the home. By 1991, this figure had increased to almost 60 percent.[11] Before 1980, African-American women were more likely than white women to be part of the work force. In 1980, the proportions of the two groups in the work force were approximately the same. [12] It was not until 1985, however, that a majority of married women with preschool-age children were employed outside the home. The impact of this trend is magnified by the fact that more than one-third of the married women with children under the age of three are now likely to be working full time. Only a decade ago, less than a quarter of these women had full-time employment.[13]

There are many reasons for this trend, and they demonstrate the connection between cultural change and public policy. Economic necessity and the desire for self-fulfillment are the major reasons married women with young children work outside the home. Employment is an empowering experience both personally and politically, but it has also created demands on government. The sheer number of women in the work force, along with their mobilization as a political force, has led to calls for action on issues as diverse as family leave, sexual harassment, pay equity, and reproductive health. In the fictionalized 1950s, June Cleaver always had time for Ward, Wally, and the Beaver. Many of the children whose family lives were very different from that of the Cleavers wished for a home in which Mother, in an attractive dress, pearls, and high-heeled shoes, was always available to lend a sympathetic ear and offer a glass of cold milk and a snack.

Today, June Cleaver has been replaced by Roseanne Connor. Television viewers sympathize with Roseanne's efforts to keep her family together while she and her husband struggle to earn enough to support their children and themselves. The Connor children (Becky, Darlene, and D. J.), unlike Wally and the Beaver, pour their own milk and snack on leftover carryout pizza. June did not have to worry about finding someone to care for Wally and the Beaver if they became ill. Care of the home and the children were her responsibility. Nor did she have to worry about juggling family and career. Her family was her career, and if she had any doubts about her life and where it was going, they were not shared with her family or her viewers. Roseanne, in contrast, has held a number of low-paying, "pink-collar ghetto" jobs, including shampoo "girl" and waitress. She is struggling to start her own business and relies on an extended family of sister, mother, and female friends to help her. Her husband shares in the care of the home and children, but she is the one more frequently seen loading the washing machine and running the vacuum cleaner. As Roseanne Connor has replaced June Cleaver in the culture, the issues that are important in the "typical" woman's life have moved from the private to the public arena. [14] The changes in women's lives have increased the demands on government to address many issues. The intersection of cultural change and public policy has a long history, which is the subject of the next section.

A BRIEF HISTORY

The impact of cultural change on public policy has led to creation of the specific notion of political and legal rights that define an individual. According to Anne Schneider and Helen Ingram, the "social construction of target populations" (their term for the "cultural characterizations or popular images of the persons or groups whose behavior and well-being are affected by public policy") can remain the same for extended periods or can be subject to continual change.[15] Because public policy has largely been based on traditional ideas of women's roles, it has served to reinforce women's subordinate status.[16] The patriarchal male has, in many instances, been replaced by the patriarchal state. Nancy Fraser has argued that women's continued dependency on welfare is ensured because they are not given the opportunity to develop job skills; they are forced to rely on the state for housing, food, and medical care for themselves and their children.[17]

But public policy can empower women and lessen their dependency on men or on the patriarchal state. Women's acquisition of political and legal rights has been the result of two distinct women's political movements, each of which had two phases. In the first phase of the first women's movement (the first six decades of the nineteenth century), women demanded basic rights. Perhaps best known is the wide range of policy demands contained in the Declaration of Rights issued by the Seneca Falls Convention in 1848. This phase culminated in the unsuccessful drive to include guarantees of legal and political rights for women in the post-Civil War amendments to the United States Constitution, which conferred the legal rights of citizenship, including the right to vote, on black males.[18]

The second phase of the first women's movement, which was dominated by disputes about both the issue agenda that should be pursued and the most appropriate means for seeking policy change, culminated in the ratification of the women's suffrage amendment to the Constitution in 1920.[19] Women have acquired other rights as a result of court decisions and the enactment of federal and state laws during the nineteenth and twentieth centuries.

From 1920 to 1960, activism was limited because there was little public interest in or support for a policy agenda of particular relevance to women. The extensive changes that took place in American society during those years, however, gave rise to a second women's movement during the 1960s, a movement that is still strong in the 1990s.[20] The first phase of this second movement consisted of raising women's political and social consciousness about policy problems and the denial of women's basic rights. As a result of their observations of the effectiveness of political action in racial minorities' pursuit of civil rights and economic equality during the 1950s and 1960s and the participation of many women in both the civil rights and the anti-war movements, women became increasingly aware of the denial of their basic rights and of the effectiveness of collective action in bringing about political and social change.[21] Books such as Betty Friedan's *The Feminine Mystique* gave expression to the dissatisfaction of many women with the roles assigned them by modern American society.[22]

Early in his presidential term, John F. Kennedy appointed an Advisory Commission on the Status of Women. In its report issued in October 1963, the commission recommended several policy changes, including the removal of restrictions on married women's control over property owned by them, increased opportunities for women to participate in politics by holding appointive and elective office, and the establishment of equal employment opportunity as a federal government policy. The commission recommended that equal employment opportunity be implemented to the extent possible through an executive order of the president, which would make the policy applicable to employees of the federal government and companies having contracts with it. The commission expected compliance with the executive order to be voluntary, however, and the recommendation specified no enforcement mechanisms.[23] The commission's recommendation made no mention of other problems confronted by women in modern society, such as access to adequate and affordable day care for the children of working mothers.

Two major policies affecting employed women were enacted into law during this period. First, a bill mandating equal pay for equal work, which had been regularly introduced in Congress since 1948, was passed in 1963.[24] Second, Title VII of the 1964 Civil Rights Act was amended to prohibit gender discrimination in employment. In an effort to kill the act, the bill's opponents offered this amendment in the belief that broadening the coverage of the employment discrimination prohibition would result in the bill's defeat. The bill was passed, however, and when enforced, the legislation proved to be an effective deterrent to gender discrimination in employment.[25]

The 1960s witnessed a rapid increase in the creation or growth of organizations that expressed the policy concerns of women and worked to gain an effective public policy on issues of particular interest to women. The founding of one of the largest such organizations, the National Organization for Women (NOW), on October 29, 1966, should be viewed as the start of the second phase of the second women's movement. NOW began when women attending the National Conference of State Commissions, sponsored by a presidential Citizen's Advisory Council, had been denied the right to propose and adopt resolutions. Realizing the need for an organization to express women's views, a group of women meeting at lunch on the last day of the conference agreed to become NOW's founding members.[26]

At its national conference in November 1967, NOW drew up a policy agenda that reflects the continuing policy concerns of this second women's movement.[27] The agenda's central issues are:

1. Enforcement of laws prohibiting gender discrimination in employment
2. Provision of adequate, quality child care for families of employed women and of students in educational and training programs
3. Maternity leave rights for employed women
4. Fair tax treatment for employed women, including tax credits or tax deductions for child care expenses and nondiscriminatory tax treatment of two-income families
5. Equal access to all fields of education.

General agreement exists on the importance of these issues, but others are more controversial. Although there is widespread public support for women's rights, an equal rights amendment (ERA) to the Constitution failed to achieve ratification by the required thirty-eight states, even though the time allowed for ratification was extended by three years.[28]

Also controversial is the demand by NOW and by other women's groups of the second women's movement that women have the right to control their own reproductive processes, including the right to an abortion. Although the Supreme Court upheld as constitutional the right to an abortion in several cases decided during the 1970s, the controversy continues and has resulted not only in a campaign for passage of laws and a constitutional amendment to prohibit abortion but in outbreaks of violence against organizations promoting the right to an abortion and against medical facilities and personnel providing abortion services.

This book focuses on the issues of the second women's movement; they highlight the relationship between cultural change and public policy.

CULTURAL CHANGE AND PUBLIC POLICY

There are three broad categories of cultural change that are relevant to women and public policy: (1) changes in the way social institutions treat women (covered in Chapters 2, 3, and 9); (2) changes in the role of women in the family (Chapters 7 and 8); and (3) changes in the economic conditions of women (Chapters 4, 5, and 6). These changes are interactive, that is, they affect one another; progress in any single area of women's lives is seldom straightforward.

It is important to remember that the policy-making process itself occurs in a cultural context and is affected by factors such as the previously discussed social construction of target populations and the culture specific to the issue. The culture of each public policy issue includes all of the thinking about the issue, the language used to discuss the issue, and the values and beliefs that are relevant to the issue.[29] Cultural changes in women's roles, for example, are part of the history of the culture of child care as a public policy issue. The entry into the work force of large numbers of women with young children has created the need for a public policy on child care. Over time, thinking about women's roles as mothers and employees has changed. As discussed in Chapter 8, the policy-making process with regard to the issue of child care has been influenced to a great extent by changes in perceptions that caring for children is women's responsibility.

THE POLICY-MAKING PROCESS

Since the policy-making process is seldom, if ever, direct, linear, or compartmentalized and can involve national, state, and local governments, it is helpful to think in terms of actions that occur in most forms of policy making.

Problem definition may occur as a result of the activities of a political movement.[30] A political movement frequently begins with the realization by a set of individuals that the problem that each thought was unique and personal is shared by others, and the problem comes to be viewed as one that the government can solve. Diagnoses of the problem's causes are developed and possible solutions are proposed; these diagnoses and symbols of them are adopted by those who identify with the political movement.[31] Political movements also stimulate increased awareness of mutual problems by those who face the objective situation that creates the demand for policy change, to increase the likelihood that an issue and the proposed solutions for its attendant problems will be placed on the public agenda. Political movements frequently find expression in protest activities, but more conventional types of political activity are usually employed to advance the movement's policy agenda, such as the mobilization of voters and the formation or co-optation of interest groups. Interest groups lobby elected and appointed officials, generate and manipulate media coverage of the issue, and mobilize group supporters to advance their issue concerns to a high position on the government's policy agenda.[32] Other forms of political activity may include endorsing candidates or referenda proposals, making campaign contributions, and doing campaign work in support of those candidates who support the preferred solutions for the policy problem.

The process by which a political movement seeks to place its issue concerns on the policy agenda of government decision makers helps to define the policy problem and thus establishes the permissible boundaries for proposed solutions to it. The process can vary with the nature of the issue, the interests involved in the policy controversy, and the scope and intensity of the conflicts surrounding the issue.[33]

Although an issue may gain the attention of policy makers and the support of policy entrepreneurs, the enactment of legislation designed to alleviate the underlying problem is not assured. In general, legislation that is perceived as involving radical change (which Joyce Gelb and Marian Palley refer to as "role change") rather than incremental change (which they term "role equity") is less likely to be enacted.[34] Unfortunately for women, many of the policy changes advocated as enhancing their status in American society are attacked by opponents as resulting in role change rather than role equity.[35]

Policy can be created and changed through a number of formal government actions, the most obvious of which is the enactment of a law. One of the most significant policy changes affecting women, however, was accomplished with the ratification of the Nineteenth Amendment to the Constitution. During the past two decades, the difficulties of obtaining policy changes by other means have resulted in extensive litigation in federal and state courts initiated by both individual women and women's groups. Significant changes have been achieved in a number of policy areas, including employment, education, pension rights, and insurance. Presidential executive orders have also had an important impact, particularly in establishing equal opportunity in employment.[36]

Policy gains achieved through the enactment of laws can be minimized or largely subverted in the processes of writing or revising the regulations that specify how a law will be put into effect (as was clear to the women who worked to gain passage of the Equal Credit Opportunity Act), which can become a battle between contending interests.[37]

The implementation of a policy, once it is established (by whatever means), can also result in the policy's enhancement, distortion, retrenchment, or defeat.[38] The objectives and standards set forth in the policy statement may be vague, too narrow to be effective or too broad to be achieved. Congress or a state legislature may have felt that it would be easier to enact a law if some of the provisions were deliberately left vague. Conversely, the provisions written during the regulation-drafting phase of the policy implementation process may be so specific that they limit or distort the policy, with the result that it fails to have the effects intended by many of its advocates.

The manner in which responsibility for policy implementation is assigned can have a substantial impact on the success of a program. If responsibility for implementing a policy is not explicitly assigned to a specific agency (or agencies), priorities in implementation and enforcement are more likely to be given to those tasks for which the agency already has explicit responsibility. If multiple agencies are assigned responsibility for implementing the program, lack of coordination among them could mean that responsibilities are carried out with different degrees of rigor or that different standards are applied by each agency. This problem has affected several policies of particular importance to women, such as employment, education, and credit.

In some cases, policy implementation may be added to the responsibilities of an agency that is already overburdened with responsibility for other policies or that must interact with a large clientele of private firms and state and local government agencies. And if the budgetary resources allocated to the implementing agencies are inadequate, or if the agencies lack appropriately skilled personnel, implementation is less likely to be effective. The activities of governmental agencies at the federal, state, or local levels that are necessary to implement and enforce a policy or law may not be forthcoming because the agency personnel charged with those tasks are only weakly committed to the policy or do not support it at all, resulting in less than optimum policy outcomes or even serious distortion of the policy's impact. Effective implementation generally requires that those who are given explicit responsibility for the task have the support of their immediate and higher-ranking supervisors. As a result of faulty communications patterns within the implementing agency, there may be a failure to convey either the policy goal as expressed by Congress or a strong commitment to the stated implementation goal. Enforcement of a policy may be thwarted as much by a lack of effort on the part of those charged with the task as by a lack of effective sanctions against those who violate the law that incorporates the policy. Indeed, such problems have impeded policy implementation in several equal rights areas. For example, many in the Office of Civil Rights in the Department of Justice, created to enforce a policy of equal rights for racial minorities, found it difficult to develop a strong commitment to equal rights for women during the 1960s and early 1970s, and the implementation of policies designed to guarantee equal employment opportunity for women suffered as a result.[39]

Also needed for effective policy implementation are mechanisms for monitoring compliance with the policy's requirements. If nondiscrimination in employment is not monitored, past patterns of job bias may be allowed to continue. Mechanisms for monitoring compliance are not effective if precise standards for measuring compliance are not established, however.

Economic, social, and political conditions can significantly affect the implementation of policy. During an economic recession, the federal, state, and local governments have fewer resources available to them and are likely to freeze or even to reduce the budgets of many agencies charged with policy implementation. A president who does not approve of a particular policy may try to hamper its implementation by ordering reductions in the budgets of the relevant administrative agencies or by having the policy's implementation regulations rewritten to reduce the policy's impact, as happened in several equal rights policy areas during the Reagan administration. In addition, social conditions may change, resulting in reduced public support for a policy and less pressure from Congress to implement it effectively. During the past two decades, inadequate implementation and enforcement have been evident in several policy areas of crucial concern to women, including education, health, employment, and credit (see Chapters 2 through 5).

Evaluation of a policy once it has been implemented can involve contention between those who advocate change and those who prefer that women continue in their traditional roles. The assessment of a policy's outcomes and of its impact on the intended beneficiaries and on others in society depends on the political values of those making the assessments. For example, some Reagan administration appointees advocated changes in the implementation of equal employment opportunity policy that would, in effect, have meant that no affirmative action requirements would be applied to employers covered by the provisions of federal laws (see Chapter 4).

MODELS OF THE POLICY-MAKING PROCESS

Since there are so many factors to consider in any discussion of public policy, it is useful to organize them in the context of a general theory or model. Students of the policy process have developed a number of models, three of which have merit for organizing our thinking about women and public policy. The utility of each model for this study is assessed in Chapter 10.

The first model suggests that policy is based on the preferences of a dominant elite, whose values are reflected in the policy outputs of government. The members of this elite hold prominent positions in the government and in major social institutions (such as religious organizations), the educational system, business, and the mass media. According to this view, the dominant elite recruits those who share its values and policy preferences, and policy therefore reflects this self-perpetuating consensus. Substantial and rapid policy change would be expected only if there were major changes in elite compositions.[40] Such changes have occurred periodically in American society as representatives of groups previously unincorporated into the elite have attained political power through the electoral process. Changes in elite compositions are likely to be more extensive in times of crisis; major changes occurred during the economic depressions of the 1890s and the 1930s.

According to the second model, which is based on a more explicit group theory, public policy is the outcome of conflict between organized groups—a balance of interests weighted by the groups' relative political strength. A group is a collection of individuals organized around an interest, broadly defined, on the basis of which representatives of the group make demands on the political system. The interest may be highly self-centered (as is the demand of oil well owners for special tax policy benefits), or more altruistic (as are the demands made by environmental groups for policies protective of the nation's natural resources). In this conflict model of the policy process, the policy reflects the interests of those groups which are dominant in a particular historical era.

The third model suggests that policy is the result of past policies, in which minor changes have occurred incrementally over time. Constraints on decision making, such as the limited availability of information about the consequences of proposed policy changes, limited time for decision making, lack of knowledge about citizens' policy preferences, and the costs of both elaborate policy-making processes and significant policy changes, force policy makers to pursue an incremental change strategy. This results in policies that are conservative in the sense of being traditional and slow to change.[41]

POLICY SILENCES

Thomas Dye has perceptively described public policy as "whatever government chose to do or not to do."[42] Governmental inaction maintains a set of conditions and is thus just as much an expression of policy as laws would be, had they been enacted. If federal marshals in Washington, D.C., do not execute arrest warrants for parents who fail to pay child support (as occurred in 1986), the public policy in the nation's capital is that parents who are legally obligated to pay child support may fail to do so without fear of punishment.[43] The traditional view of policy is that it consists of sets of laws, regulations, actions, and programs that have specified goals and that allocate values authoritatively in the society.[44] According to this view, policy reflects conscious decisions and is manifested in actions and programs. However, policy made by default, when a government passively ignores a problem and its impact on citizens, is just as significant in its consequences as policy created by deliberate action. Since there has been radical and rapid change in so many of the public policy areas that are of concern to women, policy silences are as frequent and as significant as policy that results from deliberate action.

NOTES

1. Quoted in Eleanor Flexner, *Century of Struggle* (Cambridge: Harvard University Press, Belknap Press, 1959), 15. Original source is *Familiar Letters of John Adams and His Wife, Abigail Adams, During the Revolution* (New York: Hurd and Houghton, 1876), 148-150, letter dated March 31, 1776.

2. John Tomlinson, *Cultural Imperialism: A Critical Introduction* (Baltimore: Johns Hopkins University Press, 1991), 5. For a theoretical discussion of politics and culture, see Michael Ryan, *Politics and Culture: Working Hypotheses for a Post-Revolutionary Society* (Baltimore: Johns Hopkins University Press, 1989); Douglas Tallack, *Twentieth-Century America: The Intellectual and Cultural Context* (London: Longman, 1991); and Jurgen Habermas, *The New Conservatism*, ed. and trans. Shierry Weber Nicholsen (Cambridge, Mass.: MIT Press, 1989).

3. Herbert M. Levine, *Political Issues Debate: An Introduction to Politics*, 4th ed. (Englewood Cliffs, N.J.: Prentice-Hall, 1993), 20.

4. Tomlinson, *Cultural Imperialism*, 23.

5. David C. Leege, Joel A. Lieske, and Kenneth D. Wald, "Toward Cultural Theories of American Political Behavior," in *Political Science: Looking to the Future*, vol. 3, *Political Behavior*, ed. William Crotty (Evanston, Ill.: Northwestern University Press, 1991), 194.

6. Leege et al., "Toward Cultural Theories," 193.

7. Ibid., 214.

8. "Portrait of the Electorate," *New York Times*, November 5, 1992, B9.

9. Michael deCourcy Hinds, "Elections Change Face of Lawmaking Bodies," *New York Times*, November 5, 1992, B9. See also Center for the American Woman and Politics, *Women in Elective Office 1992* (New Brunswick, N.J.: CAWP, National Information Bank on Women in Public Office, Eagleton Institute of Politics, Rutgers University, 1992), 1; and "Elect Women for a Change,"

National NOW Times, January 1993, 2. For a comprehensive tally of the 1992 election results and an analysis of their significance for women and politics, see Center for the American Woman and Politics, *1992 Post-Election Wrap-Up* (New Brunswick, N.J.: CAWP, 1993).

10. Women constitute 51.2 percent of the population of the United States, an increase from 48.9 percent at the turn of the century. Women increasingly dominate the ranks of the elderly in this country. In 1940, for example, there were 95.5 males for every 100 females aged 65 and over. By 1991, this figure had declined to 67.5 males for every 100 females in that age-group. Women also were more likely than men to predominate among the very elderly, those aged 85 and over. As of 1991, women aged 85 and over constituted 12 percent of the female population aged 65 and over. For men, the comparable figure was 6.9 percent. Women are more likely than men to be widowed. In 1970, 17.1 percent of the males and 54.4 percent of the females aged 65 and over were widowed. In 1990, the comparable figures were 14.2 percent (men) and 48.6 percent (women).

In 1970, 2.6 percent of all males aged 18 and over were divorced. By 1991, this figure had increased to 7.8 percent. The increased incidence of divorce among women is equally dramatic. In 1970, 4.1 percent of all women aged 18 and over were divorced. By 1991, this figure had increased to 10.0 percent.

The average number of children in families has declined over the last two decades. In 1970, families averaged 3.8 children. By 1991, this figure had declined to 3.18.

A major change has occurred in the labor force status of women who give birth. In 1976, 60 percent of all women were in the labor force. By 1990, this figure had increased to 71 percent. In 1976, 31 percent of those women in the labor force had given birth in the preceding year. By 1990, this figure had increased to 53 percent. All data from U.S. Department of Commerce, Bureau of the Census *Statistical Abstract of the United States, 1992* (Washington, D.C.: Government Printing Office, 1992).

11. U.S. Department of Commerce, Bureau of the Census, *Statistical Abstract,* 388.
12. Paula Ries and Anne J. Stone, eds., *The American Woman, 1992-1993: A Status Report* (New York: Norton, 1992), 309.
13. Ibid., 323.
14. The role that television characters play in America's cultural life and their ability to impact political views were dramatically illustrated during the 1992 presidential campaign by the controversy over the unmarried Murphy Brown's decision to become a mother and Vice President Dan Quayle's choice of her as a symbol of the decline in "family values."
15. Anne Schneider and Helen Ingram, "Social Construction of Target Populations: Implications for Politics and Policy," *American Political Science Review* 87 (June 1993): 334, 336.
16. Virginia Sapiro, "Gender Politics, Gendered Politics: The State of the Field," in William Crotty, ed., *Political Science: Looking to the Future,* vol. 1, *The Theory and Practice of Political Science* (Evanston, Ill.: Northwestern University Press, 1991), 175.

17. Nancy Fraser, "What's Critical about Critical Theory?" in Seyla Benhabib and Drucilla Cornell, eds., *Feminism as Critique* (Minneapolis: University of Minnesota Press, 1987), 50.
18. See Flexner, *Century of Struggle*, for a discussion of the first women's movement.
19. Ibid. See also Nancy McGlen and Karen O'Connor, *Women's Rights* (New York: Praeger, 1983), chaps. 1 and 2.
20. For a discussion of the origins of the second women's movement, see Jo Freeman, *The Politics of Women's Liberation* (New York: David McKay, 1975); and Barbara Sinclair Deckard, *The Women's Movement*, 3d ed. (New York: Harper and Row, 1983).
21. Freeman, *The Politics of Women's Liberation*, chap. 2.
22. Betty Friedan, *The Feminine Mystique* (New York: Norton, 1963). Other books that had a significant impact in the form of consciousness raising include Kristen Amundsen, *The Silenced Majority* (Englewood Cliffs, N.J.: Prentice-Hall, 1971); Germaine Greer, *The Female Eunuch* (New York: McGraw-Hill, 1971); and Robin Morgan, ed., *Sisterhood Is Powerful* (New York: Vintage, 1970).
23. President's Advisory Commission on the Status of Women, 1963.
24. Equal Pay Act of 1963, P.L. 88-38.
25. Civil Rights Act of 1964, P.L. 88-352. U.S.C. sect. 2000e-2(a)(1).
26. For a brief history of the formation and early organizational struggles of NOW, see Freeman, *The Politics of Women's Liberation*, chap. 3.
27. See, for example, the National Organization for Women Bill of Rights, App. 3, in June Sochen, *Herstory*, 2d ed. (Palo Alto, Calif.: Mayfield, 1981).
28. For a discussion of the reasons for the failure to pass the equal rights amendment, see Janet K. Boles, "Building Support for the ERA: A Case of 'Too Much, Too Late,' " *PS* 14 (Fall 1982): 572-577; Jane J. Mansbridge, *Why We Lost the ERA* (Chicago: University of Chicago Press, 1986); Mary Frances Berry, *Why ERA Failed* (Bloomington: Indiana University Press, 1986); and Jean Hoff-Wilson, ed., *Rights of Passage* (Bloomington: Indiana University Press, 1986).
29. Dvora Yanow, "Toward a Policy Culture Approach to Implementation," *Policy Studies Review* 7, no. 1, (Autumn 1987): 108-109.
30. For a discussion of agenda setting, see Roger W. Cobb and Charles D. Elder, *Participation in American Politics: The Dynamics of Agenda Building* (Baltimore: Johns Hopkins University Press, 1983); Ellen Boneparth, *Women, Power, and Policy* (New York: Pergamon Press, 1982); and John W. Kingdon, *Agendas, Alternatives, and Public Policies* (Boston, Little, Brown, 1984).
31. Harold D. Lasswell and Abraham Kaplan, *Power and Society* (New Haven, Conn.: Yale University Press, 1950).
32. For a discussion of the role of interest groups in American politics, see Jeffrey Berry, *The Interest Group Society* (Boston: Little, Brown, 1984) and Allan Cigler and Burdett Loomis, *Interest Group Politics*, 3d ed. (Washington, D.C.: CQ Press, 1991).
33. See Cobb and Elder, *Participation in American Politics*; and Boneparth, *Women, Powers, and Policy*, chap. 1.
34. Joyce Gelb and Marian Lief Palley, *Women and Public Policies* (Princeton, N.J.:

Princeton University Press, 1982), chap. 1.
35. Of course, a number of seemingly "harmless" role equity changes, such as equality of access to credit and education, can result in role change. As Machiavelli reminds us, politics is often about images and appearances.
36. See, for example, Leo Kanowitz, *Sex Roles in Law and Society* (Albuquerque: University of New Mexico Press, 1973); Leslie Friedman Goldstein, *The Constitutional Rights of Women: Cases in Law and Social Change* (New York: Longman, 1979); and Herman H. Kay, *Sex-Based Discrimination: Text, Cases, and Materials,* 2d ed. (St. Paul, Minn.: West, 1981).
37. Gelb and Palley, *Women and Public Policies,* chap. 4; M. Margaret Conway, "Anti-Discrimination Law and the Problems of Policy Implementation," in John G. Grumm and Stephen L. Wasby, eds., *The Analysis of Policy Impact* (Lexington, Mass.: Lexington Books, 1981).
38. For an extended discussion of this problem, see Jeffrey Pressman and Aaron Wildavsky, *Implementation* (Chicago: University of Chicago Press, 1974); George C. Edwards III, *Implementing Public Policy* (Washington, D.C.: CQ Press, 1980); Eugene Bardach, *The Implementation Game* (Cambridge, Mass.: MIT Press, 1977); Randall Ripley and Grace Franklin, *Policy Implementation and Bureaucracy* (Chicago: Dorsey Press, 1986); and Donald S. Van Meter and Carl E. Van Horn, "The Policy Implementation Process," *Administration and Society* 6 (February 1975): 445-487.
39. McGlen and O'Connor, *Women's Rights,* 173-178.
40. See Thomas Dye, *Understanding Public Policy,* 7th ed. (Englewood Cliffs, N.J.: Prentice-Hall, 1992), for a summary of the model. For examples of the development, elaboration, and application of the model, see C. Wright Mills, *The Power Elite* (New York: Oxford University Press, 1956); and Floyd Hunter, *Community Power Structures* (Chapel Hill: University of North Carolina Press, 1953).
41. Charles Lindbloom, "The Science of Muddling Through," *Public Administration Review,* 19 (Spring 1959): 79-88.
42. Thomas Dye, *Understanding Public Policy,* 5th ed. (Englewood Cliffs, N.J.: Prentice-Hall, 1984), 1.
43. Elsa Walsh, "Marshals' Service Revised," *Washington Post,* January 29, 1987, DC1.
44. See, for example, Randall B. Ripley and Grace A. Franklin, *Congress, the Bureaucracy, and Public Policy,* rev. ed. (Homewood, Ill.: Dorsey Press, 1980), 1-2.

SUGGESTIONS FOR FURTHER READING

Bendix, John. "Women's Suffrage and Political Culture: A Modern Swiss Case." *Women and Politics* 12, no. 3 (1992): 27-56.
Caraway, Nancie. "The Cunning of History: Empire, Identity and Feminist Theory in the Flesh." *Women and Politics* 12, no. 2 (1992): 1-18.
Clinton, Catherine, and Nina Silber, eds. *Divided Houses: Gender and the Civil War.* New York: Oxford University Press, 1992.
Cook, Elizabeth Adell. "Measuring Feminist Consciousness." *Women and Politics* 9,

no. 3 (1989): 71-88.

Gelb, Joyce. *Feminism and Politics: A Comparative Perspective.* Berkeley: University of California Press, 1989.

Henry, Charles P. *Culture and African American Politics.* Bloomington: Indiana University Press, 1990.

McCracken, Ellen. *Decoding Women's Magazines.* New York: St. Martin's Press, 1993.

Mattison, Georgia, and Sandra Storey. *Women in Citizen Advocacy: Stories of Twenty-eight Shapers of Public Policy.* Jefferson, N.C.: McFarland, 1992.

Rinehart, Sue Tolleson. *Gender Consciousness and Politics.* New York: Routledge, 1992.

Sapiro, Virginia. "The Gender Basis of American Social Policy." *Political Science Quarterly* 101, no. 2 (1986): 221-238.

———. *The Political Integration of Women: Roles, Socialization, and Politics.* Urbana: University of Illinois Press, 1983.

Tinker, Irene, ed. *Women in Washington: Advocates for Public Policy.* Beverly Hills, Calif.: Sage, 1983.

Women and Educational Policy

At the 1992 Army-Navy football game, the brigade of midshipmen from Annapolis was led onto the field by the highest-ranking member of the senior class. Chosen as brigade commander from a group of forty-three finalists who had been nominated by various officers, this person represented the United States Naval Academy's finest: an honors math major who aspired to be an astronaut and who was taking courses in electrical engineering, weapons systems, creative writing, and advanced linear algebra, as well as a postgraduate math course in complex variables. The brigade commander was Kristen W. Culler of Fayetteville, North Carolina.[1] On her uniform she wore glider and jump wings (which she had earned as an exchange student at the Air Force Academy), a ribbon acknowledging expert shooting ability, and a National Defense ribbon awarded for serving in the military during the war in the Persian Gulf.

Only two or three decades ago, the idea of a woman serving in the military, taking courses in weapons systems at a service academy, and aspiring to be an astronaut would have seemed preposterous. The accomplishments of Kristen W. Culler reflect the changes that have taken place in society, in the military, and, most importantly, in education, because it was the demonstration of her abilities in the classroom that made possible her admission to the Naval Academy, where she could take the courses she wanted to take and compete on an equal basis with the other students, in the hope of becoming an astronaut. The story of Kristen W. Culler demonstrates both the successes that women have attained and the importance of education in American society.

The primacy of education in a democratic system of government inevitably places educational controversies at the center of public attention. When individuals are denied equal access to the educational system, whether on the basis of race, ethnic origin, religion, disability, or gender, there is an immediate recognition that such denial has adverse consequences for the moral fabric of society as well as for the economy. Not only do individuals lose opportunities but society loses the opportunity to develop a better-educated, more productive, more democratic citizenry. For these reasons, education was one of the first and most important areas in which the struggle for equal opportunity for women took place. This chapter explores the cultural, theoretical, and historical context of the battle for equal educational opportunities for women, particularly in higher education; major legislation and court decisions; and some of the battles still to be fought.[2]

EDUCATIONAL POLICY IN CULTURAL AND HISTORICAL CONTEXT

Education is a unique good in a modern democratic society.[3] It is of primary importance both to the individual and to society; everyone needs at least some education, and an educated and enlightened citizenry is thought to be necessary in such a society. An important question in the current debate over federal spending is how much money to invest in America's future. Nearly everyone agrees that education is an investment, not only for the individuals who are being educated but for society as a whole.

Education is also a divisible or competitive good, in that it can be allocated to (1) some individuals or groups at the expense of others; (2) various members of society in unequal quantities; and (3) different members of society in unequal qualities. Some groups (such as women) can be and have been excluded from the educational system or allocated this good inequitably, with adverse consequences both for the individual and for society. If the admissions officials at Harvard Law School had listened to those who argued that admitting women would deny qualified men the opportunity to be considered for those positions, the Supreme Court would have been denied its second woman justice—Ruth Bader Ginsburg.

Finally, education is a good that may be consumed differently by different individuals. Individuals may choose, be socialized or encouraged to choose, or be discouraged from choosing certain types of careers. The variability in the consumption of this good can have a significant impact on a meritocratic society. If individuals are to distinguish themselves from others on the basis of their career successes rather than simply by their class, race, or gender, the educational system should be recognized as the first and most important forum in which merit can be measured.

In summary, the educational system should reflect the fundamental values of American society—individual freedom, competition, and equality of opportunity. Some scholars have argued that the American educational system tends not to equalize opportunities but rather to reinforce existing social inequalities.[4] The policy of separate but equal schooling, the creation of different curricula for different students, and the ascription of certain occupations as being the domain of one class, race, or gender have led to separate and unequal schooling and have contributed to the perpetuation of social inequality. The educational system can, however, be a major agent for change in society's complex system of social relationships. Educational policies aimed at redressing past discrimination can have dramatic consequences both for the groups that have experienced it and for society as a whole.

Throughout the history of American education, the role of women has been circumscribed in many respects. Women have been denied access to many types of educational institutions. Women students have often had strained relationships with male educators. Women's roles as wives and mothers have often been affected by both the formal and the informal arrangements of the American educational system (such as the lack of child care for women students). Despite these factors, women have continued to have an important influence on American education.[5]

Even though American women were denied the right to vote until 1920, they transmitted the values of the political culture (including an emphasis on citizenship) to the male members of society.[6] Women who desired a career usually chose teaching in elementary and secondary schools since that was one of the few areas where they had actually seen women in a career. Women teachers were thus early role models. Interestingly, many communities placed restrictions on teachers that reinforced cultural norms, such as the requirement that women teachers who married would have to give up their careers to assume the duties of wife and mother. Some people, of course, still believe that it is impossible for a woman to have both a career and a family.

The success of the suffragist movement and the increased importance of women in the work force (in part as a result of their activities during the two world wars) began to change ideas about the education of women and their role in society. (Nevertheless, in the period immediately following World War II, teaching was still considered a "woman's occupation.")

The civil rights movement of the 1960s, although primarily a movement to guarantee the rights of racial minorities, also prompted society to question some of its traditional stereotypes about women. Concepts that had originally been used solely in the discussion of racial discrimination, such as affirmative action and equality of educational opportunity, began

Table 2-1   Women as Percentage of Selected Majors, 1978-1988

Subject	1978	1988	Increase
Business	34.6	45.9	11.3
Law	30.4	42.2	11.8
Engineering	10.7	14.8	4.1
Medicine	23.2	34.9	11.7
Veterinary medicine	33.7	56.9	23.2

Source: U.S. Department of Education, National Center for Educational Statistics, *Digest of Education Statistics, 1991,* 166.

to resonate for those committed to the elimination of gender discrimination as well. As women began to test the educational system, however, they discovered that many of the attitudes and policies of the past persisted and effectively made the attainment of equal educational opportunity difficult.

THE CURRENT STATUS OF WOMEN IN HIGHER EDUCATION

The current status of women in higher education can be analyzed from two perspectives: women as students and women as faculty members.[7] As shown in Figure 2-1, the percentage of women attending institutions of higher learning has increased dramatically since the 1950s. In the first four decades of this century, the percentages were higher than those in the two decades after World War II, suggesting that the 1950s and 1960s were "lost" decades for women with respect to higher education. This decrease in percentages can be explained in part by the increase in the number of men furthering their education (and taking advantage of the GI bill) after the war. In 1988-1989, women received 52.2 percent of all bachelor's degrees awarded, 51.9 percent of all master's degrees, and 36.5 percent of all doctorates. In 1969-1970, women received 43.0 percent of the bachelor's degrees, 39.7 percent of the master's degrees, and 13.3 percent of the doctorates that were awarded.

As Table 2-1 indicates, women's choices of major area of study have changed as well. Between 1978 and 1988, the percentages of women choosing to major in fields traditionally thought of as the domain of men (such as law and medicine) increased significantly.

With regard to women as faculty members, the results are somewhat mixed. The proportion of full-time female faculty members in all institutions of higher learning increased from 23 percent in 1969-1970 to 33 percent in 1987-1988. In general, the salaries of female faculty members at all

Figure 2-1 Women Enrolled in Higher Education, 1909-1989 (percent)

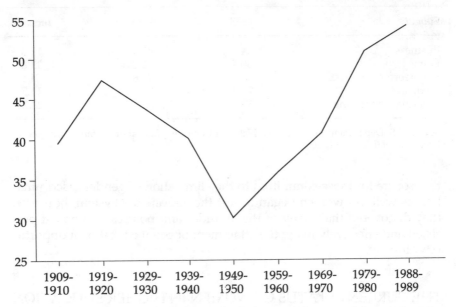

Source: U.S. Department of Education, National Center for Educational Statistics, *Digest of Educational Statistics, 1991,* 166.

levels were less than those of their male counterparts. In 1989-1990, for example, the average salary for females as a percentage of the average salary for the rank as a whole was 88.8 percent for professors, 93.3 percent for associate professors, 92.1 percent for assistant professors, and 86.9 percent for lecturers. Some of these discrepancies can be explained by differences in the number of years male and female faculty members remain in one rank as well as by differences in the percentages of male and female faculty members in the different disciplines. Variations in salary range by discipline can be significant. In 1988, women constituted approximately 45 percent of the faculty in education, 33 percent in the humanities, and 37 percent in agriculture and home economics, but only 28 percent in business, 17 percent in the natural sciences, and 2 percent in engineering.

What these statistics suggest is that women are making progress in higher education both as students and as faculty members. But there is still a long way to go in some areas, especially women's appointment to administrative-level positions (department chairs, deans, college presidents) in education. It should be remembered that in higher education, as in other fields of employment, there is generally a time lag between success at the entry level and success at the top. The successes we see now as increases in the number of women faculty members are a result of the increases in the number of women enrolled in college and teaching in various disciplines ten and fifteen years ago. One of the many hurdles that women must still overcome in higher education is gender discrimination, which is the subject of the next section.

DISCRIMINATION AGAINST WOMEN IN HIGHER EDUCATION

Women in higher education have experienced discrimination both as students and as faculty members. In general, discrimination against women as students has taken two forms. First are the institutional practices that have restricted their freedom of choice as it pertains to admission to schools, programs, and courses, as well as their eligibility for and receipt of financial assistance; and practices that have limited expenditures for programs separated on the basis of gender (specifically, sports programs). A second, more subtle (but perhaps more pervasive and more detrimental) form of discrimination against women derives from the traditional gender stereotypes that conditioned women students to seek careers and programs in certain areas but not in others (for example, women sought careers as nurses whereas men became doctors). Both forms of discrimination in higher education are the result of the interplay of four patterns of discrimination that exist in society: systemic, institutional, situational, and dispositional.[8] These patterns are evident in attitudes reflected in such statements as, "Why waste money educating women when they'll give up their careers after they get married?" and "I don't understand science and anyway, it's something boys are good at."

Systemic discrimination against women can be explained in part by the patriarchal nature of American society. Most major political figures are males (although more women have entered politics and won election to public office in recent years), as are most business executives and directors of large corporations. Although women are becoming more visible at higher levels of the educational system (Donna Shalala, secretary of the Department of Health and Human Services, was the first woman chancellor of a Big Ten university), teaching and administrative positions in institutions of higher learning are still dominated by men. Research suggests that faculty members treat female students differently than their male counterparts and that this differential treatment can have a cumulative effect that may "damage women's self-confidence, inhibit their learning and classroom participation, and lower their academic and career aspirations."[9] Such a patriarchal system provides few role models or opportunities for women interested in careers at the postsecondary level and tends to produce individual dispositions or attitudes that foster discriminatory practices against women.

Although public policies and institutional practices have begun to lessen institutional discrimination, it is still evident in admissions policies, financial aid practices, differential curricula, and personnel attitudes. Admissions practices have been patently discriminatory in some instances (single-gender institutions and quota policies) and subtle in others (institutions that discourage women from seeking admission to certain programs). Financial aid practices have been discriminatory in both type and amount of funds allocated. Discrimination has been particularly strong against married women and women pursuing their education on a part-time basis. Certain attitudes of university personnel have encouraged discriminatory practices against women by reinforcing societal stereotypes that define "suitable" programs and careers for women. The interplay of systemic and institutional discrimination has had an enormous impact on the attitudes of society and women concerning the proper role of women in society, their competence, and the relevance of higher education to women's lives.

Situational discrimination arises from expectations about the proper role of women in society. The traditional expectation that a woman's proper role was that of wife and mother constrained women's educational aspirations by encouraging women to raise a family rather than pursue a career and to defer the pursuit of an education and a career until after the children were raised. These role expectations have been strongly challenged by the women's movement and by the socioeconomic realities of contemporary life.

Dispositional discrimination against women as students has been reinforced by the dispositions of women themselves. Societal pressures and traditional gender-role stereotyping have created fears of failure and of success, feelings of passivity and dependence, ambivalence and lack of confidence with respect to educational aspirations and goals, and negative attitudes toward intellectual life in general. These dispositions have led to the continued pursuit of traditional careers and have been reinforced by educational institutions' replication of the discrimination in society, with the net result that women have been restrained from reaching their full educational and occupational potential.

In many respects, past discrimination against women as faculty members and administrators was the logical consequence of discrimination against women as students. The absence of role models in higher education; societal attitudes toward women with careers; and women's own attitudes toward their roles, their competence, and higher education's relevance, in combination with institutional and systemic discrimination, have limited women's access to higher education.

In recent years, the percentage of women in positions of authority in universities has begun to increase, although optimism in this regard should be tempered by the realization that before the passage, in 1972, of the landmark legislation known as Title IX (discussed in the next section), the percentage of women in positions of authority was abysmally low. Both the number of women college presidents and the number of women college administrators would double in the next ten years.[10] Women are still underrepresented in the upper ranks of the academic hierarchy (tenured associate professors and full professors, department chairs and program directors, deans, provosts, and presidents). However, the increase in the proportion of doctorates earned by women—from 16.0 percent of all doctorates awarded in 1972 to 35.4 percent of the total awarded in 1986—indicates that more women are pursuing careers in educational institutions, even though a larger proportion (52.5 percent in 1986 compared with 36.4 percent in 1972) now plan to use their degrees in noneducational fields.[11] These percentages provide some hope for the future, for if the percentage of women pursuing doctorates continues to increase, with the consequence that women will constitute an increasingly large proportion of the educational hierarchy, there will be more role models for women students, and more women will likely see university teaching and administration as attractive career options. An increase in the number of women holding positions of responsibility in the educational establishment will probably result in a lessening (and possibly the eventual elimination) of institutional discrimination against women.

WOMEN, EDUCATION, AND THE POLICY PROCESS

Until the early 1970s, there was no federal legislation protecting women students from gender discrimination (in terms of admissions, financial aid, and facilities) at any educational level. In that decade, however, various pieces of legislation were passed or amended to prohibit discrimination against women.

Title VII of the Civil Rights Act of 1964 was amended in 1972 to prohibit discrimination on the basis of gender at all levels of government and by all private employers, public and private educational institutions, and public and private employment agencies. The only type of discrimination that was allowed, and only in limited circumstances, was in occupational categories that could be closed to one of the sexes because of the nature of the work. Title VII established a presumption of discrimination if it could be demonstrated that any employment practice had a differential impact on persons of one sex. A 1972 amendment to the Equal Pay Act of 1963 extended its coverage to academic personnel. The Women's Educational Equity Act of 1974 created a series of programs to promote educational equity. It authorized the extension of grants and contracts to public agencies and private, nonprofit organizations that supported activities promoting educational equity, such as the training of personnel and the development of relevant materials; guidance and counseling; and the development and improvement of educational programs for adult women, especially those in the fields of vocational and educational administration. The act also established an Advisory Council on Women's Educational Programs in the Office of Education. The Public Health Services Act of 1975 prohibited gender discrimination in the admission of students to federally funded health services training programs. In 1976, the Vocational Education Act of 1963 was amended to require states receiving federal funds for vocational education programs to reduce barriers to vocational education caused by gender bias and stereotyping.

Although each of these public policies just discussed has contributed to the effort to reduce or eliminate gender discrimination in education, the major public policy instrument that changed and continues to change the relationship between women and institutions of higher learning is Title IX of the 1972 Higher Education Amendments to the Civil Rights Act of 1964. The history of this act, especially the adjudication of its implementation, demonstrates the extent to which politics and policy implementation can affect specific policy impacts and outcomes. The intended consequences of a piece of legislation may be blunted by the active obstruction or negligence of the current administration. Because the Reagan administration actively challenged the goals of Title IX and took a foot-dragging approach to its implementation, women's groups had to wage a four-year struggle to achieve equal educational opportunities.

Opponents of legislation establishing a policy can challenge it even after it has been passed; the main avenues for such challenges are the bureaucracy and the legal system. Within the bureaucracy, implementation and compliance procedures provide an opportunity for interested parties to comment on legislation and attempt to influence its effect. Within the legal system, opponents can challenge the legislation as a whole or in part, or they can challenge its applicability to specific individuals or institutions. Title IX was challenged both in the bureaucracy and in the legal system.

TITLE IX AND THE BATTLE OVER IMPLEMENTATION

The general prohibition of gender discrimination by educational institutions in Title IX aroused considerable controversy both within and outside the educational system. Although public attention was focused largely on the potential impact on intercollegiate and intramural sports programs, the legislation is sufficiently broad to have an important impact at virtually all levels of the educational system.

The provisions as originally enacted were very similar to those of Title IV of the Civil Rights Act of 1964, which barred federal aid to any institution that engaged in discrimination on the basis of race, creed, color, or national origin. Title IX empowered the Department of Health, Education, and Welfare (as it was then known) to revoke or delay funds to any institution that discriminated on the basis of gender. It also permitted the Department of Justice to file suit against any institution that refused to comply with the law. In effect, the provisions not only hit institutions where it would hurt the most—in the pocketbook—but put the full weight of the Department of Justice behind compliance.

In creating this legislation, Congress both provided some exemptions and made some omissions that have caused problems for women who seek admittance to certain types of institutions. Congress excluded from Title IX all institutions controlled by religious organizations whose fundamental beliefs are not compatible with gender equality, all military institutions whose major purpose is the training of individuals for the armed services or the merchant marine, and private undergraduate institutions. The arguments for these exclusions ranged from concerns about practical administrative feasibility to the desire to preserve an alternative educational institution's unique character. Many, including the Civil Rights Commission, argued that to allow these exemptions was to suggest that discrimination on the basis of gender was less invidious than discrimination based on race. The absence of specific provisions against gender stereotyping in text and curriculum materials (which can have a lasting influence on the individual dispositions and attitudes of women students) and against gender-specific scholarship and financial assistance led some to argue that Congress was again making a distinction between gender discrimination and racial discrimination that would hinder the elimination of the former from the educational system. The Department of Health, Education, and Welfare (HEW) suggested that to mandate the elimination of gender stereotyping could be construed as a restriction of the First Amendment right of freedom of speech and suggested that instead educators themselves should be the primary actors in the attempt to eliminate gender stereotyping from all forms of educational material. Their unwillingness to act would mean that its elimination might take decades and would occur only as more women progressed through the educational system and became primary actors.

In general, however, the thrust of Title IX was broad and powerful. Gender discrimination in vocational schools, graduate schools, and public coeducational undergraduate institutions was prohibited, and even schools that were exempted had to treat their admitted students equally.

Courses could not be provided separately to men and women. (There were a few exceptions, such as sex-education courses and physical education courses involving a contact sport.) The same prohibition applied to educational activities and athletic programs (scholastic, intramural, and intercollegiate). Providers of insurance benefits and plans could not discriminate on the basis of gender, nor (with some exceptions) could providers of financial assistance. Schools could not discriminate on the basis of pregnancy, although voluntary separate programs were allowed. Discrimination in counseling and employment was also prohibited.[12] Title IX was thus a significant step forward in the movement to achieve equal educational opportunities for women. The key to the success of any legislation, however, is the translation of policy objectives into effective action. At this implementation stage of the policy process, those who so wish may still subvert the policy's objectives.

In June 1974, HEW (the agency charged with implementing Title IX) published proposed regulations and solicited comments from the public. Many groups commented. A content analysis of the positions taken by significant groups in the field of education identified six major issues that could have important consequences for women either as students or as employees in the educational system; they concerned whether the regulations should (1) eliminate gender-bias from textbooks and curriculum materials; (2) prohibit all gender-specific courses except sex education courses; (3) prohibit gender-specific scholarship assistance; (4) require that permanent, part-time employees receive fringe benefits; (5) require that all categories of employees make equal contributions to retirement plans and be entitled to receive equal benefits; and (6) require that maternity leave be counted as a temporary disability.[13]

The position of the Women's Equity Action League (WEAL) on these six issues clearly reflected the position of most women's groups. In terms of scorecard notation, WEAL had won two (the prohibition of gender-specific courses and the requirement that maternity leave be counted as a temporary disability), lost two (elimination of textbook gender bias and equalization of retirement plans), and had minimal success on two (gender-specific scholarships and fringe benefits for permanent part-time employees).[14] Thus, by June 1975, women had made some progress in influencing the implementation of Title IX. The opposition that women would face, especially from parts of the educational establishment, arose primarily with respect to sports programs.

The sports issue is one of the most interesting for two reasons. First, any effort to change the distribution of resources for intercollegiate athletics strikes at the heart of what is and has always been a virtually all-male bastion within the educational establishment. Second, sports programs, especially at the intercollegiate level, require considerable financial resources. The proposal to require equivalence in expenditures created considerable consternation among schools with high-powered intercollegiate football programs. In December 1978, HEW issued new policy interpretations regarding Title IX and specifically its implications for intercollegiate athletics. According to a report issued by the Association of American Colleges in January 1979, an institution was presumed to be in compliance with Title IX if it could demonstrate that it (1) has "eliminated discrimination in financial support and other benefits and opportunities in its existing programs," and (2) "follows an institutional policy that includes procedures and standards for developing an athletic program that provides equal opportunity for men and women to accommodate their interests and abilities." [15] Whether discrimination in financial support had been eliminated would be determined by an assessment (by HEW) of whether the average per capita expenditures were substantially equal for those items that are "financially measurable" and for athletics. Although, on its face, the making of an average per capita expenditure calculation would appear to support the requirement of equal resources per participant, HEW allowed differences that were the result of "nondiscriminatory" factors such as the nature of the sport and differences in the "nature, level, and scope" of competition available. For those items not deemed financially measurable, comparable benefits and opportunities were required (equal access to facilities, tutoring programs, coaching, medical training services, and housing).

In addition to equalizing expenditures, to demonstrate compliance institutions had to establish and implement policies for accommodating increased interest in, and abilities relevant to, women's athletic programs. A school without such policies would have to demonstrate that it was already providing comparable opportunities at all levels, or that there was a pattern of increased participation by women at all levels, or that its athletic programs reflected regional growth or real growth patterns that influenced its manner of handling increased student interest. Again, if an institution was found to be not in compliance with the guidelines, it had to show that the disparities were caused by "nondiscriminatory factors."

According to the association's report, women's groups claimed that these interpretations gave institutions maximum flexibility to circumvent the attainment of equity in intercollegiate programs for women. They said the term "nondiscriminatory factors," including the idea of different natures, levels, and scopes of intercollegiate athletics for men and women, was so nebulous that "almost any discrepancy can be justified by the nature or level or scope of the competition concept." Women's groups also argued that the assumption that an institution is in compliance if it adopts a plan allows institutions to proceed so slowly that equity is never reached. The report stated: "Theoretically an institution can perpetually plan to increase opportunities for women, accomplish this at a very slow rate and still be in compliance." [16] The educational establishment is still dragging its feet in this area. Women constitute only about 31 percent of the students participating in athletic programs in Division I schools, but they constitute more than 50 percent of the student population. Moreover, women receive only 30 percent of all scholarship money, 23 percent of travel and game budgets, and only 17 percent of all funds allocated to recruitment.[17] Many athletic officials in the Division I schools cite the costs of football programs as the key to these inequities. They argue that since such programs include ninety-five scholarship players (far more than any other male or female sport) and are very costly, but also generate huge revenues, equity is impossible. Those who challenge this assertion argue that more than four-fifths of all Division I football programs lose money. At a time when colleges and universities throughout the United States are caught in a financial squeeze, it is difficult to see how they can come up with the money to equalize spending on women's sports, particularly when the educational establishment claims that women's sports programs do not have the following, and therefore do not have the gate receipts, of men's programs.

This argument points out another inequity. The lack of recognition of and support for women's sports programs and the virtual nonexistence of women's professional sports leagues means that few women athletes are able to parlay their college athletic experience into a professional career. One would think that the growing number of women involved in high school and college athletics would result in increased career opportunities, but women constituted a smaller proportion of women's sports coaches at the college level in 1992 (48.3 percent) than in 1978 (58.2 percent), and the number of women athletic administrators at major universities is minuscule. The fact that college athletics has been dominated by males makes it difficult for women to succeed. Donna Lopiano, the former women's athletic director at the University of Texas who is currently executive director of the Women's Sports Foundation, argues: "We have a tendency as employers to hire people who are like us. We are less likely to be able to hire blacks and women if we are white males. That's a situation we have to overcome." [18]

In summary, the ability of powerful groups within the educational establishment to utilize the traditionally slow implementation process to impede or prevent the development of timetables and regulations has hampered the movement to achieve equal opportunity for women in higher education. The less than enthusiastic Reagan administration also played a role, not only by foot-dragging in the implementation of policies but by instituting litigation to challenge Title IX.

POLICY ADJUDICATION: GROVE CITY COLLEGE'S CHALLENGE TO TITLE IX

A decision by the Supreme Court in February 1984 further complicated the picture with respect to equal educational opportunity for women.[19] Grove City College, a small Presbyterian institution in Pennsylvania, argued that since it received no federal funds other than those from the federal student assistance program (Pell grants), and since it had never discriminated against women, it did not have to comply with the regulations established to enforce Title IX and challenged the right of the Department of Education to enforce them. In effect, Grove City College challenged the implementation of Title IX but not necessarily its substance. The college refused to sign an assurance form that would have pledged it to comply with the Title IX regulations, claiming that signing the form would lead to excessive entanglement with the federal government. The college also challenged the appeals court's ruling that when the government furnished any college with indirect aid, the institution itself became the educational program in which discrimination or bias was prohibited.[20] The Supreme Court ruled 6-3 that Grove City College's interpretation was correct and that Title IX applied only to its student assistance program. The decision was perceived as a victory for the Reagan administration, which had argued that the Court should adopt this interpretation of the law.[21]

The *Grove City* decision raised many questions. Some argued that it would have minimal impact on the movement to achieve equal opportunity for women; others asserted that the ruling would mean less aggressive implementation of all antidiscriminatory provisions by institutions having programs that did not receive direct federal aid. A bill intended to reverse the impact of the Supreme Court's decision was defeated in the Republican-controlled Senate in October 1984, although it had passed the Democrat-controlled House by a vote of 375-32.[22]

With no legislation to direct it, the Office of Civil Rights of the Department of Education took a cautious approach to the enforcement of Title IX. Two years earlier, in *North Haven v. Bell*,[23] the Supreme Court had upheld the right of the Office of Civil Rights within the Department of Education (then the Department of Health, Education, and Welfare) to prohibit discrimination against women that related to their employment as teachers and administrators. But the Office of Civil Rights was reluctant to move forward in this new area because it was under increasing pressure from the Reagan administration. (Campaigning for president in 1980, Ronald Reagan had promised to eliminate the department as part of an effort to reduce the governmental bureaucracy.) Its reticence would have important consequences for cases arising from charges of discrimination

on the part of educational institutions. More than eight hundred complaints that had been filed were either dropped or narrowed because of
the Court's ruling.[24] Critics of the Department of Education contended that
it was purposely dragging its feet in the enforcement of antidiscrimination
laws. The combined effect of the Court decision, an unsympathetic administration, and a tentative administrative agency thus created a chilling
climate for attempts to achieve equal educational opportunity for women.

In the Court's decision, however, lay the seeds of successful mobilization against the *Grove City* decision. The decision had the effect of extending this new interpretation of federal government authority beyond gender discrimination and Title IX to legislation couched in similar language
that had prohibited discrimination against many groups in many settings.
Women thus found natural allies in many other groups that had suffered
discrimination. Formation of a coalition in support of legislation that
would later be known as the Civil Rights Restoration Act was difficult at
first because of the anticipated effect of such legislation on current policies
governing abortion, but a compromise was reached, and in the early
spring of 1988 Congress overrode a Reagan veto and passed the Civil
Rights Restoration Act by overwhelming margins (in the vote on the bill
itself, 75-14 in the Senate and 315-98 in the House; in the vote on the
override of the Reagan veto, 73-24 in the Senate and 292-133 in the
House).[25]

The passage of the legislation and the override of the presidential
veto were a big victory for women, but the acid test will be the vigor with
which the Office of Civil Rights reimplements Title IX and the aggressive-
ness with which women pursue equal educational opportunities through
bureaucratic, legislative, or (if necessary) legal channels.[26] Compounding
the problem for women is the current budget crisis, which makes new
initiatives highly problematic, especially those related to equity in sports
programs.[27]

LOOKING AHEAD

Although women have made strides in the effort to eliminate gender
discrimination in higher education, the task is far from complete. In such
areas as admissions policy, financial assistance, and the elimination of
single-sex courses, women's goals are approaching realization. Some
progress has been made toward the achievement of equal treatment for
women employees in the educational system, and athletic opportunities
for women, although far from equivalent, have increased dramatically. In
other areas, success is far less visible. The elimination of gender bias from
textbooks and curriculum materials, for example, is a step that has broad

implications for the elimination of gender discrimination in society as a whole. Such a change is particularly important in primary and secondary schools, where attitudes about the role of women and their relationship to society are developed and reinforced.

Curricular reform has been receiving some attention since the mid-1980s. A number of projects have recently explored the development of more gender-inclusive and multicultural curricula. The National SEED (Seeking Educational Equity and Diversity) Project on Inclusive Curriculum, for example, has organized seminars on this subject for more than 2,500 teachers from the kindergarten level through high school.[28] Many feminists have charged that the schools (particularly high schools and universities) are dominated by a male cultural standard that glorifies combat and competition, accepts if not promotes violence, and glorifies the individual as a warrior. What would happen if the schools' curriculum emphasized cooperation rather than conflict, the peaceful resolution of conflict rather than violence, and the individual as peacemaker rather than warrior? How might the high school or university curriculum be different if women's culture were the prevailing standard?

Nel Noddings suggests that the curriculum should reflect the perspectives of both men and women.[29] If women's perspectives were incorporated, similar changes would be made in such areas as citizenship education, history and the social sciences, and peace studies. In citizenship education, the emphasis on the rights of citizenship would be replaced by an emphasis on the obligations of individuals to their communities, including an obligation to exhibit "decent, responsible behavior in personal and family relationships." Noddings also argues that "if women's culture were taken more seriously in educational planning, social studies and history might have a very different emphasis. Instead of moving from war to war, ruler to ruler, one political campaign to the next, we would give far more attention to social issues." (Women's active role in many of the social reform movements of the last two centuries is often downplayed in traditional texts.) Noddings advocates an emphasis on peace and an ethic of care to replace the warrior notion that is central to the masculine culture: "social consciousness should be a central theme in social studies, literature, and science. And the study of peace must be extended beyond an analysis of nations at war to a careful and continuing study of what it means to live without the fear of violence." Such a change in the educational experience of both men and women, if implemented, could have important long-term consequences in many of the policy areas that affect women. Traditional textbooks often portray women as housewives and mothers and not as career professionals. Girls are passive and demure, whereas boys are clever, able to solve problems, and adventurous.[30] Certainly these characterizations do not reflect women's attitudes and behaviors today, or the careers available to women. Yet their continued usage provides negative stereotypes for children that may have lasting implications for the development of their role images and their educational and occupational aspirations.

But because of the nature of the problem, the protections afforded by the First Amendment, and the demonstrated reluctance of Congress and the courts to take any action to promote the eradication of negative gender stereotypes from textbooks and curriculum materials, such a change will probably require a long-term effort waged by women professionals within the educational establishment.

The elimination of gender discrimination in higher education thus depends on the tenacity with which women continue to pursue their objective of eliminating discriminatory practices in society as a whole. Although opportunities for women have increased dramatically, there are still areas influenced by past educational practices where women will have to be especially vigilant. They must still be encouraged to follow the example of Kristen W. Culler and consider traditionally male academic disciplines and fields of employment.

NOTES

1. James Brady, "In Step With: Kristen Culler," *Parade*, November 29, 1992.
2. The policies of educational institutions are being challenged in a wide variety of areas, including university admissions. In January 1994, Shannon Faulkner became the first woman to attend the Citadel, an all-male, state-run military college in South Carolina. Lower courts had ordered her admission to day classes but not to the corps of cadets or the barracks. The school, arguing that admission would destroy both its unique disciplinary environment and its educational mission, had asked the courts to intervene. On January 18, a temporary stay was granted, lifting an order that had prohibited Shannon Faulkner from attending classes. Another educational policy area is gender equity in sports. A number of women's sports teams at major (Division I) colleges and universities have filed lawsuits charging that the schools have failed to move toward gender equity in number of scholarships awarded, proportion of player opportunities in Division I sports, and quality of travel accommodations provided for players. The nature of the curriculum offered to students at various educational levels has also been challenged. See, for example, Madeleine R. Grumet, *Bitter Milk* (Amherst: University of Massachusetts Press, 1981); Mary Kay Thompson Tetreault, "The Journey from Male-Defined to Gender-Balanced Education," *Theory into Practice* 25 (Autumn 1986): 227-234; and Rebecca Grant, "The Sources of Gender Bias in International Relations Theory," in Rebecca Grant and Kathleen Newland, eds., *Gender in International Relations* (Bloomington: Indiana University Press, 1991), 8-26.

3. The following discussion of education as a good is drawn from Fred M. Frohock, *Public Policy: Scope and Logic* (Englewood Cliffs, N.J.: Prentice-Hall, 1978), 30.

4. Samuel Bowles and Herbert Gintis, "Schooling in Capitalist America," 1-14.

5. Barbara Matthews, "Women, Education, and History," *Theory into Practice* 15, no. 1 (February 1976): 47-48.

6. Ibid., 48.

7. All data in this discussion of women as students and as faculty members are from U.S. Department of Education, *National Center for Educational Statistics, Digest of Education Statistics,* (Washington, D.C.: Government Printing Office, 1991), 166, 221.

8. For an excellent discussion of these four patterns, see Ruth Eckstrom, "Barriers to Women's Participation in Post-Secondary Education: A Review of the Literature" (Princeton, N.J.: Educational Testing Service, 1972), 1-88.

9. Bernice R. Sandler, "The Classroom Climate for Women," in Sara E. Rix, ed., *The American Woman 1987-1988* (New York: Norton, 1987), 244.

10. Donna Shavlik and Judith G. Touchton, "Women in Higher Education," in ibid., 239.

11. Mariam K. Chamberlain, ed., *Women in Academe: Progress and Prospects* (New York: Russell Sage Foundation, 1991), 257.

12. This summary is abstracted from Margaret C. Dunkle and Bernice R. Sandler, "Sex Discrimination against Students: Implications of Title IX of the Educational Amendments of 1972," *Inequality in Education,* no. 3 (October 1974): 12-32.

13. For a full discussion of the analysis, see Andrew Fishel, "Organizational Positions on Title IX: Conflicting Perspectives on Sex Discrimination in Education," *Journal of Higher Education* 47, no. 1 (January-February 1976).

14. Ibid., 93.

15. Association of American Colleges, Project on the Status and Education of Women, "Update on Title IX and Sports, No. 2: HEW-Proposed Policy Interpretation Concerning Title IX and Athletics," ED 166 342, January 1979, 1.

16. Ibid., 3, 5.

17. Milton Kent, "Sports Still Falling Short on Gender Equity," *Dayton Daily News,* January 3, 1993, 9D.

18. Quoted in ibid.

19. *Grove City College v. Bell,* 465 U.S. 555 (1984).

20. In 1982, the appeals court had reversed the lower court ruling in *Grove City College v. Harris* (500 F. Supp. 253 [1980]).

21. "Supreme Court Rules Anti-Sex Bias Law Covers Only Programs that Get Direct U.S. Aid," *Chronicle of Higher Education* 28, no. 2 (March 7, 1984): 1.

22. "Bill to Overturn Grove City Rule Killed in Senate," *Chronicle of Higher Education* 29, no. 7 (October 10, 1984): 1.

23. *North Haven v. Bell,* 456 U.S. 512 (1982).

24. Courtney Leatherman, "Congress Overrides President's Veto of Civil Rights Bill, Countering High Court's 'Grove City' Decision," *Chronicle of Higher Education* 36, no. 29 (March 30, 1988): 1.

25. Leatherman, "Congress Overrides President's Veto," 24.
26. In June 1993, female athletes from four universities—Auburn, Brown, Colgate, and Temple—testified before the House Subcommittee on Commerce, Consumer Protection, and Competitiveness, chaired by Rep. Cardiss L. Collins (D-Ill.). They expressed their frustration concerning the limited opportunities they perceived to be available for female athletes. Representative Collins has proposed a bill that would require colleges to publish annual reports comparing their treatment of male and female athletes. See "Athletic Notes," *Chronicle of Higher Education* 39, no. 43 (June 30, 1993): A30.
27. The issue of equity for women in college athletics is especially problematic at the many universities with Division I football programs. With pressures to reduce college athletic budgets already requiring choices to be made between revenue-producing and non-revenue-producing sports, the additional problems posed by the goal of gender equity have generated talk of secession from the National Collegiate Athletic Association both by the College Football Association and by individual conferences. See Debra E. Blum, "Officials of Big-Time College Football See Threat in Moves to Cut Costs and Provide Equity for Women," *Chronicle of Higher Education* 39, no. 41 (June 16, 1993): A35; Douglas Lederman and Debra E. Blum, "It Wasn't on the Agenda, but Everyone Was Talking about Gender Equity," *Chronicle of Higher Education* 39, no. 20 (January 20, 1993): A46; and Debra E. Blum, "NCAA Urged to Find Stronger Incentives for Compliance with Gender-Equity Plan," *Chronicle of Higher Education* 39, no. 39 (June 2, 1993): A27.
28. Cathy L. Nelson, "The National SEED Project," *Educational Leadership* 49, no. 4 (December 1991-January 1992): 66-67.
29. This paragraph is based on Nel Noddings, "The Gender Issue," *Educational Leadership* 49, no. 4 (December 1991-January 1992): 65-70.
30. Doris Price, "Sexism in Instructional Materials," *Thrust for Educational Leadership*, no. 6 (October 1976), 7.

CHRONOLOGY

1972 Passage of the Higher Education Amendments to the Civil Rights Act of 1964. Title IX of these amendments, which were part of a series of amendments to the Higher Education Act of 1965, prohibits discrimination on the basis of gender at all levels of government and by all private employers.

1974 The Women's Educational Equity Act creates a series of programs to promote educational equity.

1975 The Public Health Services Act prohibits gender discrimination in the admission of students to federally funded health training programs.

1976 The Vocational Education Act of 1963 is amended to require states receiving funds for vocational education to reduce barriers created by gender bias and gender stereotyping.

1982 In *North Haven v. Bell*, the Supreme Court upholds the ability of the Office of Civil Rights of the Department of Education to ban discrimination against women in the employment of teachers and administrators.

1984 The Supreme Court's decision in *Grove City College v. Bell* challenges the federal government's power to withhold all financial aid from an institution for failure to comply with Title IX in one particular area. The decision is viewed as a threat to women's educational equity.

1988 The Civil Rights Restoration Act, passed over President Reagan's veto, restores the right of the federal government to withhold funds from an institution if any program or policy is found to be discriminatory.

SUGGESTIONS FOR FURTHER READING

Chamberlain, Mariam K., ed. *Women in Academe: Progress and Prospects.* New York: Russell Sage Foundation, 1991.

Davis, Diane, and Helen S. Astin. "Reputational Standing in Academe." *Journal of Higher Education* 58 (May-June 1987): 261-275.

Fishel, Andrew, and Janice Puttker, eds. *National Politics and Sex Discrimination in Education.* Lexington, Ky.: Lexington Books, 1977.

Furniss, W. Todd, and Patricia Albjerg Graham, eds. *Women in Higher Education.* Washington, D.C.: American Council on Education, 1974.

Hall, Roberta M., and Bernice Sandler. "The Classroom Climate: A Chilly One for Women?" Washington, D.C.: Project on the Status and Education of Women, Association of American Colleges, 1982.

Hearn, James C., and Susan Olzak. "The Role of College Major Departments in the Reproduction of Sexual Inequality." *Sociology of Education* 54 (1981): 195-205.

Klein, Susan J., ed. *Handbook for Achieving Sex Equality through Education.* Baltimore: Johns Hopkins University Press, 1985.

Rossi, Alice, and Ann Calderwood, eds. *Academic Women on the Move.* New York: Russell Sage Foundation, 1973.

Salamone, Rosemary. *Equal Education under Law.* New York: St. Martin's Press, 1986.

3

Women and Health Care Policy

Julie Kamper was the forty-four-year-old mother of three teenage children, a full-time store manager, wife, and community activist. While watching a television movie one evening with her family, Julie was stricken with a massive coronary and fell to the floor. She died a few hours later and was buried on what would have been her twenty-fifth wedding anniversary.

Julie's heart condition had not been diagnosed. She had led an active life and dismissed any signs of fatigue as the inevitable consequence. Unfortunately, Julie's fate is not unique among American women. Although heart disease continues to be the leading cause of death among women, little research has been done on how heart disease and its treatment affect them. Not until 1994, for example, was it confirmed that aspirin, for years known to reduce the risk of heart attack in men, would also help women. There is also the possibility that "good" cholesterol in men is "bad" for women and that dietary recommendations for lowering cholesterol may actually be harmful to women.[1]

Few areas of public policy in the United States are as complicated as those concerning women and health care or as illustrative of the relationship between culture and public policy. The complexity derives from a number of interrelated factors, including society's attitudes toward health and health care, differing views of the proper relationship between the government and free-market forces in the provision of health care, and the changing image of women in society. Moreover, health issues raise fundamental questions of justice. To what extent are individuals responsible for their own health? To what extent should society as a whole assume responsibility for health-related expenses? Such questions become even more critical when the focus is on the concerns of women and health policy.

WOMEN, CULTURE, AND PUBLIC POLICY ON HEALTH CARE

Women not only have the burden of childbearing but are penalized in some respects because the average woman is healthier and lives longer than the average man. Women also experience discrimination in that they are frequently denied access to better paying, more powerful positions in the health professions. To this day, women must deal with attitudes and health policies that have yet to recognize the particular needs of women.

The case of Julie Kamper is not unique. Women generally develop heart disease later in life than men, and the rate of heart disease among women is generally lower than that among men. As a result, physicians may not interpret women's health complaints as possible symptoms of heart disease and consequently may wait too long to begin treatment. Women referred to surgeons for bypass surgery, for example, are found to be much sicker, on average, than the males who are referred.[2]

ATTITUDES TOWARD HEALTH AND HEALTH CARE

Clearly, Americans' attitudes toward health and health care, like their attitudes concerning women, are shaped by cultural values and, in turn, shape the culture itself. What is defined as a health problem and who is viewed as having responsibility for that problem are just two of the questions that affect women and health policy. As discussed in Chapter 1, the social construction of the target population is an important factor in bringing culture and public policy together.

Health and health care are primary, variable, and divisible. Health constitutes a primary value to individuals, who want to feel good and function efficiently. Health is also a primary value to society; of particular importance is a healthy work force. As discussed later in this chapter, many private health care systems are available to individuals in their workplaces, but a disproportionate number of those not receiving such coverage are women.

Health varies among both individuals and groups. Some individuals, whether because of differences in diet, access to health care, genetic makeup, personal habits, or living conditions, have better health than others and therefore require less care. In this respect, the position of women in society has a direct bearing on their health. Poor women, for example, have less access to the kind of diet that has been shown to prevent disease. Some diseases or conditions are group-specific because of biological differences (breast cancer in women and sickle-cell anemia in blacks) or behavioral differences (black lung disease in coal miners and lung cancer in smokers). Distinctions can be made between economically necessitated behavior (a miner needs to make a living) and optional or pleasurable behavior (a smoker likes to have a cigarette). Pregnancy is an interesting group-specific condition because it is a biological difference, is behaviorally induced, and may or may not be of benefit to society. These differences in the causes of diseases and conditions are an important consideration if the argument is made that government has a responsibility to pay for the treatments of certain kinds of medical problems. (It might be argued, for example, that since society needs miners, the government should bear the cost of treating health problems that result from such employment. Smokers should assume responsibility for their own condition.) Many of women's health problems fall into this category.

Health care is a divisible good that can be allocated to some individuals at the expense of others. Although illness can result from personal contact among individuals in public places (causing spread of contagious viruses), and large-scale government action (such as massive inoculation programs) can be taken to benefit the whole society, health is also affected by individual behavior and subject to individual treatment. To complicate the matter, some individuals' health problems are a result of the actions of others (passive smoking). This situation poses questions regarding responsibility in the event that society, which may be causing or contributing to the condition, is unable to bear the cost of its treatment. Such distinctions are particularly important in a society whose health care system operates primarily according to market principles.

HEALTH CARE AS A WOMEN'S ISSUE

In the United States, health care has traditionally been considered a gender-neutral policy area. Clearly, it is not. On the average, white women outlive white men by 6.2 years, and black women outlive black men by 8.5 years.[3] As a group, women spend more time in nursing homes and visit health care practitioners more frequently than men do. (In 1990, women, who constitute 51 percent of the nation's population, made 60 percent of all visits to physicians.)[4] Consequently, women's health care costs more than men's.[5] Furthermore, for the most part, American women have primary responsibility for birth control and child care; their lives are significantly affected by decisions concerning prenatal care and abortion. Disproportionately represented among the ranks of the poor and the elderly, women are more dependent than men on government assistance for health care.

Health care is clearly a women's issue. Changes in health policy do not impact equally on men and women, and viewing health care questions as gender neutral unfairly penalizes women for their biological difference and cultural role.

What accounts for the relative absence of women's voices from public debate about the making and implementation of health care policy? The answer can be found in American society's traditional attitudes concerning women, the influence of the medical profession in public policy making, and women's roles in the field of health care.

Society's attitudes have been influenced to a large extent by the nineteenth-century image of frail, sickly women that was promoted within the medical profession. Middle-class women, whose husbands were more able to pay for medical care, were viewed as more frail and thus more in need of care than their working-class counterparts, who had fewer resources.[6] As the culture's image of women has changed, so has the image of women that has guided the medical profession. Indeed, changes in the medical profession itself, discussed in the following paragraphs, have contributed to the changing image of women.

Physicians have also had an extraordinary influence on the development and implementation of health care policy. Medical questions have often been viewed as requiring decisions that should be made by the "experts." Underrepresented among physicians (as well as among lawmakers), women have had little influence on health care policy; that is, they have not been active participants in the making of decisions concerning their own health care. The male-dominated American Medical Association (AMA) has significantly affected the making of health care policy. The AMA is generally regarded as one of the best organized and most effective lobbying groups, whose efforts have been facilitated by the extensive financial resources available to physicians and their perceived expertise.

The extent of women's employment in the health professions is deceptive. Approximately 75 percent of all health care positions are currently held by women, but they are concentrated in the low-paying, service-oriented jobs associated with the traditional roles of women—a reflection of both past discrimination and societal attitudes towards women's "proper" role of nurturers and supporters. In contrast, the positions in the health care system held primarily by males—physicians and administrators—are associated with traditional male roles of managing and decision making.[7] The channeling of women into the least desirable and least powerful positions has increased the dominance of men in the health professions and in the hierarchy responsible for making health care policy. The pattern has begun to change, however, as a result of both changing ideas of what is "appropriate" behavior for women and the elimination of barriers to medical education. Title IX of the Higher Education Amendments of 1972 and the Public Health Services Act of 1975 outlawed gender discrimination in medical school admissions. Since 1975, the number of female physicians has more than doubled.[8]

Clearly, the answer to the question of why women's voices have been relatively absent from public debate and action in the field of health care policy is complex. Traditional societal attitudes toward women and their health problems have muted women's voices. Discrimination has prevented women from occupying positions of authority in the health care field. The relative strength of the medical profession in determining health care policy has magnified the problem, resulting in the creation of a public policy that affects women but over which they have little control and to which they have little input.

GAINING A PLACE ON THE PUBLIC POLICY AGENDA

Only since the late 1960s have the specific health care needs of women become part of the public policy agenda. The Sheppard-Towner Act of 1921 addressed the health care needs of women, but only in their traditional roles as mothers and nurturers of children. In fact, prior to the depression of the 1930s, health care was largely a personal or family matter. Individuals, families, and private charities paid health care costs. The passage of the Social Security Act in 1935 marked the entry of the federal government into the field of domestic social policy, as well as the failure of efforts to obtain enactment of legislation that included a national health insurance plan. Health care was still not significantly addressed; policy makers continued to treat it as a gender-neutral area, an approach whose consequences are being felt even today by many women, particularly the elderly and the poor. Two key federal health programs, Medicare and Medicaid, became law in 1965 as amendments to the Social Security Act.[9] Congress in that year had two female senators and ten female representatives,[10] and women as a group received no special consideration.

Anything affecting Medicare and Medicaid continues to impact women more than men. Reductions in these programs hurt women more than men because women are disproportionately represented among the poor and the elderly. A 1992 study indicates that almost 60 percent of the Americans over 65 years of age are female, and among the elderly, women are twice as likely as men to be poor.[11] According to the Census Bureau, 14.2 percent of the nation's population now lives below the official government poverty level; the percentage increases to 35.6 percent for members of female-headed households in which no spouse is present.[12]

Women's health care began to be recognized as a legitimate policy area shortly after the establishment of Medicare and Medicaid. In the late 1960s, feminists organized themselves into a number of interest groups that succeeded in defining health care as a women's issue and in placing women's health issues on the policy agenda. These groups included the National Organization for Women (NOW) and the Women's Equity Action League, which have since been joined by the National Women's

Health Network, the National Breast Cancer Coalition, the National Black Women's Health Project, the National Latina Health Organization, the Native American Women's Health Education Resource Center, and the Asian Health Project. As a direct result of pressure exerted by the Congressional Caucus for Women's Issues, the National Women's Health Network, and similar groups, in 1991 the National Institutes of Health (NIH) created the Office of Research on Women's Health to ensure that women are included in medical research funded by the federal government. (Previously, such research was conducted only on male subjects.) The National Breast Cancer Coalition also achieved a significant victory in 1992 when Congress increased the funding for breast cancer research.

CONTEMPORARY WOMEN'S HEALTH ISSUES AND THE POLICY-MAKING PROCESS

A number of women's health care issues are currently receiving attention in the policy-making process. The two discussed in this section are representative and illustrate the connection between culture and public policy on women's health discussed in the previous section.

HEALTH CARE FINANCING

Health care today is big business. In 1990, health expenditures in the United States constituted 12.2 percent of the gross national product and totaled more than $650 billion. Moreover, health care costs continue to rise at a faster rate than other expenditures. The largest proportion of health care expenditures—almost 40 percent—is for hospital care. Large sums are spent on the major federal health care programs; Medicaid and Medicare together pay for 28 percent of national health expenditures.[13]

Because the delivery of health care can be profitable, corporations have been attracted to it, especially since the introduction of Medicare and Medicaid. The declining importance of independent physicians and small private hospitals and the growth of large, profit-motivated businesses has had a significant effect on health care. The "corporatization" or "privatization" of health care began in connection with nursing homes and hospitals, whose expenses were reimbursable through Medicare and Medicaid. Many corporations have now expanded to include health maintenance organizations (HMOs), resulting in the creation of a "medical-industrial complex."[14]

Ironically, the corporations that were able to expand because they could depend on the "guaranteed" customers of Medicare and Medicaid now consider these patients less attractive than patients with private health insurance because of the limitations on reimbursements for certain services under these programs. Some hospitals owned by private corporations accept Medicare and Medicaid patients reluctantly and in some instances only when relatively few private patients are awaiting care.[15] Since women are more dependent on Medicare and Medicaid than men, this trend does not bode well for them. Unless major changes are made in the health care delivery and insurance systems, the gap between the quality of health care provided to those who can pay and to those who must rely on government assistance may widen as corporations assume responsibility for a larger part of the health delivery system. The poor and the elderly may have less access to the latest medical technology, for example. As one observer has pointed out, the cutbacks in public financing for health care, coming at the same time as the rise of corporations, will most likely only intensify the two-class system in medical care.[16]

The desire of federal and state governments to control their health care expenditures has prompted proposals for changes in Medicare or Medicaid such as requiring higher user payments or reducing the services provided. The failure to concentrate instead on expansion of the financial base to ensure the sound operation of these programs will affect more women than men—in part because men eligible for Medicare are likely to be covered by private health insurance benefits that were provided during their years of employment. Women may have been denied access to jobs that provided these benefits or may have been fulfilling other roles that society views as necessary (mother or homemaker) and thus are more likely to depend now on Medicare and Medicaid. Moreover, since states have flexibility in setting eligibility requirements for Medicaid, poor women receive different treatment in different parts of the country. The eligibility standards of almost half of the states are more restrictive than they would be if those states observed the federal guidelines for defining poverty. In addition, some states limit the number of yearly visits to the doctor covered by Medicaid, which can have serious implications for women in need of prenatal care. Ironically, the young women with high-risk pregnancies who are most in need of medical help (those from low-income and minority groups) are least likely to be covered by private health insurance or adequately covered by Medicaid. Of the 56 million women of childbearing age in the United States, 14.5 million (26 percent) are not covered for maternity services; 9 million of these women have no health insurance and 5 million have no coverage for prenatal or obstetrical care.[17] About one-fourth of the pregnant women between the ages of 20 and 40 lack maternity coverage because of the waiting period required by some health insurance.[18] The unpaid medical bills of the uninsured are primarily those of maternity cases.[19]

In 1990, private health insurance paid thirty-three cents of every dollar spent for health care in the United States.[20] Women's access to private insurance is determined largely by their employment and marital status, however. Many women are denied access because they are poor and either unemployed (which they are more likely than men to be) or not covered by private health insurance provided by their own or their spouses' employers.

Moreover, women who are not in the work force on a full-time basis are not eligible for a company's health plan. Some women have low-paying jobs that do not provide health insurance, yet their income is not low enough to make them eligible for government programs.[21] Divorced women seem to be particularly likely to have problems linked to a lack of health insurance. They are about twice as likely as married women, and more likely than widows or never-married single women, to be without health insurance.[22]

Men and women pay different rates for life, health, and auto insurance as well as for retirement annuities. They also receive different levels of benefits. Women as a group spend more time in hospitals than men; the insurance industry argues that the higher rates charged women are simply commensurate with the benefits they receive. The industry also contends that women benefit from the higher rates charged young males for auto insurance and that women's groups' demands for gender-neutral insurance would ultimately work against women rather than for them. (Gender-neutral insurance is explored in detail in Chapter 6.)

Women's groups such as NOW and the Women's Equity Action League argue that these differences in insurance rates and coverage are an example of economic discrimination. To date, their attempts to persuade Congress to enact legislation to correct this and other serious inequities have failed, although certain Supreme Court decisions (discussed in Chapter 6) have not precluded the possibility.

Gender-neutral insurance raises a number of difficult questions regarding women and health policy to which there are no clear answers. Should men and women be treated equally as a matter of policy, or should women receive special consideration in acknowledgment of the particular contribution they make to society in their role as childbearers? A society must reproduce itself to survive, but to what extent should society share in the financial burden that role places on women? Should women be treated as members of a gender group, or should they be viewed strictly as individuals (as proposed by the proponents of gender-neutral insurance)? Those who oppose reductions in Medicare and Medicaid benefits point out that these programs affect the poor and the elderly and therefore a disproportionate number of women, particularly mothers and providers of child care. The defenders of gender-neutral insurance make a strong case, however, that women should be treated as individuals and that gender should not be a relevant characteristic when determining the costs and benefits of insurance.

One suggestion that would essentially make the question of gender-neutral health insurance moot is the idea of national health insurance.[23] In part, the impact of such a plan on women would depend on its scope. Some have suggested that it cover only one group—the elderly, or mothers and children, or the poor. Since women live longer than men and need more health care, the argument has also been made that they should pay more for national health insurance than men.[24]

What kinds of services would be covered by national health insurance? Would it cover nursing home care and doctors' visits? What would be the deductible and out-of-pocket expenses? Would it replace, complement, or supplement private health insurance and government plans such as Medicare and Medicaid? Would it be voluntary or mandatory? To what extent would the consumer participate in decision making?[25] There are other questions of special interest to women. Would the plan include preventive services such as Pap smears and birth control? What about counseling for victims of rape and other forms of physical abuse? If national health insurance were provided only to the poor and the elderly, it would affect women more than men. As Theda Skocpol has pointed out, plans "geared only to stably employed wage earners overlook the needs of many women and children."[26] Clearly, any discussion of alternatives should include consideration of women's issues.

ISSUES CONCERNING REPRODUCTION

The ability of women to control their reproductive lives is a major cultural change that allows women to take advantage of the educational and employment opportunities now available to them. The policy agenda with regard to women's health care includes a wide range of reproductive issues: contraception and abortion, fetal protection policies, government funding for research in obstetrics and gynecology, and the rising birth rate among unwed teens.

Since most health care in the United States is provided by private physicians, most of whom are specialists, cost largely determines women's access to reproductive health care. Governmental programs such as Medicaid and Medicare, along with clinics, make health care available to those unable to afford it and those who do not have access to private physicians.[27] Currently, the single most preferred form of contraception in the United States is sterilization. Compared with European women, American women have few contraceptive options. In part, this is a result of the climate created by the anti-abortion forces opposed to birth control, which has made research on contraception unattractive to American companies. In addition, the high cost of many contraceptives limits women's access to them. (In the United States, a form of contraception is made available to the public only if it is offered by a private company and approved by the Food and Drug Administration.) The costs of contraceptives are inflated because of high fees for product liability insurance and potentially high liability costs, such as those of the lawsuits stemming from problems with intrauterine devices (the Dalkon shield).[28] It is estimated that 12 percent of the women aged 15-44 who could become pregnant use no contraception and that this 12 percent is responsible for almost half of the unintended pregnancies.[29]

The American culture does not encourage the use of contraception. In 1873, Anthony Comstock, convinced that contraception was immoral and obscene, succeeded in his effort to have Congress pass a law prohibiting both the importation and sale of birth control devices and written material about them (or about birth control generally) across state lines. A number of states followed the federal example and passed their own versions of the "Comstock law." In 1912 Margaret Sanger began her campaign to counter "comstockery." Although she never succeeded in getting Congress to pass a law repealing the Comstock Act, she did begin to change public attitudes about birth control and women's right to control their reproductive lives.

It was not until 1965, in *Griswold v. Connecticut*,[30] that the Supreme Court recognized a married couple's right to privacy with regard to their sexual behavior and eliminated the ban on their use of contraception. In its decision in *Eisenstadt v. Baird* (1972),[31] the Court extended the right of privacy in decisions concerning contraception to unmarried couples.[32]

The controversy over contraception has not been as emotionally intense as that over abortion. Supporters of freedom of choice argue that women have a right to control their own bodies and to make the decision whether to bear a child. Defenders of the right to life position argue that abortion is murder and that it threatens the very foundation of the American family. The abortion issue arouses deeply felt passions about the family, religion, motherhood, and the right of a husband or lover to have a "say" about a woman and her unborn child.

Predictably, the two national political parties have split over the abortion issue. In the 1992 presidential campaign, the Republican party platform supported a constitutional amendment prohibiting abortion; the Democratic platform opposed it. The National Women's Political Caucus and the National Abortion Rights Action League are two of the groups supporting a freedom of choice position. Right to life supporters have been joined by a number of religious organizations including the Catholic church and the Moral Majority.

In 1973 the Supreme Court ruled in *Roe v. Wade*[33] that a woman has a constitutional right to an abortion during the first three months of pregnancy and that the right of privacy includes the decision to have an abortion, although the state's "compelling interest" in regulating abortion increases after the first trimester.[34] The Court upheld this decision later the same year in *Doe v. Bolton*.[35] In 1983, in *Akron v. Akron Center for Reproductive Health*,[36] the Supreme Court held unconstitutional certain portions of the regulation adopted by Akron, Ohio, in 1978 that some had viewed as a model of abortion regulation. The Court did, however, uphold some aspects of other state regulations concerning abortion.[37]

In 1989, the Court ruled in *Webster v. Reproductive Health Services*[38] that states may regulate abortions even during the first trimester, and in 1992, in *Planned Parenthood of Southeastern Pennsylvania v. Casey*,[39] the Court replaced the trimester condition of *Roe* with an "undue burden" test. In *Casey*, the Court ruled that spousal notification was an undue burden but that a twenty-four-hour waiting period, informed consent requirements, parental consent requirements, and reporting requirements were not.

Even before the decision in *Webster*, restrictions existed on women's access to abortion. In 1976, Representative Henry Hyde (R-Ill.) succeeded in attaching a provision to an appropriations bill that forbade or severely limited the use of federal funds for abortion; it permitted the expenditure of such funds only in cases in which the mother's life was in danger. The Hyde Amendment has been in effect in some form since then. It affects women on Medicaid as well as those dependent on the military health care system, but not women who have access to private funds or private insurance. The anti-abortion forces had attempted to prevent the expenditure of Medicaid funds for abortions since 1974, but the Hyde Amendment was their first significant victory. In 1980 the Supreme Court, in *Harris v. McRae*,[40] held the Hyde Amendment to be constitutional. Since 1981, it has been the policy of the federal government, as well as a majority of the states, that public funds can be used for abortion only when the pregnancy endangers the mother's life. In December 1993, the Clinton administration ordered states to pay for Medicaid abortions for poor women in cases of rape or incest, or when there is a threat to the woman's life. This is a significant departure from past practice and is opposed by abortion foes.

In 1991, in *Rust v. Sullivan*,[41] the Supreme Court upheld the "gag rule," which prohibited personnel in federally funded family planning clinics from providing information or counseling about abortion.[42] By executive order on January 22, 1993 (the twentieth anniversary of *Roe v. Wade*), President Clinton formally repealed the gag rule. Many proponents of a woman's right to choose support passage of the proposed freedom of choice act, which would make the principles of *Roe* apply to all women in the United States.[43] Some groups, such as NOW, however, are on record as supporting such legislation only if it permits federal funding for abortions for poor women and contains no restrictions on access to abortion by unmarried minors. In many respects, state policy on abortions has preceded federal policy. Prior to *Roe v. Wade,* some states permitted an abortion if it was performed to save the woman's life or if her physical or mental health was endangered. Since the *Webster* decision, the states have become the major arenas of policy making on the abortion issue and will likely continue to be important unless some form of the proposed freedom of choice act is signed into law.

The "abortion pill," RU-486, has not been approved for sale in the United States. Supporters of RU-486 believe that the controversy over abortion would be lessened if RU-486 were to become an option. Opposition from the conservative right is largely responsible for the continued unavailability of RU-486 for use by American women, but this situation might change since testing of the drug is supported by President Clinton.

POLICY SILENCES

The health system is in need of repair. There is too little coordination and not enough maximization of available technology. Federal health policies and programs are fragmented and at times in conflict with one another.[44] Interagency squabbling and assertion of territoriality are not uncommon in matters of health care delivery, such as in vitro fertilization.[45] Because the federal government has remained silent on the issue of in vitro fertilization research, the private sector and the medical establishment have assumed responsibility for the decisions in this critical area. The in vitro fertilization clinics that do operate in the United States are not guided by any federally funded research and operate in a patchwork climate of private regulation and limited state laws.[46]

Society's attitudes are changing in respect to both women and the health professions. Currently, AMA membership is 83 percent male and 17 percent female. If it wishes to retain its influence, the AMA will have to increase its appeal to women doctors as their number increases. In 1990, women constituted 36 percent of the total medical school enrollment.[47]

More emphasis is being placed on self-care, an approach to women's health care supported in *Our Bodies, Ourselves,* the "bible" of grass-roots efforts for the empowerment of women in health-related matters.[48] Women increasingly have turned to self-care gynecology and clinics to circumvent the sexism they encountered in the male-dominated medical profession.[49] Renewed interest in home birth is another example of the impact of the self-care movement.

As noted, women have not been routinely included in studies on heart disease. This is also true of major research studies on AIDS. Between

1986 and 1990, AIDS spread twice as fast among women as among men.[50] Over two-thirds of the AIDS cases among women are reported by those aged 20 through 39—childbearing years, when there is the additional risk of a mother passing the virus to her unborn child.[51]

Public policy must also begin to focus on the intersections of gender, race, age, and class and how they affect women's health. Black women, for example, are less likely than white women to be diagnosed as having breast cancer but are more likely to die of the disease.[52] Interestingly, black women are far more likely than white women to perform breast self-examinations at least once a week, but black women are less likely than white women to have a breast examination by a physician or a periodic mammogram.[53] Older women of any race are less likely than younger women to perform breast self-examinations, to have breast examinations by physicians, or to have periodic mammograms.[54] To what extent are these differences related to differences in access to health care services and to what extent should these issues be addressed by public policy?

Data regarding women's access to prenatal care demonstrate the necessity for greater recognition among policy makers of the diversity of women's health care needs as well as of the importance they should have on the public agenda. One-quarter of all women have no prenatal care during the first trimester of pregnancy. Among African-American and Hispanic women, however, the percentage can exceed 40 percent.[55] Lack of prenatal care, due in large part to policy silences concerning the diversity of women's needs, threatens the health of both the mother and the child and results in less healthy babies and higher health and social welfare costs later in the child's life.

The continued increase in women's political influence—as voters, candidates, officeholders, and lobbyists—will affect the future of health care policy in the United States. Women are more likely than men to support the idea that the federal government should require employers to provide health insurance. Working women of the baby boom generation are most likely to support increased government spending for long-term health care. Two-thirds of the women, in contrast to half of the men, worry about the consequences to themselves of health care costs, particularly long-term costs such as nursing home care. They see themselves as likely to be responsible for the care of elderly parents and grandparents and in the future to be in need of such care themselves.[56]

Female state legislators are more likely to work on health care bills than are their male colleagues, and they are more likely to see to it that women's health concerns are prominent on the policy agenda.[57] They also give priority to health care issues more frequently than do male legislators.[58] Changes in societal attitudes about women's roles and about health care will no doubt increase women's ability to influence health policy decisions. Women are becoming more informed consumers of health care. They must utilize their increasing political influence to encourage policy makers to adopt approaches that recognize women's diverse health care needs.

NOTES

1. The results of research focusing only on men are discussed in Leonard Abramson, "Uncaring Women's Health," *New York Times,* May 14, 1990, A17; Andrew Purvis, "A Perilous Gap," *Time,* Fall 1990, 66-67; Joan O'C. Hamilton and Peter Hong, "When Medical Research Is for Men Only," *Business Week,* July 16, 1990, 33; Joanne Silberner and Dorian R. Friedman, "Health: Another Gender Gap," *U.S. News & World Report,* September 24, 1990, 54-55; and "New Aspirin Study Has Good News, Bad News," *Cleveland Plain Dealer,* January 7, 1994, 4-C.

2. For discussions of some issues concerning heart disease, see Barbara Berney, "In Research, Women Don't Matter," *Progressive,* October 1990, 27; Sally Squires, "A Look at Research Involving Women," *Washington Post,* December 12, 1990, 9; Jerry E. Bishop, "Study Finds Doctors Tend to Postpone Heart Surgery for Women, Raising Risk," *Wall Street Journal,* April 16, 1990, B4.

3. Paula Ries and Anne J. Stone, eds., *The American Woman, 1992-1993: A Status Report* (New York: Norton, 1992), 216.

4. Cynthia Murray Taeuber, ed., *Statistical Handbook of Women in America* (Phoenix: Oryx Press, 1991), 221, 246. See also National Center for Health Statistics, *Healthy People 2000 Review* (Hyattsville, Md.: U.S. Public Health Service, 1993), 120.

5. *Health U.S., 1985* (Washington, D.C.: Department of Health and Human Services, 1985), 9.

6. Barbara Ehrenreich and Deidre English, *Complaints and Disorders,* Glass Mountain Pamphlet no. 2 (New York: Feminist Press, 1973).

7. For a discussion of historical trends in the employment of women in health care, see Susan Reverby, "Health: Women's Work," in *Prognosis Negative: Crisis in the Health Care System,* ed. David Kotelchuck (New York: Vintage Books, 1976), 171. In 1988, 20 percent of the physicians, 94.6 percent of the registered nurses, 98.7 percent of the dental assistants, and 9.3 percent of the dentists in the United States were women. See Sara E. Rix, ed., *The American Woman, 1990-91: A Status Report* (New York: Norton, 1990), 384.

8. Janet Bickel, "Women in Medical School," in Rix, *The American Woman, 1990-91,* 212.

9. Medicare is a pay supplement to social security for the elderly that is designed to help them pay the costs of institution-provided medical care. Medicaid is a public assistance program funded out of federal revenues that is designed to assist states in providing medical benefits to the indigent.

10. Congressional Quarterly, *Congress and the Nation,* vol. 4 (Washington, D.C.: Congressional Quarterly, 1977), 8.

11. Ries and Stone, *The American Woman, 1992-1993,* 211, 405.
12. U.S. Department of Commerce, Bureau of the Census, Current Population Reports, Series P-60, no. 181, *Poverty in the United States: 1991* (Washington, D.C.: Government Printing Office, 1992), 1-2.
13. Katharine R. Levit, Helen C. Lazenby, Cathy A. Cowan, and Suzanne W. Letsch, "National Health Expenditures, 1990," in *Health Care Financing: Review,* Fall 1991, 29-54.
14. Paul Starr, *The Social Transformation of American Medicine* (New York: Basic Books, 1982), 428-429.
15. Ibid., 435-436.
16. Ibid., 448.
17. House Committee on Ways and Means, Subcommittee on Health, *Health Insurance for Children and Pregnant Women,* serial no. 101-78, March 20, 1990, 2, 50.
18. Department of Health and Human Services, *Women and National Health Insurance: Where Do We Go from Here?* Secretary's Advisory Committee on the Rights and Responsibilities of Women (Washington, D.C.: Department of Health and Human Services, 1980), 8.
19. *Health Insurance: An Overview of the Working Uninsured* (Washington, D.C.: General Accounting Office, 1989), 36.
20. Levit et al., "National Health Expenditures, 1990," 29.
21. Department of Health and Human Services, *Women and National Health Insurance,* 7.
22. Marc L. Berk, *Women and Divorce: Health Insurance Coverage, Utilization, and Health Care Expenditures* (Rockville, Md.: Department of Health and Human Services, 1984), 3.
23. The managed competition plan supported by the Clinton administration is not a plan for national health insurance, but would permit individual states to adopt a state version of it.
24. Department of Health and Human Services, *Women and National Health Insurance,* 9.
25. Ibid., 4.
26. Theda Skocpol, *Protecting Soldiers and Mothers: The Political Origins of Social Policy in the United States* (Cambridge, Mass.: Harvard University Press, Belknap Press, 1992), 537.
27. Elise F. Jones, Jacqueline Darroch Forrest, Stanley K. Henshaw, Jane Silverman, and Aida Torres, *Pregnancy, Contraception, and Family Planning Services in Industrialized Countries: A Study of the Alan Guttmacher Institute* (New Haven, Conn.: Yale University Press, 1989), 78.
28. Ibid., 89.
29. Ibid., 114.
30. *Griswold v. Connecticut,* 381 U.S. 479 (1965).
31. *Eisenstadt v. Baird,* 405 U.S. 438 (1972).
32. For an in-depth discussion of these issues, see chapter 4 of Dorothy McBride Stetson, *Women's Rights in the U.S.A.* (Pacific Grove, Calif.: Brooks/Cole, 1991).
33. *Roe v. Wade,* 410 U.S. 113 (1973).
34. *Roe v. Wade* has had an effect on the number of abortions performed annually

in the United States, as well as the number of deaths resulting from abortion. In the year prior to *Roe*, approximately 600,000 legal abortions were performed. In 1980, there were 1,553,900. The number of deaths declined from 4.1 per 100,000 abortions in 1972 to 3.4 in 1973 to 0.5 in 1978. *Congressional Quarterly Weekly Report*, June 18, 1983, 1248.

35. *Doe v. Bolton*, 410 U.S. 179 (1973).
36. *Akron v. Akron Center for Reproductive Health*, 462 U.S. 416 (1983).
37. *Congressional Quarterly Weekly Report*, June 18, 1983, 1248.
38. *Webster v. Reproductive Health Services*, 492 U.S. 49 (1989).
39. *Planned Parenthood of Southeastern Pennsylvania v. Casey*, 112 S. Ct. 2791, 120 L. Ed. 2d 674 (1992).
40. *Harris v. McRae*, 448 U.S. 297 (1980).
41. *Rust v. Sullivan*, 111 S. Ct. 1759, 114 L. Ed. 2d 233 (1991).
42. The Bush administration issued a modified "gag rule," effective October 1, 1992, that exempted clinic physicians from the ban on abortion counseling and referral. On November 4, 1992, a federal appeals court, basing its decision on narrow procedural grounds, invalidated the modified ban. This effectively ended the gag rule. President-elect Clinton opposed the gag rule. *New York Times*, November 4, 1992, A1, A10.
43. For a fuller discussion of this topic, see Barbara Hinkson Craig and David M. O'Brien, *Abortion and American Politics* (Chatham, N.J.: Chatham House, 1993).
44. Robert R. Alford, *Health Care Politics* (Chicago: University of Chicago Press, 1975), 228.
45. Wendy Noble suggested this point.
46. Andrea L. Bonnicksen, *In Vitro Fertilization: Building Policy from Laboratories to Legislatures* (New York: Columbia University Press, 1989), 82.
47. Data on the AMA were obtained from a telephone interview on April 20, 1994, with a representative of the AMA membership group. The figure on medical school enrollment is from the National Center for Health Statistics, *Health United States 1991* (Hyattsville, Md.: U.S. Public Health Service, 1992), 254.
48. Boston Women's Health Book Collective, *Our Bodies, Ourselves* (New York: Simon and Schuster, 1973). See also Boston Women's Health Book Collective, *The New Our Bodies, Ourselves: A Book by and for Women* (New York: Simon and Schuster, 1984).
49. Starr, *The Social Transformation*, 391.
50. Ries and Stone, *The American Woman, 1992-93*, 221. The discussion in this paragraph and the next is based largely on this source.
51. Ibid., 230.
52. Ibid., 237.
53. Ibid.
54. Ibid.
55. National Center for Health Statistics, *Prevention Profile: Health U.S., 1991* (Hyattsville, Md.: Public Health Service, 1992), 130.
56. Ries and Stone, *The American Woman, 1992-93*, 185, 192.
57. Ibid., 162.
58. Susan J. Carroll, Debra L. Dodson, and Ruth B. Mandel, *The Impact of Women in*

Public Office: An Overview (New Brunswick, N.J.: Center for the American Woman and Politics, Rutgers University, 1991), 10, 22.

CHRONOLOGY

1921 Congress passes the Sheppard-Towner Act, which addresses the health care needs of women, but only in their traditional roles as mothers and nurturers of children.

1965 Medicare and Medicaid, federal health care programs for the elderly and the poor, become law as amendments to the Social Security Act.

1965 In *Griswold v. Connecticut,* the Supreme Court recognizes a married couple's right to privacy with regard to their sexual behavior and lifts ban on their use of contraception.

1972 Title IX of the Higher Education Amendments bans gender discrimination in medical school admissions.

1972 In *Eisenstadt v. Baird,* the Supreme Court extends the right of privacy in decisions concerning contraception to unmarried couples.

1973 In *Roe v. Wade,* the Supreme Court establishes that women have a constitutional right to an abortion during the first three months of pregnancy and that the right of privacy includes the decision to have an abortion, although the state's "compelling interest" in regulating abortion increases after the first trimester.

1973 In *Doe v. Bolton,* the Supreme Court upholds its decision in *Roe v. Wade.*

1975 The Public Health Services Act of 1975 outlaws gender discrimination in medical school admissions.

1976 The Hyde Amendment forbids or severely limits the expenditure of federal funds for abortion.

1980 In *Harris v. McRae,* the Supreme Court upholds the Hyde Amendment.

1983 In *Akron v. Akron Center for Reproductive Health,* the Supreme Court holds unconstitutional certain portions of the regulation adopted by Akron, Ohio, in 1978 that some had viewed as a model of abortion regulation.

1989 In *Webster v. Reproductive Health Services,* the Supreme Court rules that states may regulate abortions even during the first trimester of a woman's pregnancy.

1991 In *Rust v. Sullivan,* the Supreme Court upholds the "gag rule," which prohibits personnel in federally funded family planning clinics from providing information or counseling about abortion.

1992 In *Planned Parenthood of Southeastern Pennsylvania v. Casey,* the Supreme Court replaces the trimester condition of *Roe* with an "undue burden" test.

SUGGESTIONS FOR FURTHER READING

Ballou, Mary, and Nancy W. Gabalac, with David Kelley. *A Feminist Position on Mental Health.* Springfield, Ill.: Charles C. Thomas, 1985.

Behuniak-Long, Susan. "Radical Conceptions: Reproductive Technologies and Feminist Theories." *Women and Politics* 10, no. 3 (1990): 39-64.

Binion, Gayle. "*Webster v. Reproductive Health Services:* Devaluing the Right to Choose." *Women and Politics* 11, no. 2 (1991): 41-59.

Kessler, Suzanne J. "The Medical Construction of Gender: Case Management of Intersexed Infants." *Signs* 16, no. 1 (Autumn 1990): 3-26.

Meadow, Rosalyn M. *Women's Conflicts about Eating and Sexuality: The Relationship between Food and Sex.* Binghamton, N.Y.: Haworth Press, 1992.

Schultz, Jane E. "The Inhospitable Hospital: Gender and Professionalism in Civil War Medicine." *Signs* 17, no. 2 (Winter 1992): 363-392.

Woliver, Laura R. "The Deflective Power of Reproductive Technologies: The Impact on Women." *Women and Politics* 9, no. 3 (1989): 17-47.

Equal Employment
Opportunity Policy

The sweeping cultural changes that have occurred in the United States since the 1960s were largely created by, and reflect, changes that have taken place in the social and economic roles of women. The changes in the lifestyle and employment of four generations of women in one American family illustrate this revolution.

Born in 1865, Amy married a farmer at the age of twenty-five (which was considered late in life at that time) and never worked outside the home. Besides cooking, cleaning, preserving food, and caring for the garden, she raised chickens and sold the surplus chickens and eggs, along with butter she had churned, to town residents. Amy used the money she managed to save to help send her daughter, Beth, to college.

Beth, who was born in 1895, not only graduated from high school (few women even attended high school in those years), but graduated from college at the age of twenty-one. She became a teacher (one of the few occupations then open to women) and married at the age of twenty-five. But she gave up teaching as soon as she married, for middle-class married women were not supposed to work outside the home unless their husbands could not provide an adequate living for the family. Most school systems would not employ married women.

Beth's daughter, Claire, born in 1930, had two rowdy older brothers. Beth's husband managed a small grocery store and continued to work even during the most terrible economic conditions of the Great Depression, so the family was able to survive without Beth having to work outside the home. The strain of long hours and hard work took its toll, however; Beth's husband died of a heart attack in 1938. As a result of her family's influence with local decision makers (her father was a member of the community bank's board of directors) and the scarcity of language teachers, Beth obtained a job teaching English and Latin in a small community's school, despite the cultural prejudice against women work-ing.

Claire entered college in 1948, graduated in 1952, and also became a teacher. She married immediately after graduation and taught until her first child, Denise, was born in 1954. Claire stayed home with the three children until the youngest entered the sixth grade, then returned to teaching to help pay for her children's college education.

Denise graduated from college in 1976, several years after the policy of equal employment opportunity had been established as federal law. Having majored in business, she accepted a job with a large bank. She continued to work after marriage and took only a short leave following the birth of each of her two children. The children were placed in a day care center while she worked. Largely because of her talent and deter-mination, she was promoted to a regional vice presidency in 1993.

As the experiences of these four members of one family illustrate, both cultural expectations and economic opportunities have changed enormously in four generations. What has caused these changes? What problems did they create? Which problems have been resolved and which remain? This chapter addresses those questions.

EMPLOYMENT DISCRIMINATION: THEORIES OF CAUSE AND CHANGE

What causes employment discrimination and what is necessary to bring about equitable conditions in the employment market? Even those who believe that women desire and should have equitable treatment advance alternative, frequently conflicting theories about the causes of problems of economic inequity and how they should be resolved. Feminism is an ide-ology that advocates the economic, political, and social empowerment of women, but it encompasses several different points of view. Liberal femi-nists believe that "female subordination is rooted in a set of customary and legal constraints that blocks women's entrance into and/or success in the so-called public world." [1] Gender justice would then require making the rules of the game fair and ensuring that all individuals, including those who are systematically disadvantaged in the competition for social, economic, and political well-being, have an equal opportunity to compete in the economic market. Liberal feminists thus believe that if the rules of the game are defined by constitutions, laws, and the mechanisms estab-lished for their implementation, enforcement, and adjudication, and if they encourage or permit unfair policies to exist, then the constitutions, laws, and mechanisms must be changed.

Feminists who reject the tenets of liberal feminism argue that to empower women and improve their condition in society, a change in laws and public policies is not enough. Radical feminists attack the patriarchal society and its influence on the legal, economic, and political systems as the source of women's disadvantaged condition. They argue that until its manifestations are obliterated, equity for women will be impossible.[2]

Policies whose aim is to improve the economic situation of women in the United States reflect the moderate or liberal rather than radical theories. This chapter focuses on some of the employment-related problems that have confronted American women and their families and the policies proposed (and in some cases implemented) to eliminate women's disadvantages.

PATTERNS OF EMPLOYMENT

Prior to 1900, less than one-fifth of adult American women worked outside the home. Many who did were single and were expected to quit their jobs if they married. Most Americans expected men to work but considered employment inappropriate for women, especially middle-class and married women. In a time of national crisis such as a major war, however, when millions of men were drafted into the armed forces, women's employment outside the home was accepted. During World War II, large numbers of American women worked in offices, factories, and stores. After the war ended in 1945, most of them were encouraged by social and cultural norms to return to the role of full-time housewife. But by 1950, one-third of American women aged sixteen and older worked outside the home. Since then, the proportion of such women has steadily increased; in 1990, it was 57.5 percent.[3]

This pattern of increased employment outside the home was evident in all age-groups except women over sixty-five and in all categories of marital status; it was found both among women without children at home and among women with children under age eighteen. In 1980, two-fifths of the women with children younger than six years worked part time or full time; by 1990 more than half the women with children in that age-group did.[4]

What caused this increase in the proportion of women employed outside the home? Single women work to support themselves, and many married women work to help support their families. Most divorced women receive alimony infrequently and must work to support themselves and their families. For many women, jobs satisfy their psychological needs, such as a sense of accomplishment and social interaction. Although a majority of adult women now work outside the home, the patterns of women's employment remain quite different from those of men's employment. Economists have labeled this difference the "dual labor market."[5]

Patterns of employment in the United States vary by gender, race, and social class. Although the proportions of white, black, and Hispanic women participating in the labor force are almost equal, the labor force is segregated by gender and race. Moreover, there is substantial occupational concentration by gender and race; the resulting wage distribution is a major cause of economic inequality.[6] In general, women are employed in occupations that are at least 70 percent female, whereas men are employed in occupations that are at least 70 percent male. There has been a gradual change in these occupational patterns since the 1960s, but as of 1990, one-third of all employed women were concentrated in just six occupational categories: teaching, managerial, administrative, secretarial, retail sales, and banking and insurance (including such positions as teller or clerk).[7]

Women's average earnings are substantially lower than men's, in part because the occupations in which women are concentrated generally pay lower wages than do those in which men are concentrated. But women in male-dominated occupations also earn less than men of the same age with the same level of education. Whether the comparison is on the basis of hourly wages, weekly pay, or annual earnings, women earn substantially less than men.

Why do women earn less than men? The reasons, in addition to occupational segregation, are that women tend to enter and leave the labor market more frequently than men because they are expected to be the primary care providers for both children and elderly parents.[8] Furthermore, women are less likely than men to be employed full time.[9] Pay levels also reflect past employment discrimination. Prior to the 1970s, many occupations effectively excluded women; if they were hired later than men of the same age, women had less occupational seniority and therefore probably were paid less.[10] Furthermore, predominantly female occupations have tended either to be nonunionized or to have weak unions, and unionization usually results in higher wage levels.[11] The "glass ceiling" that exists in many employment settings means that women are infrequently promoted to higher-paying jobs despite the supposedly nondiscriminatory employment practices of most businesses and government agencies.[12] Although the policy is illegal, some male managers continue to believe that women do not need to earn as much as men who hold the same jobs and have the same amount of experience. In cases where employers (usually private businesses) do not make wage and salary information available to employees, wage discrimination may continue to exist.

The difference between the average earnings of men and women has been declining. As of 1988, however, women's average weekly earnings were 73.8 percent of those of men.[13] How can the increase in women's pay relative to that of men be explained? The change in the occupational characteristics of men and women workers that has occurred in the past two decades is an important factor. Other factors include a decline in employers' discrimination against women, an improvement in women's job skills (more women are employed in the higher-paying professional, technical, and managerial occupations), and a convergence in the occupational patterns of men and women (a larger proportion of women are employed in formerly all-male or predominantly male occupations). In addition, an increased proportion of women are working continuously rather than leaving the work force to raise their children. Women who work continuously have significantly higher wages than do those whose work force participation is intermittent.[14]

A HISTORY OF EMPLOYMENT POLICY

Ambivalence about women working outside the home persists even today. The conflict between support for equality and the perception that women's basic role is that of wife and mother continues to influence public policy concerning women's employment. In the nineteenth century, that policy consisted primarily of laws intended to protect working women. They regulated the kinds of jobs women could hold and the hours they could work; night shifts were prohibited or limited, and jobs that required lifting supposedly heavy weights were forbidden, even though the weight to be lifted might be less than that of a child a mother would lift in the course of normal child care.

Court decisions affirmed the constitutionality of such restrictive legislation. In 1908 the Supreme Court, in *Muller v. Oregon*, upheld the constitutionality of a state law limiting the hours of work for women. The Court's justification was the possibly injurious effect of certain working conditions on women's maternal role. The justices viewed restrictive laws as being necessary to protect women and thereby to guarantee their equality. The tortured logic of the Court's opinion includes the following statement, referring to woman's nature:

> Though limitations upon personal and contractual rights may be removed by legislation, there is that in her dispositions and habits of life which will operate against a full assertion of those rights. She will still be where some legislation to protect her seems necessary to secure a real equality of right.[15]

Policy silences with regard to women's employment continued until the 1960s. For example, before that time, employers were permitted to deny women access to many types of jobs, including the higher-paying or professional and managerial positions. Moreover, the means used by employers to recruit new employees, such as employment agencies and newspaper advertisements, frequently specified that the job was open only to men.

THE DEVELOPMENT OF EQUAL EMPLOYMENT OPPORTUNITY POLICY

The establishment of the Women's Bureau in the Department of Labor in 1920 was the first official recognition by the federal government of the existence of policy issues concerning working women.[16] Congress charged the bureau with "formulating standards and policies to promote the welfare of wage earning women." [17]

The initial stimulus for enactment of a federal law on equal employment opportunity came from leaders of racial and religious minorities in the 1930s. Recognizing the limited effectiveness of the many techniques they had tried to end discrimination against blacks and Jews by private employers, they sought government support. The first federal government action taken as a result of this request was a presidential directive issued several months before the United States entered World War II. Persuaded by civil rights leader A. Philip Randolph, head of the Brotherhood of Sleeping Car Porters, in June 1941, President Franklin D. Roosevelt issued Executive Order 8802, which forbade employment discrimination in defense industries. The first bill to prohibit employment discrimination was introduced in Congress in 1942. Many bills were subsequently introduced, but a comprehensive federal equal employment opportunity law was not enacted until 1964: Title VII of the Civil Rights Act.[18]

Several conditions were necessary for the federal government to take any action on equal employment opportunity policy. One requisite was an increase in the number of women in the work force. Another requisite was the government's assumption of a more activist role in managing the economy, which it did primarily as a consequence of the Great Depression of the 1930s. The Supreme Court, after striking down several types of economic regulatory legislation during the 1930s, accepted the constitutionality of a federal economic regulatory role. The Court also began to issue decisions more supportive of minority groups that were targets of discriminatory practices.[19]

Demand for more regulation of working conditions followed. The increased proportion of women in the labor force during and after World War II (33.9 percent in 1950—more than at any time previously)[20] focused public attention on the legal status of women in the workplace and aroused greater awareness of inequities in pay and employment opportunity. As a consequence, more workers demanded equal opportunity and equal pay for equal work.

FEDERAL LEGISLATION

Any corrective policy had to address three basic problems: unequal access to jobs, unequal pay, and discriminatory laws. Equal access to jobs would mean that an individual was judged on the basis of merit when seeking a job and not rejected because of gender or some other socio-demographic characteristic. Equal pay would mean that women who performed the same work (or substantially the same work) as men would receive equal pay. The effect (though not necessarily the intent) of existing discriminatory laws was to decrease the economic prospects of women (for example, a state law requiring a higher minimum wage for women; in 1923, sixteen states had such laws). Although these laws would appear to be beneficial to women, they actually made women less competitive for available jobs.[21] Discriminatory laws existing within both the income tax system and the social security benefits system penalized families in which both spouses worked.

The initial efforts to establish equal pay were temporary wartime measures; Congress enacted laws requiring equal pay for women during both World War I and World War II. The intent, however, was to prevent a decline in wages paid for jobs normally held by men; if women were hired at lower wages during the war, they would be retained in the jobs after the war, when the men returned from military service, because they could be paid lower wages.

The Fair Labor Standards Act of 1938 had a more lasting impact on wages for some women. It requires fair treatment for wage and hourly workers and the payment of minimum wages for certain kinds of employment. Classifying jobs on the basis of age or gender is prohibited under the law's wage order section.

Following World War II, advocates of fairness for women introduced in Congress laws requiring equal pay for jobs of *comparable worth* to the employer, but equal pay legislation was not passed at the federal level until 1963. By then a majority of states had enacted equal pay laws. The Women's Bureau of the Department of Labor, supported by President John F. Kennedy's Commission on the Status of Women, advocated equal pay legislation. Finally, a small but very significant step toward requiring gender equity in employment was taken with passage of the Equal Pay Act of 1963.[22] Note, however, that in order for the bill to be passed, its wording had to be changed from the long advocated equal pay for work of comparable worth to equal pay for *equal work*. Furthermore, this first effort at gender equity in employment addressed only the problem of pay equity for equal work.

The act provides that when an employer has men and women doing the same or substantially the same job (that is, requiring the same or substantially the same skill, effort, and responsibility) at the same location and under similar working conditions, the employees must receive equal pay. Allowable differentials in pay include those based on seniority, merit, or measures of quantity or quality of work output. In addition, a sweeping provision permits pay differentials based on "any other factor other than sex."[23]

Amendments enacted in 1972 extended the act's coverage to employees of small firms not covered by minimum wage laws and to executive, administrative, and professional workers, including teachers and other professional personnel in educational institutions.[24] Thus, teachers with the same experience doing the same work have to be paid at the same rates; women teachers with equivalent training and experience can no longer be paid less than men teachers. The act was initially enforced by the Department of Labor's Wage and Hours Division of the Employment Standards Administration, but since 1978 it has been enforced by the Equal Employment Opportunity Commission (EEOC) as a consequence of a general reorganization of civil rights enforcement.

An individual who believes he or she has suffered the type of discrimination prohibited by this act can file a complaint with the EEOC. Normally, enforcement begins with an investigation; if the evidence indicates that an employer is in violation of the act, the agency uses conciliation processes in an attempt to bring the employer into compliance. If conciliation fails, the EEOC has the authority to file suit. In addition, the complainant may file a suit on his or her own to enforce the act if the complainant has not already received back pay or if the EEOC has not filed a court suit to collect those wages. If the court finds the employer guilty of gender discrimination in determining wages, it orders the firm to stop the practice and may award up to two years of back wages to those who suffered the discrimination. If the court finds that the discrimination was willful, the employer may be ordered to pay up to three years of back wages plus an equal amount as a penalty. An employer convicted of willful discrimination may be fined up to $10,000 and, if convicted twice, may be imprisoned for up to six years.[25]

Problems arose with both the coverage and the enforcement of this law. There are ways for companies to meet the law's requirements while circumventing its intent. For example, a firm can employ only female employees in certain jobs; wage disparities cannot, therefore, be attributed to gender discrimination. One problem with enforcement has no right to a hearing and may participate in such a hearing, if held, only at the discretion of the enforcing government agency.

TITLE VII OF THE CIVIL RIGHTS ACT OF 1964

A more comprehensive measure to ensure equal employment opportunity for women by prohibiting discrimination in hiring or discharging and in determining compensation, terms, conditions, or privileges of employment, came about as an unexpected addition to the Civil Rights Act of 1964. The intent of the act as initially proposed was to end discrimination based on race or religion. There was no prohibition against gender discrimination—until the act's basic equal employment opportunity section (Title VII) was debated by the House of Representatives. As initially proposed, that bill prohibited discrimination on the basis of race, color, religion or national origin. Representative Howard Smith (D-Va.), a conservative southerner who opposed the Civil Rights Act, introduced an amendment adding gender to the list, in the belief that such a bill would be defeated. The House accepted his amendment, but contrary to his expectations, the bill passed in the Senate as well. Thus a botched legislative tactic enabled a prohibition against employment discrimination based on gender to become federal law.[26]

Congress also debated what type of employers should be subject to the Civil Rights Act's employment discrimination provisions. Should the law apply to private employers? How large did these firms have to be for it to apply to them? Should the law apply to state and local governments as well as to the federal government? As finally enacted, the law applies to the federal government, unions, firms with fifteen or more employees, and employment agencies; as amended in 1972, it also applies to state and local government agencies, small firms, and educational institutions.[27]

The enforcement of the Civil Rights Act's discrimination provisions raised several issues. Congress chose to enforce the act by means of judicial proceedings rather than administrative action such as a cease and desist order. The issue here was who could initiate binding legal action. Could suit be brought by the individual experiencing the discrimination, or must it be done by an administrative agency? As originally enacted, the law stated that if the administrative agency could not resolve the dispute through conciliation, the aggrieved individual had either to file suit or to rely on the attorney general of the United States to sue. The 1972 amendments to Title VII permit the administrative agency (the EEOC) to bring suit on the individual's behalf. A second issue was whether to require that complaints be considered on a case-by-case basis, or to permit class action suits where a pattern of discrimination by an employer was found to exist. The law permits use of class action suits, and a number of such suits have been brought against major employers. A third issue in enforcement was whether a separate administrative agency should be created to administer the law, and if so, whether it should have enforcement powers or be merely an educational agency. Congress decided to create an independent administrative agency with enforcement powers (the EEOC, established as part of the 1964 act).

For a law to be effective, it must have teeth; that is, there must be penalties for employers who violate it. The Civil Rights Act provides that those who are found guilty by the courts of violating its prohibitions against employment discrimination can be subject to judicially issued cease and desist orders. Court orders can also enforce affirmative action and require the hiring, promoting, and provision of back pay to the victims of discrimination.

Title VII of the Civil Rights Act of 1964 (as amended in 1972) is far more comprehensive than the Equal Pay Act of 1963. Under the provisions of the 1964 act, discrimination on the basis of race, color, religion, sex, or national origin is unlawful in hiring or firing; determining wages; providing fringe benefits; classifying, referring, assigning, or promoting employees; extending or assigning facilities, training, retraining, or apprenticeship; or any other terms, conditions, or privileges of employment. Both acts allow differentials in wages between men and women if they are based on a seniority or merit system, or on quantity or quality of production, or on "any other factor other than sex." The 1964 act permits sex discrimination if the employer can prove that "sex is a bona fide occupational qualification [BFOQ] reasonably necessary to the normal operation of the business." [28] Such exceptions are rare but do exist; for example, considering only women for a role as an actress is an acceptable BFOQ.

Some state laws protective of women conflicted with Title VII; according to EEOC guidelines, and as decided by the courts, such laws are invalid. Equal employment opportunity may be achieved by granting to men benefits formerly granted only to women. [29]

The first case in which the Supreme Court interpreted Title VII was *Phillips v. Martin Marietta* (1971). Ida Phillips filed suit against the Martin Marietta Corporation, which had refused to hire women with preschool children. [30] Both the federal district court and the court of appeals had concluded that such a policy did not violate Title VII's prohibition against refusal to hire on the basis of sex because, these courts reasoned, the discrimination was not *solely* on the basis of sex (which was illegal) but on the basis of sex plus having preschool children (which was not illegal). The Supreme Court rejected this narrow "sex plus" reasoning and held that discrimination on the basis of sex plus another characteristic violates Title VII. In litigation instituted by individuals and interest groups, not the EEOC, the federal courts also upheld women's employment rights. [31] The EEOC's contribution to the legal interpretation of Title VII prior to 1972 should not be underestimated, however. Many federal courts deferred to guidelines in interpreting congressional intent. The EEOC also attempted to settle some disputes out of court.

Enforcement of Title VII rests with the Equal Employment Opportunity Commission.[32] However, most of the significant Title VII litigation has been instituted by individuals after the EEOC was unable to resolve the dispute through conciliation. The EEOC has the authority to file both individual discrimination and pattern and practice suits; these are its two principal methods of enforcing Title VII. If an individual files a complaint with the commission, it investigates the complaint and tries to resolve the dispute informally. If it is unable to do so, it may seek judicial enforcement. The second, more far-reaching method is to conduct a "pattern and practice" investigation. The EEOC may conduct industrywide or companywide compliance reviews; if they suggest that a pattern of discrimination exists, it can initiate a formal investigation. If it determines that a practice of discrimination has occurred (whether intentional or not), the EEOC tries through conciliation processes to end it. If this effort is unsuccessful, the EEOC may sue the offending company. Only the U.S. attorney general or the individual worker could bring suit prior to 1972. Because the EEOC had no authority to sue, the offending party had less incentive to correct its practices voluntarily. Moreover, the number of suits filed was much lower than supporters of Title VII deemed desirable. Pattern and practice cases have been a significant stimulus for the creation of affirmative action plans to correct past discriminatory practices and to prevent their occurrence in the future.[33]

A landmark pattern and practice case culminated in 1974 with the issuance of a consent decree. American Telephone and Telegraph agreed to award $12 million in back pay and incentive payments to thousands of women and members of racial minorities who had been denied wage increases and promotions. In addition, AT & T agreed to spend $40 million for future pay adjustments and to set up an affirmative action program to redress past abuses.[34]

Title VII is the most comprehensive federal law aimed at preventing job discrimination. Its information-gathering and enforcement provisions far exceed those of the Equal Pay Act in terms of reach and the severity of penalties. An individual may file complaints under both laws and is often encouraged to do so; most of the large settlements have been pursued under both laws. Enforcement of both laws is under the jurisdiction of the EEOC.

The 1978 amendments to Title VII prohibit discrimination against pregnant women in any aspect of employment, including hiring, promotion, seniority rights, and job security. Employers who offer health insurance and temporary disability plans must include coverage for pregnancy, childbirth, and related medical conditions. Known collectively as the

Pregnancy Discrimination Act of 1978, the amendments were intended to overrule a Supreme Court decision permitting such discrimination.[35]

FAMILY AND MEDICAL LEAVE ACT

In 1993, Congress passed, and President Bill Clinton signed, the Family and Medical Leave Act, which permits employed persons to take up to twelve weeks of unpaid leave because of their serious illness, the birth or adoption of a child, or the necessity of caring for an ill child, parent, or spouse. This law applies only to employers with fifty or more employees; to be eligible, an employee must have worked for the employer for a minimum of 1,250 hours. An employee in the top 10 percent of the company's pay scale may be denied leave if the business considers that person to be an essential employee whose leave would result in "substantial and grievous economic injury" to the employer.

EXECUTIVE ORDERS OF THE PRESIDENT

Laws enacted by Congress are not the only means of attack on gender-based discrimination; the president can issue executive orders that apply to all federal agencies and departments and whose effects may also extend to private firms having contracts with the federal government. In 1965 President Lyndon Johnson issued Executive Order 11246 to prohibit employment discrimination by contractors and subcontractors holding federal or federally funded contracts. In 1967, it was amended by Executive Order 11375 to include gender as a category. The order was a response to criticisms that case-by-case examinations of complaints are not, by themselves, sufficient to ensure equal opportunity. It specified that federal government agencies that enter into contracts with private employers must require that these contractors

> not discriminate against any employee or applicant for employment because of race, color, religion, sex or national origin. The contractor will take affirmative action to ensure that employees are employed and are treated during employment, without regard to their race, color, religion, sex or national origin. Such action shall include, but not be limited to the following: employment, upgrading, demotion, or transfer; recruitment or recruitment advertising; layoff or termination; rates of pay or other forms of compensation; and selection for training, including apprenticeship.[36]

The federal government thus can use its substantial purchasing power to require federal contractors to pursue equal opportunity and affirmative action. The importance of this executive order is underscored by the fact that roughly one-third of the total labor force works for companies holding government contracts.

The Department of Labor's Office of Federal Contract Compliance Programs (OFCCP) is responsible for enforcing contract compliance. The guidelines known as Revised Order No. 4, issued by the OFCCP in 1974, strengthened Executive Order 11246. They require a contractor to analyze his or her work force to determine if women and other minorities are underemployed. If so, the contractor must draft and implement an affirmative action plan that establishes numerical goals and timetables by job classification and organization unit to correct any deficiencies. This order applies to all nonconstruction contractors with fifty or more employees and a contract of $50,000 or more and requires that each contractor develop a written affirmative action program within twenty days of the contract's commencement.[37]

A complaint may be filed with the Office of Federal Contract Compliance Programs by any person who believes he or she has been subjected to the type of discrimination prohibited by Executive Order 11246 as amended. Simultaneously, complaints may also be filed with other pertinent agencies such as the EEOC. If the contractor is found to have unlawfully discriminated, punishment may be as severe as contract cancellation and exclusion from future government contracts. Usually the contractor will remedy the situation rather than risk losing current or future contracts. Contractors are also subject to on-site compliance reviews (somewhat similar to the pattern and practice investigations conducted by the EEOC to enforce Title VII).[38] These reviews constitute the largest and most effective part of the OFCCP's enforcement effort.

The OFCCP also has the authority to conduct reviews before the final contracts are awarded. The federal government can thus avoid unwittingly supporting discrimination by granting contracts to employers who engage in discriminatory employment practices. Prior review is an efficient tool because it can reduce or eliminate the need for later enforcement proceedings; prospective contractors must promptly remedy the violation or lose the contract.

IMPLEMENTATION OF EQUAL OPPORTUNITY POLICY

Has the enforcement of equal employment laws been effective? In attempting to answer this question, we should bear in mind that implementation is a political process that can result in either an increase or a decrease in the impact of the policy underlying these laws and executive orders.

The establishment of a comprehensive equal opportunity policy began in the early 1960s. In the early 1970s, there was an increase in both the coverage and the impact of equal employment policy and laws; the result was an increase in employment discrimination complaints. Implementation efforts improved, enforcement powers were broadened and strengthened, and responsibility for enforcement was more widely dispersed. This dispersal had a significant effect on implementation, however; it produced fragmented authority, confusion, weakened enforcement, and duplication.[39] The federal government's Reorganization Plan No. 1 of 1978 was intended to remedy that situation. To increase efficiency, responsibility for implementing equal employment policy was restricted to three agencies: the EEOC, the OFCCP, and the Department of Justice.[40] But during the Reagan and Bush presidencies (1981-1992), there was a marked decrease in both effort and effectiveness of implementation and enforcement.

The early phase of equal opportunity policy implementation emphasized individual considerations of relative merit in hiring; employers had to demonstrate that use of a suspect category (race, gender, religion, or national origin) in making employment decisions was based on a bona fide occupational qualification. Enforcement of equal employment opportunity laws at this time was largely passive—initiated after the filing of complaints by individuals. The most significant increase in the impact of equal employment opportunity laws and policy occurred in the 1970s, when the implementation emphasis shifted from passive law enforcement to the initiation of affirmative action programs.

Why was this increase followed by a decrease in the policy's impact? The change was largely a result of court decisions, regulations supplementing existing law, and changes in statutory law, accomplished either by amendment of existing laws or enactment of new laws. (An example of a change in statutory law is the Higher Education Amendments of 1972, which extended Title VII coverage to teachers and administrators in educational institutions.) The policy's impact was reduced beginning in 1981 because the Reagan and Bush administrations, which were less supportive of governmental activity on behalf of equal employment opportunity, cut back the resources allocated to the implementation of equal employment policy. There was also pressure from political appointees to reduce enforcement activities and to restrict the criteria used in assessing fair employment practices.

A 1970 court decision extended the coverage of equal employment policy. In *Shultz v. Wheaton Glass Company*, the court ruled that "equal work" as defined by the Equal Pay Act need not mean identical work but only work that was "substantially equal." [41] In contrast, the decision in *Grove City College v. Bell* (1984) restricted the enforcement of equal employment opportunity law. The Supreme Court ruled that federal equal employment opportunity requirements were to apply only to the specific program or activity receiving federal aid within an educational institution.[42] The Civil Rights Restoration Act, passed by Congress in 1988, overturned the effects of the decision in Grove City College v. Bell.[43]

The Reagan administration used the Court's decision in Firefighters Local Union No. 1784 v. Stotts (1984) as a basis for its efforts to limit the enforcement of equal opportunity law. The question in this case was whether the commitments under an affirmative action program take precedence over a local government's contract with a union that allowed firefighters to assert seniority rights to jobs (Title VII of the Civil Rights Act of 1964 recognizes such rights as legitimate) when layoffs had to be made. The Supreme Court upheld the firefighters' seniority rights.[44] A conservative Court thus had provided the Reagan administration with an excuse to try to negotiate revision of a number of affirmative action programs (that included goals and timetables) previously agreed to by state and local government units. In two decisions issued on July 2, 1986, the Court endorsed the use of broad affirmative action programs to remedy the effects of past discrimination. Both race-based job promotions and court-ordered minority quotas for admission to union membership were found not to be in violation of Title VII of the Civil Rights Act of 1964.[45]

THE PROBLEM OF SEXUAL HARASSMENT

Sexual harassment is a form of gender discrimination in employment that violates Title VII of the Civil Rights Act of 1964. Employers' concern about the effects of sexual harassment on the work environment and a few well-publicized cases, such as the allegations of sexual harassment on the part of Supreme Court nominee Clarence Thomas made by his former aide, attorney Anita Hill, sharply focused public attention on this problem in the early 1990s. Sexual harassment includes unwelcome sexual advances, requests for sexual favors, and other verbal or physical conduct of a sexual nature when submission to or rejection of this conduct explicitly or implicitly affects an individual's employment, unreasonably interferes with an individual's work performance, or creates an intimidating, hostile, or offensive work environment.[46] The harasser can be the employee's supervisor, an agent of the employee, a co-worker, or a nonemployee. The victim need not be the person harassed but can be anyone offended by the conduct. The usual procedures for filing a complaint or grievance can be used. Many employers have developed extensive and mandatory educational programs to prevent the occurrence of sexual harassment in their places of business. Court decisions have clearly enunciated the principle that employers are liable for the actions of their employees when sexual harassment occurs. The standard to be used by the courts in sexual harassment cases, clarified in *Harris v. Forklift Systems, Inc.* (1993), is that of a reasonable person and the totality of circumstances of the alleged sexual harassment.[47]

CRITERIA FOR PROOF OF DISCRIMINATION

What constitutes proof of discrimination in employment? Three types of proof can be used. The first and most obvious is proof of *intent to discriminate*: a written document in which employer states such intent or an employer's verbal statement, sworn to by a witness, that there was an intent to discriminate in employment practices such as hiring, promotion, pay, or provision of benefits. Neither written nor verbal statements of intent to discriminate are likely to be available as evidence, however; few employers would be so foolish.

A second type of proof is proof of *disparate treatment*, which occurs when members of a protected category of citizen under Title VII are treated less well by employment practices than are other citizens.[48] A disparate treatment test can be applied in situations such as hiring:

1. The individual is a member of a protected category under Title VII—in this instance, a female.
2. She applies for a job.
3. She is denied the job even though she has the required qualifications.
4. Others with similar qualifications who are not members of the protected category are hired.
5. The employer's defense is that some legitimate, nondiscriminatory reason exists for rejecting the female applicant.
6. She must demonstrate that the reason given by the employer is an invalid rationalization or a cover-up.

Defenses used by employers have included business necessity, customer preference, and the co-workers' preferences. Reliance on business necessity to justify discriminatory practices requires the existence of a compelling business purpose that cannot be met by any alternative practice or procedure.[49] Business necessity has had limited acceptance by the courts as a defense in employment discrimination cases; in a few cases, however, a business necessity defense has been sustained by the evidence. The courts have not considered customer preference or co-worker preference to be acceptable defenses.

A third proof of discrimination in employment is proof of *disparate effects*. A plaintiff using this test in a gender discrimination case must show that the criteria used in employment decisions, although supposedly neutral, have disparate, negative effects on members of a protected category. For example, the height requirements formerly used by fire and police departments discriminated against both women and members of certain ethnic minorities who tend to be relatively short. The employer must show that the supposedly neutral criterion that has a disparate effect is a valid requirement for job performance. If the employer successfully makes such an argument, the plaintiff (a short person who wishes to be a member of the police force) must show that alternative criteria are available that are less discriminatory and that these criteria (a lower height requirement) would not result in the hiring of employees (members of the police force) who could not perform assigned (law enforcement) tasks. Administrative agencies' use of the disparate treatment and disparate effects tests to determine the existence of employment discrimination can facilitate the enforcement of equal employment opportunity law. The disparate impact doctrine, enunciated by the Supreme Court in *Griggs v. Duke Power Company*, (1971), requires an employer to demonstrate the existence of business necessity as a justification for the disparate effect of supposedly neutral employment selection criteria.[50]

A number of Supreme Court decisions in the late 1980s made job discrimination lawsuits harder to win. Congress attempted to enact legislation in 1990 to counter these decisions, but that bill was vetoed by President George Bush. He did sign a revised bill, the Civil Rights Act of 1991, in November 1991. This law in effect reversed the Supreme Court's June 1989 decision in *Ward's Cove Packing Co. v. Antonio*,[51] as well as eight other Supreme Court decisions relating to discrimination in employment.[52] It once again placed the burden of proof in disparate effect cases on the employer. The law also reinstated the principle, established in *Griggs v. Duke Power Co.*, that hiring and promotion discrimination requirements must be related to job performance. The law did not, however, clearly define the business necessity defense that employers may use in such cases.

EFFECTS OF EQUAL OPPORTUNITY POLICY ON WOMEN'S EMPLOYMENT

The Equal Pay Act of 1963 was intended to narrow the disparity between the wages of men and women who perform equal work; the purpose of Title VII of the Civil Rights Act of 1964 and Executive Order 11246 as amended by Executive Orders 11375 and 11478 was to increase employment opportunities for women and minorities. If these laws have been effective, we should find that pay disparities have narrowed, and that significant numbers of women and minorities have entered professions previously restricted for the most part to white men.

Some changes have occurred in occupational patterns. There has been an increase in the proportion of the total work force that is female and a gradual increase in the proportion of women who are employed in nontraditional fields. For example, in 1988, 8.7 percent of the workers in skilled trades were women, compared with 8.1 percent in 1983; but only 2 percent of all employed women were in these occupations.[53] Although more women now hold management positions than at any previous time, there are few in top-level administrative posts. In 1978, 26 percent of the persons holding management positions were women; the proportion had only increased to 39.3 percent by 1988. In that year, women managers constituted only 10.8 percent of all women employed, and women held only 1 or 2 percent of the top-level administrative positions. Women are more likely to be managers in fields in which many women are employed at lower levels, such as health care, personnel, and education.[54] This failure of women to be promoted to the managerial ranks has been referred to as the "glass ceiling." Lynn Martin, secretary of labor in the Bush administration, focused public attention on the glass ceiling problem and advocated that private employers initiate policies to help women attain high-level management positions.[55] She also focused attention on the dearth of women in high-level federal management positions.[56]

Occupations with a high proportion of women tend to have low hourly wages. As the proportion of women in a job category decreases, hourly wages generally increase. Another way to analyze this segregation is to examine the occupations with the highest earnings by women and determine whether they are predominantly male or female. Data collected in 1981 indicate that of twenty such occupations, only one—registered nurse—also had a high percentage of female workers (96 percent). Conversely, all of the twenty highest-paying occupations for men were male intensive.[57] This is a further indication that occupations that are predominantly female are lower paying. And compared with job categories that are predominantly male, job categories in which women predominate are the lowest paid; the study's author noted that "the pay for women librarians is just above that of men working as precision machine operatives, a classification which is in the bottom third of the male earnings ranking." [58] Thus, pay disparities are explained, at least in part, by the jobs women hold.

Equal employment opportunity for women was guaranteed by Title VII of the Civil Rights Act of 1964. The act was designed to open to women occupations from which they had previously been excluded, by making it illegal for employers to refuse to hire on the basis of gender. Women have made limited progress in gaining entry to such occupations. For example, in 1970 only 1.6 percent of all engineers were women; by

1980 this proportion had nearly tripled to 4.3 percent, and by 1989 it had increased to 8.8 percent.[59] Although this percentage represents an improvement, it is still low, considering the proportion of the work force that is female.

Given the concentration of women in the low-paying occupations, we would expect women's earnings to be substantially below those of men. This is in fact the pattern that still exists in the United States. In 1939, the median annual earnings of women who worked full time, year round, were 58 percent of the median annual earnings of men. By 1983, women's median annual earnings had increased to 63.6 percent of men's and by 1988 the figure was 66 percent. Some argue that women are less likely to work continuously throughout a year and that annual wages should thus not be used as the basis for comparison. If median weekly earnings are used for comparison (correcting for this problem), the picture improves slightly: women's median weekly earnings were 65 percent of men's in 1984 and 70 percent in 1988, compared with 62 percent in 1967.[60]

It should be emphasized that gender differences in earnings are partly the result of differences in occupational distribution rather than differences in earnings from the same job. If disparities are the result of differences in occupational distribution, the equal pay provisions of Title VII and the Equal Pay Act cannot solve the problem of unequal pay caused by job segregation.

THE CONCEPT OF COMPARABLE WORTH

Obviously, many problems must still be resolved to ensure equal employment opportunity and equal pay for women. One such problem is the segregation of women in low-paying occupations. Although Title VII prohibits employers from refusing to hire women solely on the basis of gender, the fact is that most women continue to hold jobs in predominantly female occupations. Equal pay requirements are irrelevant when the aim is to raise the wages of women in these occupations. Thus, occupational segregation contributes significantly to wage and salary differentials.

Attempts to resolve this problem have resulted in a rethinking of the concept of equal pay for men and women. The concept of equal pay as defined by the 1963 legislation has already evolved, as a result of court decisions, to mean equal pay for substantially equal work. One reconceptualization is that Title VII's prohibition against discrimination in compensation should be construed as requiring equal pay for work of comparable value to the employer. This "comparable worth" approach seeks to compare the value and compensation of different jobs in terms of their worth to the employer.

Equal pay for work requiring equivalent skill levels, effort, and responsibility would eliminate the problem of pay inequities arising from gender-based occupational distributions—that is, the association of certain professions with "women's work." Assume that an employer, as a result of a job evaluation study, assigns 226 points (based on skill, effort, and responsibility) as the value of the job of senior carpenter (a predominantly male job) and 226 points to the job of senior legal secretary (a predominantly female job) but pays the carpenter twice as much per month as the secretary. Pay equity advocates insist that the discrepancy is attributable to gender discrimination and that Title VII's prohibition against discrimination in pay requires that the secretary be paid the same as the carpenter.

Most job evaluation studies undertaken to determine comparable worth reveal not just isolated instances of wage disparity, such as that between the job of secretary and the job of carpenter, but across-the-board disparities. In a study undertaken in 1973 by the state of Washington that was subsequently used against that state in litigation, a 20 percent disparity was found to exist between 62 predominantly (over 70 percent) female job classifications and 59 predominantly male job classifications.[61] Librarians, nurses, secretaries, and other women who are generally paid less than men with similar education and training will no longer confront such wage disparities if the principle of comparable pay for work of comparable worth is translated into law. Occupational segregation (which relegates women to low-paying jobs) would be eliminated because pay scales based on the comparable worth of a job in a segregated occupation would be more appropriate to the skill level, effort, and responsibilities associated with assigned tasks. This solution still presents many problems, including sensitive political ones; whether a comparable worth standard should be instituted through new legislation or negotiation, or by means of litigation, is not yet clear.[62]

All three methods are being attempted. Several bills introduced in Congress address the pay equity issue; one would direct the EEOC to establish guidelines prohibiting employers from paying women less than men if the work of both is comparable. Many states—either of their own volition or because they were pressured by employee labor unions or threatened by litigation—have ordered job evaluation studies, set up pay equity task forces, or in some other way have begun to collect data on wage discrimination. A few states and some localities have both reevaluated their job classifications and appropriated money to institute some form of pay equity. Minnesota has appropriated $40 million to equalize the pay of employees in predominantly female jobs; Washington has appropriated $42 million and New York is planning to spend $36 million.

In the most publicized litigation concerning the issue of comparable worth—*American Federation of State, County, and Municipal Employees v. Washington State* (1983)—a federal district court found that the state had violated Title VII in paying employees in predominantly female jobs less than those in predominantly male jobs, even though the state's own evaluation scheme indicated that the same number of points should be assigned to each job category. But the court of appeals overruled that decision in 1985 and held that the state could follow prevailing private market wages in setting salaries even if to do so meant that women would be underpaid.[63] Since the state did not create the market disparity, said the appellate court, it did not have to correct the disparity. However much the concept of "comparable worth" is ridiculed (one Reagan administration appointee referred to it as the "looniest idea since looney tunes"), it is likely to be the main issue in future disputes over wage discrimination.

THE OUTLOOK FOR WOMEN

Beginning in 1963, Congress legislated major policy changes designed to establish equal employment opportunity and equal pay in the work force. Although modest gains have been made for women in the equalization of wages and employment opportunity, it is impossible to determine conclusively whether such gains are attributable to government policies. Many women undoubtedly benefited from these policies and laws when complaints were filed. The impact of both varies with the vigor with which the policies are implemented and the laws enforced.

A number of factors could affect future implementation of equal employment opportunity policy. They include changing political conditions (the installation of a conservative administration), organizational change, the adequacy of staff and resources, and the extent and seriousness of commitment. Changes in some of these factors do not appear to have inhibited the policy's effectiveness in the past. The laws, regulations, and executive orders designed to create equal employment opportunity established clear standards and objectives. The problems of interagency coordination and intraorganizational communications that existed in the early years of the policy's implementation were reduced as a result of organizational changes and the assignment of responsibility for policy implementation to three federal agencies during the 1970s. These agencies established appropriate mechanisms to carry out their responsibilities but were hampered in the use of mechanisms such as EEOC suits and OFCCP compliance reviews by lack of staff and other resources. The lack of commitment of the Reagan and Bush administrations to the success of equal employment opportunity policy, as evidenced by the administrations' opposition to the use of the disparate treatment and disparate effects tests, class action suits, and pattern and practice investigations initiated by federal agencies, limited the effectiveness of policy implementation during the 1980s and early 1990s. An agency's civil service personnel may have been committed to the effective implementation of equal employment opportunity policy, but opposition by the political appointees who headed some agencies at that time hindered the achievement of policy goals. Although the long-run benefits to society deriving from equal employment opportunity are demonstrable, these appointees often perceived conflicts with other, more highly valued goals, such as governmental noninterference with market forces and a decrease in government regulation of business.

The rhetoric of Reagan and Bush administration officials was replete with expressions of support for equal employment opportunity, but they sought to effect a major change in the policy and its implementation. Their litigation activities, attempts to induce renegotiation of consent agreements with state and local government agencies, proposed revisions in Executive Order 11246, modification of the regulations governing the enforcement of laws and executive orders (as well as the enforcement of the regulations themselves), and reductions in the budgets and staffing of federal agencies were all means to this end. The result was that it became difficult, if not impossible, to identify and remedy patterns of employment discrimination through administrative processes. It is ironic that this problem arose at the same time that significant changes were taking place in the composition of the work force and the electorate.

Have federal enforcement activities played a role in changing patterns of employment? Federal contract compliance review activities have been successful in increasing employment opportunities for women and minorities. Analyzing data on changes in total employment from 1974 to 1980 to determine the effects of federal contractor status and of being the object of a compliance review, researcher Jonathan Leonard concluded that "over a 6-year period the employment of members of protected groups grew significantly faster in contractor than in non-contractor establishments." He also concluded that "compliance reviews have played a significant role over and above that of contractor status." [64]

Future policies will probably be better directed as a result of experiences with these federal laws and executive orders. Furthermore, if vigorously enforced, equal employment opportunity laws and policy at least provide redress for those who have suffered discrimination, even if they do not substantially alter employment trends. There are those who argue that this is all that can be hoped for in a government policy. Others will continue to work for much more.

NOTES

1. Rosemarie Tong, *Feminist Thought: A Comprehensive Introduction* (Boulder, Colo.: Westview Press, 1989), 2.
2. Ibid., introduction.
3. See Paula Ries and Anne J. Stone, eds. *The American Woman, 1992-1993: A Status Report* (New York: Norton, 1992), Table 6-1, 308; and U.S. Department of Labor, Bureau of Labor Statistics, *Working Women: A Chartbook*, Bulletin no. 2385, 1991, Table A-2, 39.
4. U.S. Department of Labor, Bureau of Labor Statistics, *Working Women*, Table A-3, 39.
5. For a discussion of the dual labor market as it affects women, see Barbara Bergmann, *The Economic Emergence of Women* (New York: Basic Books, 1986).
6. National Committee on Pay Equity, "The Wage Gap," in Paula Rothenburg, *Race, Class, and Gender in the United States* (New York: St. Martin's Press, 1992), 129-135. See also Rita Mae Kelly, *The Gendered Economy* (Newbury Park, Calif.: Sage, 1991).
7. See Ries and Stone, *The American Woman, 1992-1993*, Table 6-13, 340.
8. U.S. Department of Labor, Women's Bureau, *Facts on Working Women*, no. 90-3, October 1990, 6.
9. Thomas Nardone, "Part-Time Workers: Who Are They?" *Monthly Labor Review*, February 1986, 13-19.
10. For example, in 1972 only 4.0 percent of the lawyers, 10.1 percent of the physicians, and 1.9 percent of the telephone installers and repairers were women; in 1990, 20.6 percent of the lawyers, 19.3 percent of the physicians, and 11.3 percent of the telephone installers and repairers were women. U.S. Department of Labor, Bureau of Labor Statistics, *Working Women*, Table A-9, 43.
11. Ries and Stone, *The American Woman 1992-1993*, Table 7-6, 369.
12. Secretary of Labor Lynn Martin took the lead in attacking the glass ceiling problem that exists in both the federal government and private enterprise. See U.S. Department of Labor, Office of the Secretary, *Report on the Glass Ceiling Initiative*, August 1991; and *Pipelines of Progress: A Status Report on the Glass Ceiling Initiative*, 1992.
13. U.S. Department of Labor, Women's Bureau, *Facts on Working Women*, no. 90-3, October 1990, Table 4.
14. Elaine Sorenson, *Exploring the Reasons behind the Narrowing Gender Gap in Earnings*, Report no. 91-2 (Washington, D.C.: Urban Institute Press, 1991), 2-9, 14.
15. *Muller v. Oregon*, 208 U.S. 412 (1908), 421.
16. U.S. Department of Labor, *1975 Women's Handbook*, 1975, 311.
17. U.S. Department of Labor, Women's Bureau, *Employment Goals of the World Plan of Action: Developments and Issues in the United States*, 1980, 17.
18. Title VII, Civil Rights Act of 1964, 78 Stat. 255 (1964).
19. For a discussion of changes in the pattern of the Supreme Court's decisions, see Judith A. Baer, *Women in American Law* (New York: Holmes and Meier, 1991); Richard P. Claude, *The Supreme Court and the Electoral Process* (Baltimore: Johns Hopkins University Press, 1970); Leslie Friedman Goldstein, *The Con-*

stitutional Rights of Women (Madison: University of Wisconsin Press, 1988); and Susan Gluck Mezey, *In Pursuit of Equality: Women, Public Policy, and the Federal Courts* (New York: St. Martin's Press, 1992).

20. U.S. Department of Labor, Bureau of Labor Statistics, *The Female-Male Earnings Gap: A Review of Employment and Earnings Issues*, 1982, 5.

21. U.S. Department of Labor, Women's Bureau, *Employment Goals*, 18.

22. 77 Stat. 56 (1963).

23. 77 Stat. 57, sec. 3(d).

24. Equal Employment Opportunity Amendments of 1972, 42 U.S.C. sec. 2000e et seq., Supp. III (1973); Higher Education Amendments of 1972, 20 U.S.C. sec. 1681 et seq., amending the Fair Labor Standards Act of 1938, 29 U.S.C. sec. 201 et seq. (1970).

25. U.S. Commission on Civil Rights, *A Guide to Federal Laws and Regulations Prohibiting Sex Discrimination*, rev. ed., Clearinghouse Publication no. 46 (Washington, D.C.: Government Printing Office, July 1976), 31-34.

26. Dorothy McBride Stetson, *Women's Rights in the U.S.A.: Policy Debates and Gender Roles* (Pacific Grove, Calif.: Brooks/Cole, 1991), 165.

27. U.S. Commission on Civil Rights, *A Guide to Federal Laws and Regulations*, 12. Both laws also prohibit discrimination against an individual who has opposed any unlawful employment practice or made a charge, testified, assisted, or participated in any investigation, proceeding, or hearing arising under Title VII. 78 Stat. 253 (1964).

28. 78 Stat. 256, sec. 703(e).

29. U.S. Department of Labor, *1975 Women's Handbook*, 292-293.

30. *Phillips v. Martin Marietta*, 400 U.S. 542 (1971).

31. Nancy McGlen and Karen O'Connor, *Women's Rights* (New York: Praeger, 1983), 177.

32. Responsibility for enforcement of equal employment opportunity for federal employees was not transferred to the Equal Employment Opportunity Commission until Reorganization Plan no. 1 of 1978 became effective.

33. U.S. Commission on Civil Rights, *A Guide to Federal Laws and Regulations*, 14-15.

34. *Equal Employment Opportunity Commission v. American Telephone and Telegraph Company*, 506 F.2d 735 (3d Cir. 1974). The detailed "Amended Final Report of the Consent Decree" (February 2, 1979) is evidence that progress has been made in eliminating segregation in employment: "Since the Decree was entered, the total number of employees within the Bell System was increased from 793,715 to 799,785: a percentage increase of 0.8 percent. While total employment remained relatively stable, significant progress was made for women in positions where they had been excluded or under-utilized. Women now comprise 28.6 percent of the management employees (Affirmative Action Job Classifications 1, 2, 3), as compared with 22.4 percent in 1973. More specifically in the top level management (AAJC 1) women increased from 11.2 percent to 21.1 percent, and in entry level management the increase was from 30.8 percent to 35.2 percent. In craft positions (AAJC's 6, 7, 8, 10) women now represent 9.5 percent of these employees, as compared to 2.8 percent when the Decree was entered."

35. Congressional Quarterly, *Congressional Quarterly Almanac 1978* (Washington, D.C.: Congressional Quarterly, 1979), 597-599. The decision overruled was *General Electric Co. v. Gilbert*, 97 S. Ct. 401 (1976).
36. Executive Order 11246, 3 C.F.R. 169 (1974).
37. Revised Order No. 4, "Affirmative Action Program Guidelines of the Office of Federal Contract Compliance Programs," in U.S. Commission on Civil Rights, *A Guide to Federal Laws and Regulations*, 27.
38. The complaint must be filed within 180 days of the alleged discrimination. Revised Order No. 4. Appendix II, in ibid., 14-15.
39. For a discussion of implementation, see Dvora Yanow, "Tackling the Implementation Problem: Epistemological Issues in Implementation Research," in *Implementation and the Policy Process: Opening Up the Black Box*, ed. D. J. Palumbo and D. J. Calista (Westport, Conn.: Greenwood Press, 1990), 213-227; and D. J. Palumbo and D. J. Calista, "Introduction: The Relation of Implementation Research to Policy Outcome," in ibid., 3-17.
40. U.S. Equal Employment Opportunity Commission, *Twelfth and Thirteenth Annual Reports*, 1981, 30; *Public Papers of the President of the United States, Jimmy Carter*, Book 1, 1978 (Washington, D.C.: Government Printing Office, 1979), 405-406.
41. *Shultz v. Wheaton Glass Company*, 421 F.2d 259 (3d Cir. 1970).
42. *Grove City College v. Bell*, 465 U.S. 555 (1984).
43. 20 U.S.C. 1681-1687, 1988 ed. (Washington, D.C.: Government Printing Office, 1989).
44. *Firefighters Local Union No. 1784 v. Stotts*, 467 U.S. 561 (1984); see also 42 U.S.C. secs. 2000e-h.
45. *Local No. 28 of the Sheet Metal Workers' International v. Equal Employment Opportunity Commission*, 106 S. Ct. 3019 (1986); *Local No. 93, International Association of Firefighters v. City of Cleveland and Cleveland Vanguards*, 106 S. Ct. 3036 (1986).
46. U.S. Equal Employment Opportunity Commission, "Facts about Sexual Harassment," December 1990.
47. *Harris v. Forklift Systems, Inc.*, 114 S. Ct. 367 (1993).
48. U.S. Commission on Civil Rights, *A Guide to Federal Laws and Regulations*, Appendix I, "Sex Discrimination Guidelines of the Equal Employment Opportunity Commission."
49. Ibid.
50. *Griggs v. Duke Power Company*, 401 U.S. 424 (1971).
51. *Ward's Cove Packing Co. v. Antonio*, 1093 S. Ct. 2115 (1989).
52. Congressional Quarterly, "Compromise Civil Rights Bill Passed," *Congressional Quarterly Almanac 1991* (Washington D.C.: Congressional Quarterly, 1992), 251-261.
53. U.S. Department of Labor, Women's Bureau, "Women in the Skilled Trades and in Other Manual Occupations," in *Facts on Working Women*, no. 90-5, January 1991.
54. U.S. Department of Labor, Women's Bureau, "Women in Management," in *Facts on Working Women*, no. 89-4, December 1989.
55. U.S. Department of Labor. *Report on the Glass Ceiling Initiative*.

56. U.S. Department of Labor, *Pipelines of Progress.*
57. Nancy F. Rytina, "Earnings of Men and Women: A Look at Specific Occupations," *Monthly Labor Review,* April 1982, 30.
58. Ibid., 29.
59. U.S. Department of Labor, Bureau of Labor Statistics, *The Female-Male Earnings Gap;* U.S. Department of Labor, Women's Bureau, "Earning Differences between Men and Women," in *Facts on Working Women,* no. 90-3, Table 2, 3.
60. U.S. Department of Labor, Bureau of Labor Statistics, "Earnings Differences between Men and Women," Table 1, 2. See also Sorenson, *Exploring the Reasons.*
61. For details of the study by the state of Washington, see Helen Remick, "Comparable Worth in Washington State," in Rita Mae Kelly and Jane Bayes, eds., *Comparable Worth, Pay Equity, and Public Policy* (Westport, Conn.: Greenwood Press, 1988), 223-236. A study of Minnesota's efforts to institute a standard of comparable worth is described in Sara M. Evans and Barbara J. Nelson, *Wage Justice* (Chicago: University of Chicago Press, 1989).
62. For a discussion of some of the economic and political problems presented by mandatory comparable worth solutions, see Henry L. Aaron and Cameron M. Longy, *The Comparable Worth Controversy* (Washington, D.C.: Brookings Institution, 1986); Equal Employment Advisory Council, *Comparable Worth: A Symposium on the Issues and Alternatives* (Washington, D.C.: EEAC, 1981); and U.S. Commission on Civil Rights, *Comparable Worth: Issues for the '80s,* vols. 1 and 2, 1984.
63. *Washington v. American Federation of State, County, and Municipal Employees,* 770 F.2d 1401 (9th Cir., September 5, 1985).
64. Jonathan S. Leonard, "The Impact of Affirmative Action on Employment," *Journal of Labor Economics* 2 (October 1984): 451. Note that *Special Analysis J, Civil Rights Activities, Budget of the United States Government, Fiscal Year 1986,* Executive Office of the President, Office of Management and Budget (1985), includes quotations selected from Leonard's articles and from a report he made to the Department of Labor that conveyed a misleading impression of the conclusions he drew from his research.

CHRONOLOGY

1908 In *Muller v. Oregon,* the Supreme Court upholds the constitutionality of legislation designed to protect women employees.

1920 The Women's Bureau of the Department of Labor is established.

1941 President Franklin Delano Roosevelt issues Executive Order 8802 prohibiting employment discrimination in defense industries.

1963 Congress passes the Equal Pay Act, which prohibits gender discrimination in the determination of wages and salaries for the same job in the same location.

1964 Title VII of the Civil Rights Act of 1964 prohibits discrimination on the basis of sex in all aspects of employment by the federal government, unions, firms with fifteen or more employees, and employment agencies.

1965 President Lyndon Johnson issues Executive Order 11246 prohibiting discrimination in employment practices by federal or federally funded contractors and subcontractors.

1967 President Johnson issues Executive Order 11375, which extends Executive Order 11246 to include discrimination on the basis of gender.

1972 The protections of Title VII of the Civil Rights Act of 1964 are extended to employees of state and local governments, small firms not covered by minimum wage laws, and educational institutions.

1978 Congress passes the Pregnancy Discrimination Act, which prohibits discrimination against pregnant women in any aspect of employment, including hiring, promotion, seniority rights, and job security.

1988 Congress passes the Civil Rights Restoration Act, in effect reversing the Supreme Court decision in *Grove City College v. Bell* (1984), which had limited the impact of equal employment opportunity laws and executive orders on educational institutions.

1991 Congress passes the Civil Rights Act of 1991, which overturns the interpretation of the law in a number of Supreme Court decisions that had the effect of weakening civil rights laws.

1993 Congress passes, and President Bill Clinton signs, the Family and Medical Leave Act.

SUGGESTIONS FOR FURTHER READING

Aaron, Henry L., and Cameron M. Longy. *The Comparable Worth Controversy.* Washington, D.C.: Brookings Institution, 1986.

Baer, Judith A. *Women in American Law.* New York: Holmes and Meier, 1991.

Bergmann, Barbara. *The Economic Emergence of Women.* New York: Basic Books, 1986.

Goldstein, Leslie Friedman. *The Constitutional Rights of Women.* Madison: University of Wisconsin Press, 1988.

Kelly, Rita Mae. *The Gendered Economy.* Newbury Park, Calif.: Sage, 1991.

Kelly, Rita Mae, and Jane Bayes, eds. *Comparable Worth, Pay Equity, and Public Policy.* Westport, Conn.: Greenwood Press, 1988.

MacKinnon, Catharine A. *Sexual Harassment of Working Women.* New Haven, Conn.: Yale University Press, 1979.

Mezey, Susan Gluck. *In Pursuit of Equality: Women, Public Policy, and the Federal Courts.* New York: St. Martin's Press, 1992.

Economic Equity:
Credit, Housing,
and Retirement Income

Food, clothing, shelter, and medical care are basic necessities for all Americans. The changing economy forces more men and women to focus on how to provide these necessities for themselves and their families. This chapter focuses on three economic problems that most women and their families face: obtaining credit to purchase or rent housing and to acquire other necessities; gaining access to housing; and preparing to obtain an adequate retirement income to pay for the basic necessities, including medical care, in their later years.

THE PROBLEM OF CREDIT DISCRIMINATION

In the early 1970s, three women in three different communities applied for credit; all were denied. A young high school teacher, who was the sole wage earner in her family (her husband was a full-time college student with no income), applied to a national retail chain for a credit card. The retail chain insisted that the credit card be issued in the husband's name, not hers.

A husband and wife applied for a mortgage loan at their local bank. They planned to include the wife's income from her job as a secretary in their loan application to determine how large a loan they could finance with their combined incomes. The bank insisted that the wife state what birth control practices she would use so that she could assure the lender that she would not be quitting her job to have another child. Even when she did, the lender would count only half the wife's income for the purposes of figuring the maximum loan for which the couple was eligible.

A single woman, employed as a teacher, applied for a mortgage loan to buy a house. Her application was rejected by several lenders, not because her income was inadequate or because she had a record of not paying her bills, but because she was female and might quit her job. In contrast, single male applicants who had similar credit records were granted loans to purchase homes. Although these cases might seem ridiculous to us, they represent what were considered normal credit practices in the years before 1974.

Women were not the only victims of credit discrimination. Retired persons were denied credit because they were unemployed, even when their incomes from pensions and investments were more than sufficient to pay their debts and allow them to live comfortably. Members of minority races were denied credit merely because of their race. Persons seeking to purchase or improve property in older neighborhoods were denied credit because of the neighborhood in which the property was located (a practice called redlining).[1]

In the dominant culture of that period, there was a presumption that women, the elderly, and minority race members were not creditworthy. For example, mortgage lenders automatically denied loans to single women because they were assumed to be unable to repay large loans with long repayment schedules. Because loans generally were not made to single women, lenders had little evidence to support that belief, but that did not deter them from continuing the practice until it was made illegal. Lenders considered it easier to deny credit to all applicants in some categories of race, gender, and age than to evaluate the credit record of each applicant individually.[2]

According to the 1972 report of the National Commission on Consumer Credit, discrimination against women (as well as the elderly and minorities) by credit-granting institutions and firms was widespread and included:

1. More frequent denial of credit to single women than to single men.
2. Denial of credit to a married woman in her own name.
3. Unwillingness to count a wife's income at full value in joint applications for credit.
4. The requirement that a male cosigner assume joint responsibility for a loan made to a woman.
5. The requirement that a single woman with a credit account who got married had to reapply for credit in her husband's name; the credit cards that had been issued in her maiden name were then canceled.
6. Denial of credit to a widowed or divorced woman, who usually had no credit history of her own because all credit cards and loans had been in her husband's name.[3]

To eliminate these practices so that credit would be made available to all Americans simply on the basis of their ability to repay their debts, a federal law was needed. The underlying principle of the Equal Credit Opportunity Act, which was passed in 1974 and took effect in 1976, is that creditworthiness should be judged on the basis of an individual's ability to repay debts and record of having met financial obligations, not on such irrelevant characteristics as gender, marital status, race, or age.[4]

Has the goal of equal opportunity to obtain credit, based solely on the creditworthiness of an applicant, been attained? Has the law enacted at the federal level ended discrimination in the granting of credit? Even if a law is adequate, effective regulations must be written to ensure that it is properly carried out, thus creating an environment in which there is fair access to credit.

ENFORCEMENT OF THE EQUAL CREDIT OPPORTUNITY ACT

Enactment of a law is only the first step in the policy process; subsequent steps are just as important. The second step is the drafting of effective regulations by the bureaucracy to govern the law's enforcement. Third, effective measures for enforcing the law and the regulations must be established and funded. Fourth, compliance must be monitored, and if necessary, action taken to force compliance. In the process, a need for changes in the law, its regulations, or the enforcement mechanisms may be discovered by those administering the policy or by those whom the law affects.

The drafting of regulations necessary to carry out the Equal Credit Opportunity Act of 1974 was assigned to the Federal Reserve Board. A dozen federal agencies, each of which regulated a particular type of lending institution or credit-granting business, were given responsibility for enforcing the law and the regulations.

The Equal Credit Opportunity Act established the principle that neither gender nor marital status can be used in the evaluation of an applicant's creditworthiness. A spouse's income is not to be discounted in establishing the amount of credit for which a couple is eligible. Alimony, child support, and separate maintenance may be considered in evaluating creditworthiness only if the borrower so wishes.

As originally enacted, the legislation was limited in scope; it did not make discrimination based on age, race, national origin, or religion illegal. The omission of age discrimination generated strong protests from interest groups lobbying for the elderly. Younger people, both those working and those attending college, also suffered discrimination in their attempts to gain access to various forms of credit, such as credit cards. A less obvious but no less serious problem was that the law did not preempt state laws that limited married women's right to enter into contracts. Nor did it have a mechanism for coordinating the activities of the dozen federal agencies assigned responsibility for enforcing it. Furthermore, the law did not authorize the U.S. attorney general to investigate or bring suit against those firms engaging in discriminatory lending practices. Although the law authorized the filing of court suits by victims of credit discrimination, the statute of limitations for filing civil suits (one year) was too short. In addition, the low levels of damages available to the plaintiffs in a class action suit ($100,000 or 1 percent of the lender's net worth, whichever was less) limited the use of such suits.[5]

Not only was the law inadequate, but problems arose in drafting the regulations necessary to carry it out. The drafting of such regulations is an intensely political process—a battle in which the victories won in the legislative arena can be lost, as they were in this case. The Federal Reserve Board's first draft of Regulation B, issued in April 1975, reflected strong proconsumer sentiment. However, in response to many adverse comments from lenders, the board issued a revised draft of Regulation B in September 1975 that was more favorable to their interests. Representatives of some women's groups, already mobilized to lobby the regulation drafters, made tactical errors in responding to lenders' complaints. Nevertheless, their protests ultimately prompted the board to issue a final draft of Regulation B in October 1975 that was more favorable to consumers' interests than the second draft, but not as favorable as the first had been. As a result of the failure of consumer groups, and particularly women's groups, to lobby effectively, the regulations were less favorable than they otherwise might have been.[6]

In its final draft of the regulations, the Federal Reserve Board narrowed the law's coverage so that it applied not to all types of credit but only to consumer credit. As passed by Congress, the 1974 act applied to business or commercial credit as well as to consumer credit. The committee report accompanying the Senate version of the bill clearly indicated that business credit was to be covered, thus prohibiting "discrimination based on sex or marital status in extensions of credit for commercial purposes."[7] However, Regulation B exempted commercial credit from some notification and record-keeping requirements. In 1976, amendments to the law authorized the Federal Reserve Board's post hoc exemption of certain types of business credit transactions from the relevant provisions of the act if the Fed considered those provisions unnecessary. These waivers of some of the regulations' requirements for business credit applications made it much more difficult to challenge an unfair denial of credit to a creditworthy business loan applicant. Thus women, older persons, or minority race members who applied for a loan to open a store, create a business, or set up a law practice or a medical practice could be the victims of credit discrimination because banks or other lending institutions were not required to keep records similar to those required for applications for consumer credit.

The regulations for enforcement of the Equal Credit Opportunity Act required only that an appropriate statement be made to the credit applicant if credit were denied or terminated and if the credit applicant requested it. The statement did not have to be in writing, nor did it have to explain why credit was being denied. No time limit was specified for action on the credit application (a "reasonable time" was the term used in the regulations). Critics pointed out that these provisions would permit credit discrimination to persist. For example, if no reason for credit denial were given, an individual could not correct faulty records. Of course, not having a written reason for credit denial would make it difficult for the individual to file a suit alleging discrimination in the granting of credit.[8]

REVISIONS OF THE EQUAL CREDIT OPPORTUNITY ACT

Obviously, both the Equal Credit Opportunity Act of 1974 and the regulations drafted to put it into effect had serious deficiencies. For this reason, in 1976 Congress enacted significant amendments to the act that went into effect in 1977.[9] These amendments extended the coverage of the act to protect credit applicants from discrimination on the basis of race, color, national origin, age (provided that the applicant has the legal capacity to contract), receipt of income from public assistance, or the applicant's exercise of rights under the Consumer Credit Protection Act of 1968. Inquiries may be made about an applicant's age as long as a negative score is not assigned in a credit evaluation system to an elderly applicant because of age. Thus, younger applicants may be scored lower than older applicants on the basis of age. Applicants who receive any part of their income from any government assistance program may not be rejected merely for that reason. Applicants for credit must be notified within thirty days of the action taken on their credit application.

The amendments create stronger enforcement procedures. The statute of limitations for filing suits is increased from one year to two and the maximum damages that can be obtained in class action suits are increased from $100,000 to $500,000, or 1 percent of the lender's net worth, whichever is less. The amendments authorize the U.S. attorney general to investigate and file suits against those firms identified as engaging in discriminatory lending practices.[10]

Congressional hearings held during the 1980s revealed the need for further changes in the Equal Credit Opportunity Act. In a report on women business entrepreneurs issued in 1988, the House Select Committee on Small Business pointed out that whereas women owned less than 5 percent of the nation's businesses prior to the 1970s, they owned 30 percent in 1988 and were expected to own 50 percent by the year 2000.[11] Clearly, gender discrimination in the granting of business and commercial credit adversely affects a significant and growing proportion of America's business firms.

In response to reports of discrimination by lenders in providing credit to women business owners, in 1988 the 100th Congress enacted H.R. 5050, one section of which was intended to increase women's access to business and commercial credit.[12] That section of the law provides that no exemptions to the enforcement regulations are allowed except those that would not materially affect the law's intent or be detrimental to the achievement of its goals, and such a decision is to be made by the Federal Reserve Board only after holding a public hearing on the potential effects of the exemption. No exemption may granted for longer than five years. The amendments also require that lending institutions keep all data and records relating to a commercial or business loan application for at least one year; the Federal Reserve Board can require that records be kept for a longer time. Furthermore, individuals denied a commercial or business loan must be notified in writing that they have the right to request a written statement of the reasons for denial of credit. Thus, fourteen years after the enactment of the initial legislation, women gained the protections necessary to ensure fair access to business and commercial credit. Women are now recognized as being more than just consumers in the American economy.

IMPACT OF THE EQUAL CREDIT OPPORTUNITY ACT

The protections afforded by the Equal Credit Opportunity Act significantly affect access to credit. Credit now must be made available to individuals regardless of their age, gender, or race provided they have the ability to pay their debts. For example, one requirement of the law is that a woman be permitted to establish a personal credit history by having credit issued in her own name, and a married woman may have her name added, if she wishes, to credit card accounts listed solely in her spouse's name. Prior to the law's enactment, credit accounts were listed in the husband's name, regardless of whether the wife used the account or contributed to the payment of the debt. Under the law, as amended, all credit card holders must be notified that a credit account may be listed in both spouses' names. Having the account in both spouses' names facilitates obtaining credit in the event of a divorce or the spouse's death.[13]

The Equal Credit Opportunity Act enables an individual to obtain a loan without a cosigner, based strictly on the individual's creditworthiness, unless others with similar credit histories and similar abilities to repay any loan extended would be required to have a cosigner. Thus, no woman can be required to have a cosigner for a loan or credit account unless a man would also be required under similar conditions to have a cosigner for a loan.

Certain previously accepted discriminatory credit practices are banned outright. A creditor may not ask a woman applicant about birth control practices or future intentions concerning the bearing or rearing of children. However, information may be requested concerning the ages of an applicant's children.

A creditor may not inquire whether any of an applicant's income is derived from alimony, child support, or separate maintenance. But if a credit applicant does voluntarily report income from those sources, the creditor may evaluate the probability of income from that source being received on a regular basis. Age may be considered in evaluating creditworthiness, but only if an elderly applicant is not assigned a lower score on the basis of age than the score assigned to applicants in any other age category. (The act defines elderly as age 62 or older.)

Unresolved Credit Discrimination Problems

Unfortunately, not all credit practices that are inequitable have been eliminated. In April 1993, the Office of the Comptroller of the Currency increased its efforts to monitor the credit extension practices of banks under its supervision to determine if the requirements concerning nondiscrimination in lending were being met. It found that some financial institutions still fail to apply fair credit evaluation standards with regard to women, minority group members, and young credit applicants. Such practices (now illegal) include refusal to count a woman's alimony or child support payments as income, requiring a woman to have a cosigner to qualify for a loan, and applying a higher rate of interest for loans made to young people than to other borrowers.[14]

Among the unresolved problems in assuring equal opportunity for access to credit are (1) the failure of banks, credit card issuers, and other lenders to develop feasible and fair methods of evaluating loan applicants' creditworthiness; (2) the need to monitor public utilities and health care providers, which are currently exempt from the act's provisions; (3) the continued application of state "necessities" and "family expense" laws, which are not preempted by the act; (4) the continued practice of redlining; and (5) inadequate, ineffective enforcement of the act either by federal agencies or as a result of private litigation.[15]

Assessing the Implementation of Equal Rights Policy

Ten conditions have been suggested as potentially contributing to successful equal rights policy implementation:

1. The policy goals have been clearly stated.
2. Precise standards have been established to determine compliance.
3. A mechanism has been created to monitor compliance.
4. An agency has been assigned responsibility for implementing the policy.
5. Those responsible for implementation are committed to promoting civil rights.
6. Those responsible for enforcement enjoy the support of their superiors.
7. The policy beneficiaries are organized and cohesive and thus can effectively support implementation.
8. The efforts of the various agencies responsible for achieving a policy goal are administratively coordinated.
9. The cost-benefit ratio of the situation favors compliance.
10. The federal government is an active participant on behalf of minorities.[16]

When we assess the implementation of policy under the Equal Credit Opportunity Act, we find that only some of these conditions are present. The policy goal of access to credit based on creditworthiness is clearly stated. Implementation and enforcement are assigned to a number of federal agencies, and each agency's responsibilities are clearly specified.

In general, the federal agencies are responsible for monitoring banks, retail stores, and other credit institutions to ensure that they are using the correct forms and procedures and meeting the standards for compliance that have been set, as discussed earlier. Unfortunately, the actual monitoring of access to credit has not been thorough. Agencies have been hampered in part by a lack of the information necessary to evaluate lending patterns. For example, the law forbids collection of data on the marital status or gender of applicants except when they are applying for mortgage credit. The law should be changed to require the collection of that data for all types of loans so that patterns of credit discrimination can be identified and enforcement of the law facilitated.

During the first decade after enactment of the Equal Credit Opportunity Act, personnel in the federal agencies charged with the law's enforcement perceived no career benefits to be gained from, and considerable role conflict as a result of, the addition of such enforcement to their existing responsibilities. Furthermore, they perceived their supervisors as giving it a low priority. In some agencies that problem was resolved by changes in career advancement requirements and the creation of new career paths, thus facilitating the advancement of those engaged in equal rights policy implementation and law enforcement.[17] The absence of cohesive organizations lobbying for equal credit policy implementation undoubtedly contributed to the low priority given to the law's enforcement. The lack of coordination among implementing agencies was also a problem.

Unfortunately, in cases where credit discrimination did occur, enforcement of the Equal Credit Opportunity Act often proved difficult. The difficulties encountered in enforcing the act invited its violation. To a considerable extent, any gains in achieving equal access to credit can be attributed to market forces, which encouraged in lenders to conform to the law not because it was the law but out of self-interest. Once lenders recognized the creditworthiness of groups that had been discriminated against, such as women, minorities, and the elderly, they realized that a higher number of qualified credit customers could result in increased profits. They also wished to avoid the unfavorable publicity that would follow when discriminatory practices were discovered.

THE PROBLEM OF HOUSING

After twelve years of marriage, Elaine's husband decided that he wanted to end the union; he moved out of the house and filed for a divorce. For eight of those years, Elaine had not worked but stayed home to care for the children. As part of the divorce settlement she received child support payments for the two children and half the family's assets, but the house had to be sold to pay the husband his share of the accumulated equity in it. Elaine obtained a job as a teacher and then searched for a dwelling for herself and the children. Both she and the children wanted to continue to live in the same neighborhood, so the children would not have to change schools and could maintain their friendships with their classmates. However, the search for affordable housing in that area proved unsuccessful.

Elaine's search illustrates the four problems faced by women and their families in obtaining housing—the four A's of availability, adequacy, affordability, and accessibility. Unfortunately, these problems are faced not only by newly divorced women and their families but by all women—married, single, heads of household, and especially the elderly who live alone.

Availability refers to the type and total number of housing units for purchase or rent. Scarcities may exist in the absolute number of units necessary to meet demand or in the type of units desired in terms of size, price, and amenities. *Adequacy* means that the housing unit meets minimal standards of repair, safety, appliances, and amenities. *Affordability* is determined by the cost to rent or purchase the housing unit. In some areas of the United States, such as the Washington, D.C., metropolitan area, housing units are generally more expensive. *Accessibility* refers to housing that, in addition to being available, adequate, and affordable, is located near or within easy commuting distance to work, schools, friends, shops, services, and recreational facilities.

The key question is whether women and their families have the financial resources necessary to obtain shelter that meets all four criteria—especially the married women and their families whose personal disposable income has been affected by changes in the economy.[18] Approximately 60 percent of the elderly single women who own their homes do not have adequate financial resources to pay property taxes, maintenance, and utilities.[19] And as the story of Elaine illustrates, a recently divorced woman may receive the house as part of the divorce settlement, but the cost of mortgage payments, maintenance, utilities, and taxes may be more than her income can support. If the house is sold and the proceeds divided as part of the divorce settlement, finding alternative housing that permits the custodial parent and the children to maintain social ties may be difficult.

About 17 percent of all households of more than one person are headed by women; another 15 percent of such households consist of single women.[20] According to census data, women are financially responsible for one-third of all households, and about three-fifths of all married women work outside the home. Thus women clearly make a significant financial contribution to meeting basic family needs, including housing, in a substantial majority of the households in the United States.

The income distributions for both female heads of households and single female households are such that housing costs are a serious problem for a significant number of them. Families with incomes below the poverty line are faced with rents higher than they can afford. The accepted standard is that a household should not spend more than 30 percent of its income for housing, but the housing costs of the poor may exceed that figure. Americans on average spend one-fifth of their income on housing; in 1985, those who rent spent an average of 28 percent of their income for housing.[21] Many women must spend a substantially larger percentage of their income to obtain shelter, however. In 1985, one-fifth of all renters spent 50 percent or more of their income on housing.[22]

Several federal programs address the problem of access to housing, but two are most significant in providing financial aid to the poor, including women. The government provides subsidized housing in large housing projects to individuals and families unable to afford the rents that prevail in the local real estate market. Prior to 1980, this was the most common type of federal subsidy for low-income families and individuals.[23] Since 1980, federal housing policy has emphasized a program known as Section 8, under which the government provides a subsidy to individuals and families of limited means so that they can obtain rental housing in the community. The federal government supplies the difference between 25 percent of the recipient's income and the fair market cost of the rental unit, thus enabling the individual to take advantage of rental housing available on the local housing market.[24] No owner is required to rent to someone who receives housing assistance under the Section 8 program, but an owner who chooses to do so may be required to improve units that are in disrepair.

The funding available through these two programs is sufficient to aid only a small proportion of the households needing housing assistance. Inadequate funding is a major cause of the homeless problem that currently exists in the United States.

Although such rental housing assistance is not insubstantial in cost, it should be borne in mind that most of the federal government's housing assistance takes the form of subsidies to homeowners; thus it goes not to the poor but to the upper and middle classes. These subsidies are of two types. The first is the allowed deduction of the state and local property taxes paid by a homeowner from the homeowner's gross income in calculating the adjusted gross income on which federal income tax is paid. The more valuable the home and the higher the property tax rate, the bigger the tax subsidy provided to the homeowner. The second type of subsidy is the allowed deduction of interest paid on a home mortgage from the homeowner's gross income in figuring the adjusted gross income on which federal income tax is paid. These two types of deduction from adjusted gross income (which are classified as tax expenditures in the federal budget) are available both for the principal residence and for one vacation or second home. Together, these two types of subsidy constituted 81 percent of all federal housing assistance in 1985.[25]

Federal, state, and local governments may also provide other forms of housing assistance. They frequently make small grants or loans available to those individuals who earn enough from their jobs to pay monthly rent but cannot afford the rental deposit (frequently the first and last months' rent plus a security deposit) and the cost of having utilities connected—so that they can obtain rental housing. Governments also purchase substandard housing and resell it at a low price to urban homesteaders who agree to rehabilitate the housing and reside in it for a minimum number of years.

THE PROBLEMS OF RETIREMENT INCOME AND THE FEMINIZATION OF POVERTY

Andrea and her husband had looked forward to their retirement; having worked for many years, they had planned to travel to visit family members. The sole source of income for each of them, however, was a social security pension. Although they owned their home free of any debt, this income had not even proved sufficient to pay for all basic necessities such as food, utilities, and any medical expenses not covered by health insurance. Thus in their retirement years they were plagued by unrelenting concerns about being able to meet their expenses. When her husband died, Andrea received a pension equal to his social security benefit—but it left her even more impoverished than before.

Elderly women constitute one of the two groups of American women whose economic predicament has contributed to the feminization of poverty. (The other is single heads of household.) It has been estimated that 15 percent of all women age 65 and older have incomes that place them below the government-defined level of poverty. Women also constitute two-thirds of the near-poor elderly (those with incomes ranging from 100 percent to 125 percent of the poverty threshold).[26] What has caused this pattern of impoverishment for older American women?

As a group, the elderly have three potential sources of income: (1) old-age pensions provided under the Social Security program (the government requires almost every employed person in the United States to contribute a part of his or her wages or salary and requires a matching contribution from the person's employer); (2) private pensions, provided to retirees as a benefit by their former employer; and (3) savings and investments made by the retirees during their working years.

The Social Security system pension plan was designed for the families of the 1930s, not for the modern American family. In the 1930s, the average family consisted of a husband who was employed, a wife who was a homemaker, and children. Today less than 10 percent of American families fit this description.[27] Now the majority of women work outside the home, although they continue to be the primary caregivers for both children and other adults in the household. Furthermore, households consisting of single women and headed by single women constitute about one-third of all households.

Old-age and survivors insurance, provided under the Social Security program, was intended to be only a supplement to income from private pensions and from the savings invested during a retiree's lifetime. It was not expected to be the only source of income during retirement. Unfortunately, only a minority of Americans—less than one-quarter of the retired women and less than one-half of the retired men—receive payments from a private pension. And on average, the pensions that women do receive are about half as large as those received by men.[28] Even among those individuals who are still employed, only 37 percent of the women and 42 percent of the men are enrolled in a private pension system.[29]

Many elderly women do not have income from a private pension or sufficient assets to supplement their social security income, whether it is based on their own earnings or on those of their husbands. In general, women are less likely to be enrolled in a private pension plan. Many of them have worked only part time, in lower-paying jobs, or for small businesses—types of employment that usually do not provide benefits such as pension programs. (About 90 percent of large corporations have pension plans for employees, whereas only 23 percent of small businesses do.)[30] Furthermore, women change jobs and also enter and leave employment more frequently than men; they follow a husband when he moves to a new job, or they leave employment to care for children, an elderly parent, or an ill or injured family member.

Although the private business or government agency where a woman is employed may provide a pension plan as an employee benefit, she may have difficulty qualifying for an adequate pension. Under the Employee Retirement Income Security Act of 1974 (ERISA), a person who works full time for one company for at least five years qualifies for a pension benefit that is not forfeited if the employee leaves that employer (that is, the employer "vests" pension rights in the employee)—provided, of course, that the company has a pension plan.[31] Unfortunately, women's average length of time with one employer is less than five years, which suggests that many women change jobs too frequently to earn a pension, even if it is offered by their employer.[32] Moreover, even if an individual works for one employer for five years, he or she must reach the age, or the combination of age and years of employment, specified in the pension plan before becoming eligible to draw benefits.

One economic change that has been occurring in many companies since the late 1980s is "downsizing" (a reduction in employment). Companies are also exporting manufacturing jobs to lower-cost sites, either in another state or in another country. Many individuals affected by these changes are laid off from jobs whose pension benefits become available when they reach retirement age, but the earned benefit will be less because they will have worked fewer years for the company. Alternatively, many individuals are offered early retirement with a significantly smaller pension than they would otherwise receive, and companies are not required by federal law to offer benefits to surviving spouses of individuals who take early retirement. Many companies that have found it necessary to downsize have engaged in a form of age discrimination—they have laid off individuals who have worked for the company not quite long enough to earn a full pension.

Many elderly women are entitled to receive survivor's benefits from their deceased spouse's private pension. However, the spouse may have agreed to waive his wife's right to such benefits in order to draw a larger pension while he was alive. In 1984, ERISA was amended to require both husband and wife to sign the waiver form before either can waive the survivor's benefits. Sometimes, however, the waiver form is written in such obscure legalese that many couples do not understand what they are doing when they sign it.

Many employers—both public and private—have promised pension benefits to their employees but have not funded the pension plans sufficiently to cover these commitments. Because of the potential problems created by this behavior, in 1974 Congress included in ERISA a provision establishing the Pension Benefit Guarantee Corporation to insure the pension benefits promised by private firms. The corporation acts as an insurance company, collecting a premium from each firm to cover promised benefits in case the business fails and the firm has not adequately funded the pension benefits promised to its employees. The insurance premiums are supposed to be large enough to cover any deficiencies arising when firms terminate their pension plans or go into bankruptcy. The Pension Benefit Guarantee Corporation has not received sufficient funds to cover unfunded obligations, however; approximately 15 percent of the companies having pension funds have not adequately funded their plans to cover promised benefits.[33] Also contributing to the corporation's liability is the termination of pension plans by companies that have been merged, consolidated, or liquidated.[34]

An individual may work for a firm that fully funds its pension obligations, but a decision to change employers means that the individual starts anew in earning the right to a pension. (ERISA specifies that an employer must vest pension rights in an employee only after that employee has worked for the company for five years.) Frequent job changes and short lengths of employment with several different employers thus result in either a small pension or no pension at all. Some have suggested creation of a "portable" pension plan, so that an individual who changes employers frequently can continue to pay into, and accumulate benefits from, the same plan. An example is the Teachers Insurance and Annuity Association, a pension plan available to many college and university professors and to employees of other nonprofit institutions.

To encourage individuals to provide for their own retirement, the federal government has created several types of pension plans into which an individual may invest savings for that purpose. They include individual retirement accounts (IRAs), Keogh plans, and simplified employee plans. The IRA is intended for individuals earning $25,000 or less and married couples earning $32,500 or less jointly. The money the wage earner contributes to an IRA is not taxed until after he or she retires and begins withdrawing money from the account, nor is the income earned by money invested in the account taxed before retirement. The rules concerning who may invest in an IRA and when the money may be withdrawn without penalty have changed over time. Those eligible to participate in IRAs have generally found them to be a good means of providing for retirement. Unfortunately, IRAs are not used by the individuals least likely to participate in a pension plan where they work—those earning the lowest wages and those who work part time.

Almost every person who works for a public or a private employer now pays into the federal government's old-age and survivors insurance program. Although this was originally intended to be an insurance fund, it has in fact become an income transfer fund because of the cost of benefits paid to current retirees. The money paid by individuals now employed is used to pay the benefits of those now retired. In the early 1990s, the Social Security trust fund accumulated a surplus, but it was used to help offset the deficit spending that was necessary to sustain other federal government programs.

At the present time, an individual can draw a full benefit against his or her earnings at age 65 or a reduced benefit with earlier retirement; the minimum age for retirement with a social security pension is 62.[35] However, for individuals born in 1937 and after, full pension benefits are available only to those retiring at age 67 or older. Beginning in 1991, calculation of the monthly benefit was to be based on thirty-five years of earnings of at least $520 for each fourth of a year. A woman who was not employed during the childbearing and child-caring years might have fewer years of earnings. The five years of an individual's working life in which earnings were lowest (including zero earnings if no income was earned) are dropped in the calculation of earnings against which the benefit is drawn. It has been suggested that the ten years in which earnings were lowest be dropped in calculating the benefit earned, since many women with family care responsibilities will not have had thirty-five years of employment.

A woman whose husband is eligible for social security benefits can, at age 62, receive a social security benefit equal to one-half of her husband's. Thus, if she would receive more by drawing against her husband's benefits than she would by drawing against her own earnings, she may opt to receive a social security benefit based on her husband's earnings rather than on her own, even though she has for many years paid part of her wages into the Social Security fund. If the husband dies, a widow over the age of 65 receives 100 percent of his benefit. If she is younger than 65 but older than 60, a widow receives 71.5 percent of the spouse's benefit. If a spouse dies, the widow or widower under the age of 60 receives no benefit unless she or he is disabled or has children under the age of 18 living at home. From the time the youngest child reaches the age of 18 until the widow or widower reaches the age of 60, the surviving spouse is not entitled to receive social security benefits. If the widow or widower is disabled, she or he may not collect benefits until the age of 50. A woman who is divorced may draw against her ex-husband's benefit if the marriage lasted more than ten years.

Clearly, the feminization of poverty reflects both women's employment patterns and their dual roles of wage earner and family caregiver. A change in women's employment patterns could alleviate this problem in the future—if (1) women work for an employer who provides employee pension benefits, and work long enough to acquire pension rights; and (2) their pension benefit is adequate and is not devalued substantially by inflation; or (3) they are paid enough that they can accumulate assets sufficient to yield an income that will sustain them in their retirement years.

This chapter has focused on three problems that women and their families face in seeking economic equity. Progress is slowly being made in the continuing struggle at both the federal and state levels to put into effect policies that will ensure equal economic rights. Eternal vigilance is the price of liberty;[36] it is also the price of ensuring equity in public policy. Those who support equal rights continue to propose legislation intended to reduce or eliminate discriminatory policies. Continuous monitoring of the policy process, both by individual citizens and by groups representing them, is the price to be paid for gaining and maintaining equal rights for women.

NOTES

1. National Commission on Consumer Finance, *Consumer Credit in the United States* (Washington, D.C.: Government Printing Office, 1972).
2. Richard F. Nielson, "Implications of the Equal Credit Opportunity Act Amendments of 1976, "*Journal of Consumer Affairs* 11 (Summer 1977): 168.
3. National Commission on Consumer Finance, *Consumer Credit in the United States,* 152-153.
4. Equal Credit Opportunity Act, 15 U.S.C. sec. 1691, 1988 ed. (Washington, D.C.: Government Printing Office, 1989).
5. See M. Margaret Conway, "Discrimination and the Law: The Equal Credit Opportunity Act," in Marian Lief Palley and Michael B. Preston, *Race, Sex, and Public Policy* (Lexington, Mass.: Lexington Books, 1979) 77-78.
6. For a discussion of the politics of the regulation-drafting process, see Joyce Gelb and Marian Lief Palley, *Women and Public Policies* (Princeton, N.J.: Princeton University Press, 1987), 81-86.
7. Senate Committee on Banking, Housing, and Urban Affairs, *Truth in Lending Amendments,* S. Rpt. 278, 93d Cong., 1st sess., 1973, 18.
8. Conway, "Discrimination and the Law," 77-78.
9. 15 U.S.C. secs. 1691-1691e.
10. Although the 1976 extension of the Equal Credit Opportunity Act made it

clear that the law was to be applicable to the extension of business credit, specific exemptions from the act's provisions regarding business loans were granted to creditors. Creditors considering applications for loans to businesses could inquire about the marital status of business owners, did not have to notify applicants of a denial of credit or of their right to be told the reason for the credit denial, and did not have to keep credit application records for more than ninety days. Also, separate accounts for each spouse did not have to be maintained in business credit actions. Continued discrimination against women who sought credit for the purpose of establishing, operating, or expanding a business led to congressional proposals to amend the act; however, the 99th and 100th Congresses adjourned without passing such an amendment.

11. House Select Committee on Small Business, *Hearings,* 100th Cong., 2d sess., July 24, 1988.
12. For a discussion of the legislation, see Congressional Quarterly, *Congressional Quarterly Almanac 1988,* "Women's Business Ownership Act" (Washington, D.C.: Congressional Quarterly, 1989), 582. For the details of the law, see 100th Congress, P.L. 100-533, secs. 301 and 302.
13. A survey of eight large creditors (three major banks, three large retailers, one travel and entertainment company, and one oil company), conducted by the Federal Reserve Board two years after the effective date of the Equal Credit Opportunity Act, found that spouses had been slow to exercise the right to establish separate credit accounts. Only 11 percent of the customers requested, after notification of this right, that a separate credit history be established for the spouse. Federal Reserve Board, "Exercise of Consumer Rights under the Equal Credit Opportunity and Fair Credit Billing Acts," *Federal Reserve Bulletin* (May 1978), 363-365.
14. "How to Fight Lenders' Age and Sex Bias," *Money Magazine,* February 1994, 42-46.
15. See Conway, "Discrimination and the Law," 82-84; and M. Margaret Conway, "Antidiscrimination Laws and the Problems of Policy Implementation," in John G. Grumm and Stephen L. Wasby, *The Analysis of Policy Impact* (Lexington, Mass.: Lexington Books, 1981), 35-42.
16. Charles S. Bullock III and Charles M. Lamb, *Implementation of Civil Rights Policy* (Monterey, Calif.: Brooks/Cole, 1984), 16.
17. Conway, "Antidiscrimination Laws," 38-39.
18. Cushing N. Dolbeare and Anne J. Stone, "Women and Affordable Housing," in *The American Woman, 1990-1991: A Status Report,* Sara E. Rix, ed. (New York: Norton, 1990), 94-97, 114; Delores Hayden, *Redesigning the American Dream* (New York: Norton, 1984), chap. 9.
19. Dolbeare and Stone, "Women and Affordable Housing," 114.
20. Eugenie Ladner Birch, "Women and Shelter Issues," in Sara Rosenberry and Chester Hartman, *Housing Issues of the 1990s* (New York: Praeger, 1989), Table 4.1, 89. See also Dolbeare and Stone, "Women and Affordable Housing," Table 2.1, 99.
21. Dolbeare and Stone, "Women and Affordable Housing," 108.

22. Ibid.
23. Ibid., 114.
24. Ibid.
25. Ibid., 121.
26. House Select Committee on Aging, Subcommittee on Retirement Income and Employment, *Hearings, How Will Today's Women Fare in Yesterday's Traditional Retirement System?* Testimony of Cynthia M. Taeuber, chief of Age and Sex Statistics Branch, Population Div., Bureau of the Census, U.S. Department of Commerce, Committee Pub. No. 102-873, 101st Cong., 2d sess., March 26, 1992, 8-9.
27. House Select Committee on Aging, Subcommittee on Retirement Income and Employment, *Hearings,* Cedar Rapids, Iowa, Testimony of Rev. Kathleen Clark, 101st Cong., 2d sess., July 2, 1990, 1.
28. U.S. Department of Labor, Pension and Welfare Benefits Administration, *Trends in Pensions,* 1989.
29. U.S. Department of Commerce, Bureau of the Census, *Statistical Abstract of the United States, 1992* (Washington, D.C.: Government Printing Office, 1992), Table 575, 363. This is a substantial decline from the levels of the mid-1980s. For a comparison, see *Social Security Bulletin* 52, no. 10, October 1989.
30. U.S. Department of Commerce, Bureau of the Census, *Statistical Brief,* SB 93-6, April 1993.
31. Originally, the law required ten years of employment for vesting, but this was reduced to five years by the amendments to ERISA contained in the Tax Reform Act of 1986. The vesting period is still ten years for multiple employer plans.
32. House Select Committee on Aging, Subcommittee on Retirement Income and Employment, *Hearings, Women in Retirement: Are They Losing Out?* Testimony of Louise D. Crooks, president of the American Association of Retired Persons, 101st Cong., 2d sess., May 22, 1990.
33. Albert R. Karr, "Risk to Retirees Rises as Firms Fail to Fund Pensions They Offer," *Wall Street Journal,* February 4, 1993, A1.
34. Jeff Gerth, "House Panel Hears Troubles of Pension-Insurance Fund," *New York Times,* February 3, 1993, C1.
35. The following discussion of social security benefits draws largely from Sara E. Rix, "Who Pays for What? Ensuring Financial Security in Retirement," in Christopher L. Hayes and Jane M. Deren, eds., *Pre-Retirement Planning for Women: Program Design and Research* (New York: Springer-Verlag, 1990), 14-15.
36. This is a frequently quoted paraphrase of a statement by John Philpott Curran in his "Speech upon the Right of Election" (1790).

CHRONOLOGY

1972 National Commission on Consumer Credit issues report detailing patterns of discrimination by institutions and firms granting consumer and business credit to women, the elderly, and minorities.

1973 Congressional Joint Economic Committee holds hearings on problem of credit discrimination.

1974 Congress passes the Equal Credit Opportunity Act.

1974 Congress passes the Employee Retirement Income Security Act to regulate private pension plans and to increase the security of retirement income from such plans.

1976 Equal Credit Opportunity Act becomes effective. Congress enacts amendments to it prohibiting discrimination on basis of race, color, age, national origin, receipt of income from a public assistance program, and exercise of rights under the Consumer Credit Protection Act.

1977 Amendments to the Equal Credit Opportunity Act become effective.

1988 Congress extends the Equal Credit Opportunity Act to apply to business and commercial credit.

SUGGESTIONS FOR FURTHER READING

Birch, Eugenie Ladner. "Women and Shelter Issues." In Sara Rosenberry and Chester Hartman, *Housing Issues of the 1990s.* New York: Praeger, 1989.

Conway, M. Margaret. "Discrimination and the Law: The Equal Credit Opportunity Act." In Marian Lief Palley and Michael B. Preston, *Race, Sex, and Public Policy.* Lexington, Mass.: Lexington Books, 1979, 75-85.

———. "Antidiscrimination Laws and the Problems of Policy Implementation," In John G. Grumm and Stephen L. Wasby, *The Analysis of Policy Impact.* Lexington, Mass.: Lexington Books, 1981, 35-42.

Dolbeare, Cushing N., and Anne J. Stone. "Women and Affordable Housing." In Sara E. Rix, ed., *The American Woman, 1990-1991: A Status Report.* New York: Norton, 1990.

Gelb, Joyce, and Marian Lief Palley. *Women and Public Policies,* chap. 4, "Women and Credit Discrimination." Princeton, N.J.: Princeton University Press, 1987.

Rix, Sara E. "Who Pays for What? Ensuring Financial Security in Retirement." In Christopher L. Hayes and Jane M. Deren, eds., *Pre-Retirement Planning for Women: Program Design and Research.* (New York: Springer-Verlag, 1990.

Gender and Insurance

Robert H. Jerry II

On her sixty-fifth birthday, Sara decided to retire after forty years of work at the Slowmobile Automobile Company. Dave, one of her co-workers, also decided to retire on his sixty-fifth birthday. Sara and Dave had for the past twenty years participated in the retirement plan offered by Slowmobile, and each had contributed to their plan the maximum amount allowed by law. Incredibly, Sara and Dave had the same job at Slowmobile and had received identical raises year after year. They were close friends, and they shared with each other a great deal of information about investments, financial planning, and their salaries.

During a quiet moment at a retirement party thrown by their friends at work, Sara and Dave discussed their future plans, and Dave commented that he was glad he had participated in the retirement plan because the $1,200 per month annuity payment was going to come in very handy. Sara expressed surprise, because her annuity payment was only $1,000 per month.

After the party, the more Sara thought about their conversation, the angrier she became. The next day, she visited Slowmobile's manager and asked why Dave was receiving a larger pension than she. "Well, he's a man," explained the manager, "and men get larger payments under the plan."

The next time Sara saw Dave, she told him about her visit with the personnel manager and emphasized how upset she was. When they compared their other retirement benefits, they found that for the past ten years they had contributed identical payments for a term life insurance policy offered by the employer. Also, each had made a payment on the last day of employment, as they were allowed to do under the provisions of the term life insurance policy, for a $10,000 fully paid-up whole life insurance policy. Dave was surprised to learn that he had paid more for the whole life insurance policy than Sara, even though the policy had the same face value as Sara's. Then Dave discovered that upon his death, the proceeds received by his beneficiaries under the term life insurance policy would be less than those received by Sara's beneficiaries. Dave was upset, and Sara was confused.

This time, Dave and Sara visited the personnel manager together, and they asked why they were not being treated equally. The manager replied, "Because you aren't the same. One of you is a man, and one of you is a woman. Sara, the odds are that you will live longer than Dave, and that makes a big difference."

Sara then said to the manager, "My good friend Carla is African-American, and I am white. She has worked here as long as I have. I read in the newspaper the other day that African-Americans have a shorter life expectancy than whites. Do you charge Carla more for life insurance than you charge me, and do you give Carla a higher monthly pension payment?" The manager replied, "No, we don't. That's different."

Dave said, "Now I'm really confused. Why is it different? Why do you treat Sara differently than me?" The manager said, "You need to talk to my boss. I'm already late for a meeting." [1]

THE QUESTION PRESENTED

In an important article on insurance law published over three decades ago, Spencer Kimball observed that "insurance is a small world that reflects the purposes of the larger world outside it." [2] To those who have noted that insurance companies often charge men and women different premiums for the same coverage (or provide different coverages for identical premiums), Kimball's observation has a certain poignancy. For more than a decade, an important question has been the subject of vigorous debate: Should insurers be allowed to use gender to calculate insurance premiums and benefits? This chapter analyzes the various arguments in the debate and considers the public policy implications of implementing a gender-neutral rating system.

THE BASICS OF INSURANCE RATING

The importance of insurance has long been recognized, but many people do not thoroughly understand insurance's risk-transferring and risk distribution characteristics. A common misconception is that insurance is nothing more than a wager between the insured, who bets the "premium" that some tragedy will occur during the term of the policy, and the insurer, who bets that the event will not occur. The insurer "gives odds," in that it promises to pay the insured many times more than the premium should the specified but uncertain event occur. But to view insurance as simply a wager is to ignore the *security* that the insured purchases with the premium payment. Confronting an uncertain future where great financial hardship is possible, the insured purchases certainty by paying an insurer to assume the risk of a loss. Even if the loss does not materialize, the insured receives a valuable product—the peace of mind of knowing that the financial burden of the potential loss will be borne wholly or partly by the insurer.

Another misconception is that the insured should always pay a premium calculated according to his or her risk and no more. This statement has some merit because the insured's premium should be a function of that individual's risk. Thus, a daredevil pilot should pay more for life insurance than a college professor.[3] Pilots have a riskier profession, and professors, on the average, live longer. An important reason that insurers differentiate between daredevil pilots and college professors when pricing life insurance is that the administrative costs of distinguishing between the two professions are low. When the differentiating characteristics are more expensive to measure, it may not be sensible for the insurer to divide a group of insureds into high-risk and low-risk subgroups. For example, individuals who consume moderate amounts of alcoholic beverages tend to live longer than heavy drinkers; thus, in theory, moderate drinkers should pay less for life insurance than heavy drinkers. Yet it might cost an insurance company large sums of money to distinguish accurately between moderate drinkers and heavy drinkers, partly because many insureds will claim to drink only in moderation when they in fact overindulge. If the costs of distinguishing between heavy drinkers and moderate drinkers exceed the savings a low-risk moderate drinker might receive on the insurance premium, the moderate drinker is actually better off when categorized with, and charged the same premium as, a high-risk heavy drinker.

When no distinction is made between heavy drinkers and moderate drinkers in a life insurance policy, it is fair to say that the low-risk moderate drinkers to some extent subsidize the high-risk heavy drinkers. This conclusion encourages another misconception: that insurance is designed to make the good risks subsidize the bad. On the contrary, insurers will *always* attempt to distinguish between good risks and bad risks—college professors and daredevil pilots, for example—so long as the costs of making the distinction are less than or equal to the premium reduction that the insurer can offer a differentiated, low-risk subgroup. The lower the insurer can make the premium for a particular group, the more likely the insurer will attract members of that group as customers. If it is economically feasible to offer coverage at a lower cost to some identifiable group, some insurer will attempt to do so.

When these commonly held misunderstandings about insurance are eliminated, a relatively simple definition remains: An insurance policy is a contract under which an insurer, in exchange for the payment of a fee, assumes a risk and distributes it among a group of similarly situated risks. Parties do not form contracts in the absence of mutual benefits, and an insurance policy is no exception. The applicant for insurance desires to obtain security from a possible loss. Suppose an individual calculates that the chance of an automobile accident causing $5,000 in damages is one in one hundred—an "expected loss" of $50. Because most individuals prefer to avoid risk (are risk averse), this individual may be willing to pay $60 to know with certainty that the possible loss of $5,000 will not be borne by him. If an insurer can locate one hundred similarly situated individuals willing to pay $60 to transfer their risk to the insurer, the insurer will receive $6,000 and will assume each individual's risk. With a pool of one hundred insureds, it is probable that one insured will suffer a $5,000 loss. After reimbursing this loss, the insurer will have a $1,000 profit. In short, each party to the insurance contract benefits: the insured trades risk and gets certainty, and the insurer makes a profit by assuming that risk and distributing it across a pool of similarly situated risks.

The price at which an insurer is willing to assume a risk depends on the expected loss (the probability that a loss will occur multiplied by the potential amount of the loss) plus a reasonable sum for administrative expenses, including a reasonable profit. Thus, the amount of an insurance premium should equal the present monetary value of the expected loss plus the insurer's administrative costs (including profit). Determining the *exact* value of an expected loss for a particular individual would be prohibitively expensive because it would require highly detailed, time-consuming measurements. Therefore, insurers group *similar* risks together and charge each individual in the group the same premium. Insurers will divide the group into distinct subgroups as long as the cost of measuring a differentiating factor is less than the premium reduction the insurer can offer the members of a differentiated subgroup.[4]

THE USE OF GENDER AS A RATING CRITERION

Many insurers currently use gender as a criterion for calculating premiums and benefits in life insurance, annuities, health and disability insurance, and some kinds of casualty insurance. In these kinds of insurance, gender is an inexpensive way to distinguish between low-risk and high-risk insureds.

In life insurance, insurers use gender for such calculations because women, as a group, have longer life spans than men, as a group. In the United States, women at every age have a lower incidence of death than men and a longer average life expectancy.[5] Thus, for life insurers, women are better risks than men. To obtain a death benefit of a stated sum, a woman, because of her longer average life expectancy, will make more periodic premium payments than a man. Therefore, from the insurers' perspective, a woman's periodic payment should be lower than a man's; otherwise, the woman would pay more than the man for an equivalent death benefit. If a woman's periodic premium payment for life insurance equaled a man's, the woman, because of her longer average life span, would make cumulatively more premium payments than the man. If the woman pays more money, her estate or beneficiary should receive a larger benefit.[6]

In annuities, insurers also use gender to calculate premiums and benefits, but the relationships are exactly the opposite of those in life insurance. Life insurance provides an individual with security against the risk of premature death, which can impose a hardship on those who depend upon the insured. An annuity provides an individual with security against the risk of having inadequate assets and income to pay for the expenses associated with a long life. Because women, on the average, are likely to live longer than men, they are likely to collect annuity benefits for a longer time. Thus, from the insurers' perspective, women are worse risks as annuity purchasers than men. Women's longer average life expectancy means that a woman will collect more periodic payments than a man; if a man and woman are to be paid equal *total* benefits, either the woman's payments should be smaller or the woman's contributions to fund the annuity should be larger. If the man and the woman make equal contributions and receive equal periodic payments, the woman's annuity would have a higher present value than the man's, which is the opposite of the situation in life insurance, where equating premiums and benefits would cause the man's life insurance policy to have a higher present value.

In other kinds of insurance, statistics show that men and women can be differentiated with regard to risk. Women often pay more than men for identical health and disability insurance coverage, primarily because of the cost of maternity care. Young women generally pay less than young men for identical automobile insurance coverage. Young men, on the average, have more traffic violations, more minor traffic accidents, and nearly twice as many fatal accidents as do young women.

The economic rationale set forth in the preceding section suggests that an insurer will differentiate between men and women only if the administrative costs of making the distinction are less than the premium reduction the insurer is able to offer women. In the case of gender, the differentiating criterion is both simple and inexpensive to measure. Therefore, gender is a widely used criterion in setting insurance rates and benefits. From the insurers' perspective, this is fair. Insurance is the business of discriminating between better risks and worse risks; to charge individuals of one gender more than individuals of the other gender for the same insurance product is *discriminating*, but not *discriminatory*, because the higher price reflects the insurers' assumption of a proportionately greater risk.

EXISTING AND PROPOSED RESTRICTIONS ON THE USE OF GENDER IN INSURANCE RATING

The federal government has the authority to mandate that insurance be marketed on a gender-neutral basis but has not yet exercised this power. In general, most regulation of the insurance industry is done at the state level; only a few states currently restrict the use of gender in insurance rating, however. Legislation has been proposed in Congress that, if enacted, would prohibit the selling of insurance policies whose premiums or benefits are calculated on the basis of gender.

CURRENT FEDERAL REGULATION

Several federal statutes explicitly prohibit gender discrimination in such areas as employment, credit, and education.[7] Also, the Supreme Court has frequently construed federal statutes that lack explicit prohibitions on gender discrimination as implicitly requiring equal treatment of men and women.[8] But there is currently no federal statute that explicitly prohibits gender discrimination in insurance or that could be broadly construed as requiring the marketing of all insurance on a gender-neutral basis. In two cases, however, the Supreme Court has construed Title VII of the Civil Rights Act of 1964 as prohibiting gender discrimination in connection with employer-provided pension plans.[9]

The first case, *Los Angeles Department of Water and Power v. Manhart*,[10] was decided in 1978. Pension benefits under the retirement plan offered by the Los Angeles Department of Water and Power were funded by contributions by both employer and employees. After studying mortality tables and reviewing the records of its own employees, the department concluded that its female employees, on the average, lived a few years longer than its male employees. As a result, the cost of a retirement pension for an average female exceeded the cost of the same pension for an average male. Therefore, the department required female employees to make monthly contributions that were about 15 percent higher than those of comparably situated male employees. Since the contributions were deducted from the employees' paychecks, the department's female employees had less take-home pay than its male employees.

In 1973, Marie Manhart and four other female employees of the department, on behalf of all of its past and present female employees, sued the department for requiring females to make larger contributions than those made by males to receive identical monthly retirement benefits. The plaintiffs claimed that this discrimination violated Title VII of the Civil Rights Act of 1964, which makes it an unlawful employment practice "to discriminate against any individual with respect to his compensation, terms, conditions, or privileges of employment, because of such individual's race, color, religion, sex or national origin." [11]

The department argued that the women were assessed larger contributions not because of their gender but because of their greater longevity, but the Court rejected this argument:

> [A]ny individual's life expectancy is based on a number of factors, of which sex is only one. . . . [O]ne cannot "say that an actuarial distinction based entirely on sex is 'based on any other factor other than sex.' Sex is exactly what it is based on." [12]

The Court ruled that even though women as a group live longer than men, the department's practice of requiring females to make larger contributions to its pension plan than males violated the Civil Rights Act. The Court reasoned that the act protects *individuals,* not groups, and that requiring individual women to pay more than individual men for an equal benefit violated federal law.

Five years later, the Supreme Court faced a closely related question in *Arizona Governing Committee v. Norris:* whether Title VII also prohibits an employer from providing its employees with a retirement plan that, although funded by equal contributions from men and women, provides men a higher monthly benefit than women. The Court, following the logic of *Manhart,* held that the employer providing such a plan also violated Title VII. [13]

According the logic of these two Supreme Court decisions, it is a violation of Title VII for an employer to provide its employees any kind of insurance fringe benefit—such as a retirement plan, a life insurance policy, or some other kind of insurance product—unless identical benefits are provided to both men and women and unless contributions, if any, are the same for both. These two decisions do *not* require insurance companies to offer their products to the public on a gender-neutral basis, however. Within the limits of applicable state law, insurers are free to sell, and private individuals are free to buy, annuities and insurance policies that give different benefits to men and to women or for which men and women are charged different prices. Thus, although an employer may not lawfully provide the employee with an insurance policy whose benefits or contributions are calculated with reference to gender, the employer can give the employee a sum of money, and the employee can use the money to purchase an insurance policy whose price or benefits are calculated on the basis of gender-distinct tables.

CURRENT STATE REGULATION

Only a few states have statutes that restrict gender-based insurance rating. Montana is the only state with a statute generally prohibiting the use of gender as a criterion in establishing premiums and payments.[14] Four states prohibit the use of gender in establishing automobile insurance premiums.[15] A few states have laws prohibiting gender discrimination with respect to the renewal of policies, but these statutes are not broad enough to affect rating practices.[16] Several states have statutes that explicitly prohibit discrimination in insurance on the basis of race, color, creed, or national origin, but these statutes do not mention gender discrimination.[17] All states have statutes or regulations prohibiting "unfair insurance practices," but these statutes and regulations have been applied only to prohibit discrimination among persons classified as belonging to the same group; the use of particular standards in establishing the classification is therefore not prohibited.

In a 1984 decision, the Pennsylvania State Supreme Court upheld the state insurance commissioner's determination that the equal rights amendment to the state constitution prohibits auto insurance companies from basing their rates on gender. In *Hartford Accident and Indemnity Co. v. Insurance Commissioner*, a twenty-six-year-old unmarried male with a clean driving record successfully challenged Hartford's rates, because the company had charged him $148 more in annual premiums than a similarly situated female with identical coverage.[18] At the opposite end of the spectrum, California in 1978 enacted a statute prohibiting the use of gender-neutral rating for individual life insurance policies and annuities. The statute was amended in 1983 to exempt from the prohibition life insurance policies and annuity contracts that are provided as fringe benefits by employers and that are subject to the requirements of Title VII of the Civil Rights Act of 1964.[19]

PROPOSED FEDERAL LEGISLATION

In a number of Congresses since 1980, legislation has been proposed that would prohibit discrimination in insurance on the basis of race, color, religion, gender, or national origin. Legislation introduced in the 99th Congress would have prohibited discrimination in both the writing and selling of insurance policies and annuities.[20] The most controversial aspect of the bill was its prohibition on insurers' use of gender-based mortality tables, or any other form of gender-based grouping, in establishing insurance premiums and payments. The bill would also have required that existing unequal insurance contracts of similarly situated men and women be "equalized" by either increasing premiums or increasing coverages. Because the legislation would not have abrogated existing contracts, equalization would be achieved in most instances by increasing the lower coverages. The bill did not pass, but there may be renewed interest in the proposal now that one political party controls both Congress and the White House.

PUBLIC POLICY IMPLICATIONS OF GENDER-BASED RATING

The debate over gender-based insurance rating is best understood by considering two questions. Does fairness require equal treatment of individual men and women in providing insurance? If so, can society afford the costs associated with ignoring gender in the pricing of insurance?

WHAT DOES FAIRNESS REQUIRE?

For insurers, gender is a low-cost tool for differentiating between high risks and low risks. Indeed, an insurer failing to use the cheapest and most accurate measures of risk will be competitively disadvantaged, because other insurers will be able to attract the best of the insurer's risks (that is, the lowest risks and thus the most profitable) by offering them a lower premium for the same coverage. From the insurers' perspective, the operation of these market forces is neither unfair nor inequitable; to the extent that gender correlates with risk, using gender as a criterion in establishing insurance premiums and benefits is not a discriminatory practice.

Because men are charged premiums that cover the insurers' costs of assuming their risks, and women are charged different premiums that cover the costs of assuming their risks, the insurers' perspective achieves "group equality." Proponents of gender-neutral insurance rating contend, however, that for some purposes the group is an improper unit for assessing whether equality is achieved; for these purposes, they argue, the individual is the proper unit of measurement. Insurers must be allowed to classify individuals into groups, but they should not be allowed to group individuals on the basis of race, religion, national origin, or gender, even if these characteristics are accurate predictors of loss. Indeed, utilizing such characteristics is unsound to the extent that "causality" has any value in setting rates and benefits. Arguably, it is fairer for insurers to use rating criteria that are within the insureds' control and that are therefore more likely to be related causally to loss (such as miles driven, smoking, or eating habits) than to use criteria that insureds cannot control (such as race and gender).

Thus, the fundamental disagreement between those who support gender-neutral rating and those who oppose it concerns what "equality" requires with regard to insurance. Aristotle's concept of equality suggests that like cases should be treated alike and different cases should be treated differently. But Aristotle's framework does not resolve the problem of deciding when cases are alike. A person who sought to distinguish fruits from vegetables would conclude that apples and oranges are "alike." A person who sought to distinguish citrus fruits from other kinds of fruits, however, would conclude that apples and oranges are "different." In a literal sense, no two individuals are alike because each is a unique combination of characteristics, but this does not mean that people are inherently "unequal."

For some purposes individuals should be treated equally, and for other purposes they should be treated differently. In contemporary society, when distinctions among individuals are required, the specific characteristics having relevance for a particular purpose are identified. Depending on what is being measured, a judgment is reached about whether individuals should be treated equally or differently. Thus, it is evident that the term "equality" standing alone has no substantive meaning; it must be accompanied by a supplementary standard that describes whether, for a particular purpose, individuals are similar.[21]

A few simple examples clarify this distinction. For the purpose of deciding who is entitled to vote in public elections in the United States, income is considered irrelevant. In this context, all individuals are treated equally regardless of income. For the purpose of deciding who should be taxed to pay the costs of government programs, however, income is deemed to be relevant. Accordingly, the wealthy are taxed at higher marginal rates than the poor: the wealthy and the poor are treated unequally, and this is believed to be entirely proper. For the purpose of deciding who is eligible for an education in the nation's public schools, a physical handicap is not considered a relevant characteristic. For the purpose of deciding who is eligible for a driver's license, however, some physical handicaps (such as vision impairment or blindness) are highly relevant. For this one purpose, unequal treatment is not questioned. In these examples, a consensus exists as to the appropriateness of unequal treatment. But a consensus on the permissibility of using gender to differentiate between individuals for purposes of insurance rating has yet to emerge.

The group perspective with regard to equality accepts the notion that insurance is inherently discriminating; the very nature of insurance requires dividing a group of potential insureds into smaller categories and pricing each category according to its risk. Thus, a person with a history of heart disease should pay more for life insurance than a healthy person, a daredevil pilot should pay more for life insurance than a college professor, and so on. According to the group perspective, charging women and men the same price for an equivalent amount of life insurance would be discriminatory against women, because they are lower risks than men for this kind of insurance and therefore should be charged less for identical coverage. Equality is achieved only if those with similar risks are grouped together and are charged the same premium for the risks being transferred to the insurer.

The individual perspective rejects the premise of the group perspective's defense of gender-distinct insurance rating. The group perspective contends that treating men as a group differently from women as a group achieves "equality," but the individual perspective rejects the fairness of differentiating between men and women in the first place. According to the individual perspective, risk correlates with many criteria, not just gender. Some of these criteria have a causal relationship to loss, which calls into question the fairness of using gender as a proxy for these other criteria.

Life expectancy, for example, depends on many things, such as residence, race, occupation, eating and smoking habits, and heredity. Although it is true that the average woman in the United States currently lives longer than the average man, it is not clear that the female gender will always enjoy a longevity advantage. At certain times in history in certain places in the world—even in the United States at particular times for particular age-groups—female mortality rates have exceeded those of males.[22] If race, gender, and residence are used together to measure life expectancy, other possible categorizations emerge; for example, a nonwhite, male resident of South Carolina has a life span shorter than that of the average male resident of the United States.[23] Gender is no more (and no less) valid as a rating criterion than race or residence, but insurers do not use these other criteria to price life insurance policies and annuities. Similarly, automobile accidents correlate with gender, but they also correlate with the number of miles driven, the number of traffic citations the driver has received, the age of the driver and of the automobile, and whether the automobile has safety devices.

Even if gender is a proxy for other criteria that predict whether a loss will materialize, it is an imperfect one. Not all women have the "average" characteristics that predict of a longer life, for example. The death ages of 84 percent of 65-year-old men and women are the same, yet all men and women pay different premiums or receive different benefits simply because the death ages of 16 percent of such men and women cannot be matched. The 84 percent "overlap" group costs a life insurer or annuity provider the same amount, yet all the women in this overlap group pay more for annuities (and less for life insurance) than do the men.[24] Not all young women have the characteristics—such as fewer miles driven and fewer traffic violations—that make young women, on the average, low-risk drivers.

The individual perspective, which holds that individuals should be rated as to risk without regard to gender, makes a superior case for achieving the "fairness" traditionally valued by society.[25] According to this perspective, it is unfair to treat individuals differently on the basis of characteristics outside their control—such as race, national origin, color, and gender—even if such characteristics are related to risk. Nonwhites, on the average, have a shorter life expectancy than whites, but because contemporary society views racial discrimination as being especially repugnant, no one contends that nonwhites should pay more for life insurance or receive a premium reduction for annuities. Society also values equal treatment of individuals without regard to differences in religious beliefs. If evidence were produced indicating that Catholics have a shorter life expectancy than non-Catholics, no one would seriously suggest that Catholics pay more for life insurance or receive a premium reduction for annuities. According to proponents of the individual perspective, insurers should not be allowed to use gender as a criterion in establishing insurance benefits and premiums any more than they should be allowed to use race, color, national origin, or religion.

THE COSTS OF GENDER-NEUTRAL INSURANCE

Contemporary society generally presumes that individuals are entitled to be treated equally; those who desire to differentiate among individuals must overcome that presumption. In many areas, the presumption is successfully rebutted. For example, college admissions officers favor applicants who demonstrate superior aptitude on validated texts and have better academic records in high school; similarly, those who wish to become airline pilots must meet minimum physical requirements. In these areas, unequal treatment is tolerated because the costs of equal treatment are excessive, and in some instances unaffordable. For this reason, there will never be such a thing as age equality in life insurance; allowing sixty-year-olds to purchase life insurance policies on the same terms as twenty-year-olds would destroy the market for life insurance—an unacceptable cost. Society has at other times made a choice to absorb the costs of eschewing an actuarially sound rating criterion. Prior to the 1960s, for example, insurers used race as a criterion in the pricing of insurance. Today, a more enlightened society views the practice of race-based rating as unacceptable, and the minimal costs associated with abandoning it are thought to be worth incurring.

According to this framework, men and women should be treated equally in the insurance context, as are individuals of different races, unless the costs of equal treatment are so substantial that society simply cannot afford the price of equality. What, then, are the costs of gender-neutral insurance?

A requirement that insurance be priced without regard to gender would redistribute wealth to some extent, as happens whenever one group is asked to pay more for a product and another group's payment is reduced. Men would pay less for automobile and life insurance, and women would pay more. Women would pay less for annuities, health insurance, and disability insurance, and men would pay more.[26] Over time, these changes would affect the distribution of wealth between men and women.

The magnitude of these redistributive effects is often exaggerated, however. To the extent that insurance is already gender neutral, no redistribution would occur. Currently, about 90 percent of health insurance, probably more than 50 percent of life insurance, most auto insurance for adult drivers, and some disability insurance is gender neutral.[27] With regard to annuities, wealth would be distributed from men as a group to women as a group, but, interestingly, many individuals would feel no effect—for example, married individuals who take the "joint-survivor option," which allows the annuity to be paid to the annuity holder and his or her beneficiary so long as *either* lives. Some of these benefits are already being calculated according to what is, in effect, a merged table. Also, to the extent that insurers shift from gender to other rating criteria that happen to correlate with gender, the redistributive effects between the genders would be reduced. For example, young men drive more miles than do young women; if miles driven were substituted for gender as a rating criterion, young men would pay more for automobile insurance than would young women.

The redistribution of wealth that would accompany gender-neutral rating would not reduce society's total wealth. But some individuals would be adversely affected, whereas others would benefit. The extent of the overall redistribution and the nature of the impact on individuals are difficult to calculate; both would depend in large measure on the extent to which men and women of different income levels bought particular kinds of insurance. For example, automobile insurance rates would increase for young women, but their health insurance rates would decline. More women of limited financial means would be able to afford health insurance, but fewer would be able to afford automobile insurance. Whether this would be a net positive effect or a net negative effect is impossible to know—whether, for example, the net effect on poor men would be to make health insurance more inaccessible than automobile insurance is made accessible. The needs and problems of the poor, whether men or women, would be dealt with more efficiently by a national policy specifically concerned with incomes than by a privately controlled insurance system whose principal concern is distributing risk, not distributing income.

Conversion to a system of gender-neutral rating would entail some administrative costs. The American Academy of Actuaries has estimated the costs of developing new gender-neutral policies and revising old policies to be about $1.3 billion, less than 4 percent of the insurance industry's total administrative costs for one year.[28] If gender-neutral rating principles were applied only to insurance contracts issued in the future, and existing contracts were not changed, the administrative costs would amount to only $465 million, an easily affordable sum.[29]

Implementing a gender-neutral system would have some efficiency costs. For example, to the extent that women would pay more for automobile insurance, they might purchase less coverage than they would if gender had been used as a rating criterion. Conversely, men might be induced to purchase more automobile insurance coverage than the "optimal" amount—and women might purchase more disability insurance than they need—because the price of the product does not reflect its true cost. Gender-neutral insurance would have some efficiency gains, however. If criteria such as miles driven, prior accidents, traffic citations, and age of the automobile are substituted for gender in setting automobile insurance rates, more accurate pricing would occur, resulting in efficiency gains (although prices would perhaps be slightly higher overall because of the increased difficulty of measurement). The overall efficiency effects of gender-neutral insurance are difficult to estimate, but it is doubtful that there would be any unacceptable efficiency costs.[30]

If gender-neutral rating principles are applied retroactively to existing insurance contracts, some life insurers and annuity providers might face insolvency in the short run. To equalize existing policies, most insurers would either increase benefits or reduce premiums for the currently disadvantaged gender. Increasing premiums for the currently advantaged gender is not a desirable alternative, because doing so would breach existing contracts and would no doubt prompt considerable policyholder litigation. Whether benefits are increased or premiums are decreased for the currently disadvantaged gender, the average level of insurers' liability would increase without a corresponding increase in assets, thus creating unfunded liabilities for some insurers. Some states require life insurers to carry full reserves to back up the actuarial value of their liabilities; thus, insurers that fail to increase premiums could face insolvency in the short run.[31] These problems would not exist in the areas of health and casualty insurance because such policies are written for much shorter terms. But these adverse effects can be avoided entirely if gender-neutral rating principles are applied prospectively only.

The Supreme Court acknowledged the difficulty of requiring gender-neutral rating retroactively in *Arizona Governing Committee v. Norris,* in which it held unlawful under Title VII of the Civil Rights Act of 1964 an employer-sponsored pension plan funded by equal contributions from men and women that provided men a higher monthly benefit than women. A majority of the Court noted that holding employers liable retroactively "would have devastating results" and that "liability should be prospective only." [32] The decision in a 1984 case allowed a retroactive remedy for female annuitants under a pension plan, but in the circumstances of that case the contractual rights and the legitimate expectations of the male annuitants would not have been impaired by the retroactive remedy.[33]

In short, there is no indication that gender-neutral rating—particularly if required prospectively—would have any serious costs. Abolishing gender-based rating would have some economic effects, but none of them appear to be unaffordable. In fact, the only nonsensical system is the current one; insurance provided by employers as a fringe benefit must be gender neutral to comply with Title VII of the Civil Rights Act of 1964, but insurance sold elsewhere can be priced on the basis of gender-distinct tables. This incongruity is explored in the next section.

THE IRONIES OF THE STATUS QUO

Assuming that consumer behavior is rational, the effect of the *Manhart* and *Arizona Governing Committee* decisions, in the absence of across-the-board use of gender-neutral rating, is ironic: market forces will result in the same differentiation between men and women that Title VII seeks to eliminate. Consider the following illustration. Husband (H) and wife (W) are the same age; they work for the same employer and receive the same fringe benefits. Assume that tax considerations are irrelevant. H and W can take their pension contributions either in a lump sum at retirement or in the form of an annuity. The best prediction by H and W is that they will live to their full life expectancies. To maximize their joint lifetime income, W should elect the employer-provided annuity, since that annuity is calculated on the basis of merged actuarial tables that understate her life expectancy, thus providing her with a larger annuity than she would obtain in the open market. H should elect the lump-sum payment and use this sum to purchase an annuity in the open market where annuities are calculated on a gender-distinct basis, providing him with larger monthly benefits than he would obtain with the use of merged tables.

If all similarly situated insureds make the same choices as H and W, the secondary effects will be as follows. Because of the principle of adverse selection (in any group of insureds, a disproportionate number of high risks will exist because these are the individuals who get a better bargain), the insureds opting for the employer's retirement plan's benefits will be predominantly women, and those choosing an open-market annuity will be predominantly men. Because men, on the average, die at an earlier age, the benefits provided under the open-market annuity will eventually exceed those provided by the employer's annuity. And as more women (who, on the average, live longer) choose the employer's plan, the benefits paid out on a monthly basis per retiree will gradually decrease as female retirees outlive their male counterparts. Eventually, the benefits provided in the employer's annuity will be the same as those provided to women when gender-distinct tables are used, and the benefits provided under open-market annuities will approximate those offered to men under the employer's retirement plan when gender-distinct tables are used. In short, in circumstances where existing law requires that insurance rates be calculated on a gender-neutral basis if the insurance is provided as an incident to employment, but does not require all insurance products to be marketed on a gender-neutral basis, market forces will inevitably result in the same differentiation between men and women that Title VII seeks to avoid. A requirement that *all* annuities and insurance policies be priced without regard to gender will eliminate these distortions. If either less accurate or more costly risk-measuring criteria are substituted for gender, however, overall administrative costs will rise, which will cause consumer prices to increase. As discussed earlier in this section, the available evidence suggests that these costs will be relatively moderate and thus well within the range of affordability. But a consensus does not currently exist in society on the question of whether these costs should be paid.

Abolishing the use of gender as a criterion in insurance rating will have economic effects, but they do not make gender-neutral rating impractical or unaffordable. The fundamental questions are: Does society *want* to treat individual men and women equally for insurance purposes? Or is society satisfied with a system that only requires equal treatment of men as a group and women as a group? Is the goal of treating individual men and women equally worth the moderate costs associated with gender-neutral rating? Is society willing to endure the redistributive effects of a gender-neutral system to achieve equality among individuals? These are the public policy questions currently being addressed in Congress and in some state legislatures. Whatever the outcome, such questions will be resolved by reference to the values and goals of the "larger world" outside the "small world" of insurance.

NOTES

The author expresses his appreciation to Amy Freeman, a 1993 graduate of the University of Kansas School of Law, whose research assisted in updating an earlier draft of this chapter. Portions of this chapter are based on two of the author's earlier publications: Robert H. Jerry, II, *Understanding Insurance Law* (New York: Matthew Bender, 1987), 84-90; and Robert H. Jerry, II, and Kyle B. Mansfield, "Justifying Unisex Insurance: Another Perspective," *American University Law Review* 34 (1985): 329-367.

1. As interpreted by the U.S. Supreme Court (see text accompanying notes 10-13 infra), Title VII of the Civil Rights Act of 1964 prohibits Slowmobile from differentiating between Sara and Dave in the matter of employee benefits. If Sara sued Slowmobile, the company would (in all probability) be required to provide Sara with an annuity benefit equal to that provided Dave. If Dave sued Slowmobile, he would (in all probability) obtain a judgment from a court requiring Slowmobile to give him a life insurance policy with the same face value Sara received. If Slowmobile gave Sara and Dave identical lump-sum bonuses on their retirement, however, Sara could purchase from an insurer a fully paid-up life insurance policy for less money than Dave would have to spend for the same policy. By the same token, Dave could purchase from an insurer an annuity for less money than Sara would have to spend for the same annuity. This chapter explores how this peculiar state of affairs evolved.
2. Spencer L. Kimball, "The Purpose of Insurance Regulation: A Preliminary Inquiry in the Theory of Insurance Law," *Minnesota Law Review* 45 (1961): 524.
3. The higher risk involved in providing life insurance to a pilot of experimental airplanes can be dealt with by inserting an "exclusion" in the policy: coverage will not be provided if death occurs while the insured is piloting an airplane. With such narrowing of the coverage provided the pilot, the premiums charged the pilot and the professor would be the same.
4. For an explanation of this economic principle, see Ejan MacKaay, *Economics of Information and Law* (Boston: Kluwer-Nijhoff, 1982), 176-179. For a discussion of the impact of gender-neutral rating generally, see Robert Carney and Donald Hardigree, "The Economic Impact of Gender-Neutral Insurance Rating on Women," *Journal of Insurance Issues and Practices* 13 (1990): 1-23.
5. U.S. Department of Commerce, Bureau of the Census, *Statistical Abstract of the United States, 1992* (Washington, D.C.: Government Printing Office, 1992), 76-79. On the basis of preliminary data for 1990, the Census Bureau estimates the average life expectancy for males to be 72.0 years and for females, 78.8 years; the average is 75.4 years. In compiling these data, the bureau treats women collectively as a homogeneous group; in fact, division into subgroups (according to race, geography, or economic class, for example), reveals differences

in women's average life span.

6. Most individual life insurance policies are sold on a gender-distinct basis, which means that the payments for and benefits provided under the policies are calculated according to gender-distinct actuarial tables. Some insurers create separate actuarial tables for men and women based on actual mortality data. Other insurers calculate a table for men and then "set back" the table a few years for women. For example, because women, on the average, live about six years longer than men, an insurer might use a five-year setback, which means charging a sixty-year-old man the same life insurance premium as that charged a sixty-five-year-old woman. Thus a woman aged sixty would pay less for a life insurance policy than a man of the same age.

7. See, for example, 42 U.S.C. sec. 2000e (1989 and Supp. 1992) (employment); 29 U.S.C. sec. 206(d) (1989)(equal pay in the workplace); 42 U.S.C. sec. 2000e(k) (1989) (pregnancy discrimination in employment); 15 U.S.C. sec. 1691 (1982 and Supp. 1992) (credit applications); and 20 U.S.C. secs. 1681-1686 (1991)(educational programs receiving federal assistance).

8. See, for example, *Califano v. Westcott,* 443 U.S. 76 (1979)(AFDC provisions of the Social Security Act); *Califano v. Goldfarb,* 430 U.S. 199 (1977) and *Weinberger v. Wiesenfeld,* 420 U.S. 636 (1975) (Social Security Act provisions concerning widows and widowers); *Frontiero v. Richardson,* 411 U.S. 677 (1973) (application of two federal statutes to spouses of armed forces personnel). Compare *Manufacturer's Hanover Trust Co. v. United States,* 775 F.2d 459, 85-2 U.S. Tax Cas. (CCH) 13,640 (2d Cir. 1985) (in a 2-1 vote, the Court held that the Internal Revenue Service may use gender-distinct actuarial tables; the decision is largely moot, however, because the IRS switched to gender-neutral actuarial tables in 1984).

9. 42 U.S.C. sec. 2000e (1989 and Supp. 1992).

10. *City of Los Angeles Department of Water and Power v. Manhart,* 435 U.S. 702 (1978).

11. U.S.C. sec. 2000e-2(a)(1) (1989).

12. *City of Los Angeles Department of Water and Power v. Manhart,* 435 U.S. 702, 712-713 (1978), quoting *Manhart v. City of Los Angeles Department of Water and Power,* 553 F.2d 581, 588 (9th Cir. 1976), and the Equal Pay Act, 29 U.S.C. sec. 206(d) (1989).

13. *Arizona Governing Committee for Tax Deferred Annuity and Deferred Compensation Plans v. Norris,* 463 U.S. 1073 (1983).

14. See Montana Code Annotated, sec. 49-2-309 (1985).

15. Hawaii Revised Statutes, sec. 294-33 (1976); Massachusetts Annotated Laws, chap. 175E, sec. 4(d) (Michie/Law. Coop., 1984); Michigan Compiled Laws Annotated, sec. 500.2027(c) (West, 1983); North Carolina General Statutes, sec. 58-124.19(4) (1982).

16. In addition to the four states mentioned in note 15, Arkansas, Colorado, Florida, Kentucky, Maryland, North Dakota, and Washington (among others) have such statutes.

17. Some of the states having such statutes are Arizona, California, Connecticut, Illinois, and New Jersey.

18. *Hartford Accident and Indemnity Co. v. Insurance Commissioner*, 505 Pa. 571, 482 A.2d 542 (1984).

19. California Insurance Code sec. 790.03(f) (West, 1986).

20. House Committee on Energy and Commerce, *A Bill to Prohibit Discrimination in Insurance on the Basis of Race, Color, Religion, Sex, or National Origin*, H.R. 1793, 99th Cong., 1st sess., 1985.

21. See H. L. A. Hart, *The Concept of Law* (Oxford: Clarendon Press, 1961), 155. For an in-depth discussion of the significance of equality, similarity, and difference in American law, see Martha Minow, *Making All the Difference: Inclusion, Exclusion, and American Law* (Ithaca, N.Y.: Cornell University Press, 1990).

22. See Lea Brilmayer, Richard W. Hekeler, Douglas Laycock, and Teresa A. Sullivan, "Sex Discrimination in Employer-Sponsored Insurance Plans: A Legal and Demographic Analysis," *University of Chicago Law Review* 47 (1980): 505, 539-559. For a critical analysis of this article, see George J. Benston, "The Economics of Gender Discrimination in Employee Fringe Benefits: *Manhart* Revisited," *University of Chicago Law Review* 49 (1982): 489-542.

23. Brilmayer et al., "Sex Discrimination," 512 n. 32.

24. House Committee on Energy and Commerce, Subcommittee on Commerce, Transportation, and Tourism, *Hearings, Nondiscrimination in Insurance Act of 1983*, Testimony of Dr. Mary Gray, national president of the Women's Equity Action League, H.R. 100, 98th Cong., 1st sess., February 22, 1983, 212-213.

25. For a more detailed presentation of this argument, see Robert H. Jerry II and Kyle B. Mansfield, "Justifying Unisex Insurance: Another Perspective," *American University Law Review* 34 (1985): 329-367. The argument is examined in a broader context in Leah Wortham, "Insurance Classification: Too Important to Be Left to the Actuaries," *University of Michigan Journal of Law Reform* 19 (1986): 349-423.

26. With regard to health insurance, the premiums for all individuals would reflect the costs of pregnancy benefits; thus, a cost would be imposed on those who do not bear children, whether male or female, and a benefit would redound to women who bear children.

27. Of the health insurance in force in 1990, 51 percent was sold by commercial insurers on a group basis. Health Insurance Association of America, *Source Book of Health Insurance Data* (1991), 24. Presumably, all commercial group insurance, which is sold for the most part in employer-employee settings, is gender neutral. Blue Cross-Blue Shield groups account for about 39 percent of all health insurance (ibid.), and this insurance is almost entirely gender neutral (although gender, age, and other factors can enter the picture when a premium is quoted to the employer whose employees will be covered). Currently, about 40 percent of all life insurance is sold on a group basis. American Council of Life Insurers, *1993 Life Insurance Fact Book Update* (1993), 13. If individual life insurance that is sold on a gender-neutral basis is added to this figure, an estimate that 50 percent of all life insurance is gender neutral is reasonable. A 1984 report by the General Accounting Office put these figures at 87 percent for health insurance and about 50 percent for life insurance. Comptroller General of the United States, *Economic Implications of the Fair Insurance Practices Act*,

Report to Sen. Orrin G. Hatch et al., GAO/OCE-84-1, App. I, April 6, 1984, 19. A modest increase in these percentages in the last ten years would be expected, given national trends favoring group underwriting, and it is highly unlikely that these percentages would have declined. The following discussion of gender-neutral rating is based on the 1984 GAO report.

28. The comptroller general found no reason to consider the figure either inflated or too conservative.
29. Comptroller General of the United States, *Economic Implications of the Fair Insurance Practices Act,* Report to Sen. Orrin G. Hatch et al., GAO/OCE-84-1, App. I, April 6, 1984, 28.
30. Ibid., 24-27.
31. Ibid., 4, 7-18.
32. *Arizona Governing Committee for Tax Deferred Annuity and Deferred Compensation Plans v. Norris,* 463 U.S. 1073, 1107 (1983).
33. See *Spirt v. Teachers Insurance and Annuity Association,* 735 F.2d 23 (2d Cir.), cert. denied, 105 S. Ct. 247 (1984).

CHRONOLOGY

1961 In *Hoyt v. Florida,* the Supreme Court rules unanimously that a state law that included men on a jury list unless they requested an exemption but exempted women unless they volunteered for jury service is valid. This case is representative of a long line of precedent—decisions that, consistent with public norms that often treated women differentially from men, upheld laws discriminating on the basis of gender whenever the law was viewed as having a rational relationship to a legitimate government purpose.

1963 Congress passes, and President John F. Kennedy signs, the Equal Pay Act of 1963, which prohibits gender discrimination by employers in the payment of wages.

1964 Congress passes, and President Lyndon B. Johnson signs, the Civil Rights Act of 1964.

1971 In *Reed v. Reed,* the Supreme Court departs from the approach it followed in cases through *Hoyt* and invalidates an Idaho statute requiring that men be given preference over women as appointees to be administrators of estates.

1972 Congress passes the equal rights amendment to the Constitution, and the process of state ratification begins.

1973 In *Frontiero v. Richardson,* the Supreme Court declares that classifications based on gender are suspect, thus making explicit what was implicit in *Reed,* and holds unconstitutional under the due process clause of the Fifth Amendment a federal statute providing that spouses of male members of the armed services are dependents for purposes of obtaining military benefits, but that spouses of female members are not dependents unless they are in fact dependent on their wives for more than one-half of their support.

1975 North Carolina enacts a statute forbidding the use of gender as a criterion in the setting of auto insurance rates.

1978 Congress passes, and President Jimmy Carter signs, the Pregnancy Discrimination Act of 1978, which prohibits such discrimination in employment.

1978 In *Manhart v. City of Los Angeles Department of Water and Power*, the Supreme Court holds that the department's practice of requiring women to make larger contributions to its pension plan than men violates Title VII of the Civil Rights Act of 1964.

1978 California enacts a statute prohibiting the use of gender-neutral rating for individual life insurance policies and annuities.

1980 Legislation is introduced in Congress (but not enacted) that would prohibit discrimination in insurance on the basis of race, color, sex, or national origin.

1982 The equal rights amendment to the Constitution is ratified by thirty-five states, three states short of the number needed for ratification by the June 30, 1982, deadline.

1983 The equal rights amendment is reintroduced in Congress, but in the House of Representatives falls six votes short of the two-thirds majority needed for passage.

1983 In *Arizona Governing Committee v. Norris*, the Supreme Court holds that Title VII of the Civil Rights Act of 1964 prohibits an employer from providing its employees with a retirement plan that, although funded by equal contributions from men and women, provides men a higher monthly benefit than women.

1983 California amends a statute enacted in 1978 to exempt from its coverage life insurance and annuity contracts issued in the employment setting, which are subject to the requirements of Title VII of the Civil Rights Act of 1964.

1984 The Internal Revenue Service switches to gender-neutral actuarial tables.

1984 The Pennsylvania Supreme Court upholds the state insurance commissioner's determination that the equal rights amendment to the Pennsylvania constitution prohibits auto insurance companies from basing their rates on gender.

1985 Montana becomes the first state to prohibit the use of gender as a criterion in establishing insurance premiums and payments in insurance and retirement plans. The Montana statute had been enacted in 1983, but by its own terms did not become effective until 1985.

1992 An administrative law judge in Maryland rules that the Maryland equal rights amendment bars the use of gender-based rates by life insurance companies.

1993 A Maryland circuit court judge overrules the 1992 decision of the administrative law judge and strikes down a Maryland insurance department order barring an insurer from charging gender-based rates for life insurance coverage.

SUGGESTIONS FOR FURTHER READING

Abraham, Kenneth S. *Distributing Risk: Insurance, Legal Theory, and Public Policy.* New Haven, Conn.: Yale University Press, 1986.

Benston, George J. "Discrimination and Economic Efficiency in Employee Fringe Benefits: A Clarification of Issues and a Response to Professors Brilmayer, Laycock, and Sullivan." *University of Chicago Law Review* 50 (1983): 250.

———. "The Economics of Gender Discrimination in Employee Fringe Benefits: *Manhart* Revisited." *University of Chicago Law Review* 49 (1982): 489.

Brilmayer, Lea, Richard W. Hekeler, Douglas Laycock, and Teresa A. Sullivan. "Sex Discrimination in Employer-Sponsored Insurance Plans: A Legal and Demographic Analysis." *University of Chicago Law Review* 47 (1980): 505.

Brilmayer, Lea, Douglas Laycock, and Teresa A. Sullivan. "The Efficient Use of Group Averages as Nondiscrimination: A Rejoinder to Professor Benston." *University of Chicago Law Review* 50 (1983): 222.

Comptroller General of the United States. *Economic Implications of the Fair Insurance Practices Act.* Report to Senator Orrin G. Hatch et al., GAO/OCE-84-1, April 6, 1984, 19.

Jerry, Robert H. II, and Kyle B. Mansfield. "Justifying Unisex Insurance: Another Perspective." *American University Law Review* 34 (1985): 329.

Kimball, Spencer L. "Reverse Sex Discrimination: *Manhart*." *American Bar Foundation Research Journal* 1979: 83.

Women and Family Law: Marriage and Divorce

Earlean M. McCarrick

As a presidential candidate in 1952 and 1956, Adlai Stevenson had to bear the stigma of divorce. How, the common reasoning went, could he "run the country" if he could not even "run" his own family? On television at that time was a situation comedy—"Father Knows Best"—that is representative of the "happy family with happy problems" sitcoms of that era and is still seen in reruns today. In this story, set in the mythical town of Springfield, Jim Anderson works all day and then comes home to his immaculately groomed and dutiful wife, Margaret, who has spent her day cleaning the house and preparing the family's evening meal. The three Anderson children, Betty, Bud, and Kathy, experience only those innocuous problems that were considered appropriate for family viewing in the 1950s—whom to date, what to wear to the prom, and what to get Dad for Christmas. Jim was a kind father who was stern when he had to be in dealing with his family's crises; in the end, he "knew best."

As a presidential candidate in 1980 and 1984, Ronald Reagan was asked few questions about, and received virtually no criticism of, his divorce from his first wife, Jane Wyman, and his subsequent remarriage to Nancy Davis. The fact that his divorce went virtually unnoticed may be partly attributable to the longevity and obvious success of his second marriage; a more likely explanation is the change in attitudes about divorce. In the 1980s, the popular television sitcom "Kate and Allie" depicted the experiences of two divorced women in New York City raising three children who faced problems common to those growing up at that time—separation from their fathers; experimentation with drugs, alcohol, and premarital sex; and crime. Kate and Allie were raising their children in a cultural environment different from that of Springfield. They had jobs, started a business, and expected the children to fend for themselves by cooking a meal once in a while. Most of the time, though

124

not always, they "knew best."

The television depiction and public expectation of the average family of the 1950s is obviously vastly different from that of the 1980s and 1990s. The women's movement, increasing economic opportunities for women, changes in divorce laws and in attitudes toward divorce and single-parent households—indeed, a reevaluation of what exactly a "family" is—have generated a new and different set of problems for the government to resolve. The government has established, by law, a series of responsibilities and rights that apply to those in a legally sanctioned union. When problems concerning living situations arise, the government often becomes involved in the resolution of such issues as property division, child custody, and spousal support rights. The traditional notion of marriage conforms to Judeo-Christian ideas of this union as a lifelong commitment between a male and a female for the purpose of producing and nurturing children. Most of the changes with regard to marriage and divorce discussed in this chapter relate to more traditional views of union that the state has recognized. As we shall see, however, cultural changes appear to be far ahead of the state in this area of relationships.

This chapter explores two of the most fundamental aspects of family law: the creation of a union (the marriage) and its dissolution (the divorce). Significant changes have occurred in both of these broad areas during the past century and a half, and many of them have been the result, either directly or indirectly, of changes in the legal status of married women (such as laws conferring on them the previously denied rights to own property and to enter into contracts) and changes in women's socioeconomic status and role (as a result of increased educational and economic opportunities that allow women to pursue careers and thus to be financially able to get out of an unsatisfactory marriage), as well as changes in societal attitudes toward alternative living arrangements (increased acceptance of cohabitation and unmarried parenthood). All of these factors (law, economics, and attitudes) have contributed to changes in the "family landscape."

The legal status of women has changed significantly in the twentieth century and especially in the past few decades. Most of us would now view as antiquated the nineteenth-century notion that a woman should lose her legal identity upon marriage. Yet until recently, wives were often subordinates in the eyes of the law; it thus reflected and contributed to cultural attitudes that denigrated the accomplishments of women. Today, in large part because of the pioneering efforts of those attending the women's rights convention at Seneca Falls, New York, in 1848 (which concluded with the adoption of a Declaration of Sentiments patterned after the Declaration of Independence) and the revival of the women's movement in the 1970s, a woman is generally viewed as an equal partner in a marriage union. Increasingly, the law is reflecting that view.

Changes in economic opportunities have also altered the attitudes of many women toward both marriage and divorce. Women who can earn enough to support themselves are not under the same pressure to marry that many women felt a century ago. Society expected a woman to forego education, marry young, stay at home, and become a "domestic engineer," condemned to remain in the marriage. To leave the marriage, a woman needed marketable skills that would enable her to exist financially on her own. Today, young women have the opportunity to acquire an education and thus the financial independence necessary to make important choices such as whether to marry and whether to remain married.

Attitudinal changes have had and will continue to have an impact on marriage and divorce. Divorce is no longer a stigma and government no longer makes it difficult. Single-parent families are now not only more frequent but more commonly accepted. Indeed, the growing number of alternative living arrangements increases the likelihood that the concept of family will continue to undergo transformation as the law evolves, taking into account these new arrangements.

An interesting example of the impact of an alternative living arrangement on the individuals seeking the rights and responsibilities of marriage is the experience of Sharon Kowalski and Karen Thompson, two Minnesota women who are committed to one another. In the United States, the law does not recognize same-sex marriages. (Sharon and Karen cannot, for example, file joint tax returns.) In 1983, Sharon was injured in an automobile accident that left her severely disabled. Her father, who did not accept her relationship with Karen, became her legal guardian and prevented Karen from visiting her. After more than three years of litigation, Karen finally secured the right to visit Sharon. Had Karen and Sharon been a legally married, heterosexual couple, they would not have had to endure involuntary separation. Court decisions such as the one in this case will contribute to the redefinition of family as other "rights" associated with marriage (such as pension benefits and social security benefits) are made the subject of litigation.

LAWS AND PUBLIC POLICIES GOVERNING MARRIAGE

American public policy regarding marriage is rooted in English common law. The common law doctrine that had the most serious economic and legal consequences for women was coverture; by the act of marriage, a woman in effect committed legal suicide. Under this doctrine, a woman's legal identity was suspended during marriage. As Supreme Court Justice

Hugo Black aptly but disapprovingly described coverture, the husband and wife became one, but the husband was the one.[1]

When her legal identity merged with that of her husband (symbolized by the assumption of his surname), the wife's ownership and control of her property, including her earnings, passed to him. She lost the right to enter into contracts; without it, she could not engage in a business or profession. Nor could she bring suit.

At various times throughout the second half of the nineteenth century, state legislatures removed many of these disabilities stemming from coverture. These statutes, which were collectively known as the Married Women's Acts, varied in content from state to state, but most conferred on wives the right to own and control property, to conduct a business, to enter into contracts, and to sue. The acts were egalitarian in theory, and were an improvement over the common law doctrine of coverture, but they did not make married women their husbands' equals. If a woman followed tradition and worked inside the home (as an unpaid housekeeper and childrearer) rather than outside the home, her new right to own property, for example, had little practical significance because few women had money or property of their own. Even if a woman worked outside the home, her wages were likely to be a small fraction of her husband's. More fundamentally, coverture had reflected society's attitude that women were subordinate socially, economically, and legally, and that attitude was unaffected by the Married Women's Acts. Nonetheless, they represented the most important changes that would be made in the status of married women until the 1970s.

MARITAL PROPERTY LAW

Two kinds of marital property law govern spousal rights of ownership, control, and disposition of property acquired during marriage: separate property law and community property law. *Separate property law* is derived from English common law; its fundamental principle is that each spouse owns and controls all property that he or she acquires during the marriage. *Community property law* is derived from the civil law of France and Spain; its principal tenet is that the "community," consisting of husband and wife, owns everything acquired during the marriage. Forty-two states are separate property law states; the other eight (Arizona, California, Idaho, Louisiana, Nevada, New Mexico, Texas, and Washington) are community property law states.

With passage of the Married Women's Acts in the nineteenth century, married women in separate property law states acquired the right to own and control the property they brought to the marriage and that which they acquired during the marriage. The husband would, as before, own what he brought to the marriage as well as that which he acquired during the marriage. And because the husband owned his earnings and everything bought with his money, he had the legal right to control the family assets, since the wife, in her traditional role, had no assets. Many separate property law states offered some legal protection to the non-wage-earning spouse, however; they prohibited either spouse from selling the family home without the consent of the other. Further, most of these states gave a widow (or widower) a share (one-third to one-half) of the estate of a deceased spouse. In addition, the law in these states permitted joint ownership of property. If spouses chose joint ownership, each had equal control over the assets of both.

In community property law states, property acquired during marriage is considered to belong to the community and thus to both spouses; a bank account in the name of one spouse belongs to the community and thus to both. Until the reforms of the 1970s, however, the law authorized the husband to control the assets of the community.

Beginning in the 1970s, the community property law states experimented with various techniques to increase the wife's managerial control. One technique was to give each spouse control over his or her earnings; control over the remaining property resided with both. Another was to permit either spouse to manage the community property, subject to the restriction that neither could commit more than one-half of that property without the consent of the other.

A MARRIED WOMAN'S DOMICILE

Domicile refers to a person's permanent legal residence and is a matter of individual choice. Under common law, however, a married woman was required to reside in the place chosen by her husband unless his choice was clearly unreasonable. Most state courts held that the rule followed from the common law obligation of a husband to support his family, combined with the notion that all family members must share one domicile. Her refusal to do so constituted desertion and was grounds for divorce; it could prevent the award of alimony and weaken her bargaining power in property settlement negotiations.

Because various rights and obligations are tied to domicile, a woman's eligibility to vote, to hold public office, to attend a state university on the same terms as a state resident, or her ability to gain access to a state's courts might be affected if her husband's domicile changed or was different from hers, as would her jury duty and tax-paying obligations. If the change of domicile was from a community property law state to a separate property law state, her community property rights might be endangered.

Although domicile and residence are for most people the same, they need not be. United States senators are domiciled in their home states, though most live in the Washington, D.C., area for most of the year. Similarly, a married woman may be domiciled in her husband's state but live apart from him (with his consent) in another state. She might be denied the right to run for public office or to seek a divorce in the state in which she resides because her domicile is in the state in which her husband resides. If they are living together in the same state but the husband's domicile is in a different state, her domicile may change to his; if, for example, a woman student domiciled in state *A* marries a fellow student living in the same state but domiciled in his parents' home in state *B*, her domicile may automatically change to his. She could thus become an out-of-state resident and be required to pay out-of-state tuition without leaving her home state.

Whether the domicile requirement is still applicable, and if so, whether it imposes serious legal disabilities, is unclear. Many states permit a married woman to acquire a separate domicile for specified reasons; both the list of states that are relaxing the domicile rule and the list of exceptions to it are growing longer. Some state statutes allow a separate domicile for all purposes; all states allow a separate domicile for some purposes (such as voting, holding public office, jury service, taxation, probate, and eligibility for in-state tuition). Further, when the rule has been challenged in state courts, the tendency has been to discard or modify it. In 1973 a Massachusetts state court, in a case concerning domicile for state income tax purposes, abolished the rule on the grounds that it was obsolete.[2] Nor is the rule likely to withstand federal judicial scrutiny under the Equal Protection Clause or state judicial scrutiny in those states that have added an equal rights amendment to their constitutions. Moreover, because state courts have consistently rejected the common law principle obligating husbands to support their wives, the domicile rule no longer has any legal underpinnings.

LEGAL SURNAME OF A MARRIED WOMAN

Common law permits an individual to choose whatever name he or she wishes so long as it is not used for fraudulent purposes. Custom dictates that a woman adopt the surname of her husband upon marriage. Whether the common law required her to do so has been a matter of some dispute. The courts have provided two answers. One answer is that she is required to do so. In an oft-cited 1881 case, a New York court announced unequivocally that when a woman marries, her legal name becomes that of her husband and that "her maiden surname is absolutely lost and she ceases to be known thereby."[3] Most state courts traditionally followed this rule; for example, in 1945 an Illinois court held that a married woman is legally required to use her husband's surname in order to vote.[4] When state courts have so interpreted the common law, federal courts have permitted them to do so; in the early 1970s, a federal judge upheld a state's requirement that a married woman use her husband's surname in order to obtain a driver's license.[5] The other answer is that the common law permits a married woman to retain her birth name. In a leading 1972 case, Maryland's highest court held that it was by custom, not by law, that a married woman adopted her husband's surname.[6] The trend has been to permit married women to retain their premarriage names.

Even if states require women to change their names, it is not certain that the federal courts will continue to permit them to do so. The Supreme Court has begun to scrutinize gender-based distinctions more closely. The Court traditionally held that gender-based legislation was valid if the gender distinction had a reasonable basis. Since the mid-1970s, however, the Court has adopted a more stringent test. To withstand a constitutional challenge, gender-based distinctions must substantially advance important governmental interests. If states insist that women, but not men, change their names upon marriage, federal courts now demand better reasons than custom and administrative convenience. The most successful argument against such a state requirement is probably one that has been asserted by the courts in Maryland—that the common law makes no such requirement. If a state has an equal rights amendment, the requirement may well be in conflict with that state's constitution.

SUPPORT OBLIGATIONS IN AN ONGOING MARRIAGE

Common law required a husband to provide his wife with "necessaries." This support obligation stemmed from a married woman's legal disabilities: suspension of her legal identity, loss of her property to her husband, the husband's right to her services, and her incapacity to enter into contracts. Few wives have ever sought judicial enforcement of this obligation during an ongoing marriage. Most litigation concerning the necessaries doctrine has been instituted by creditors seeking to collect a debt incurred by a wife. Until the 1970s, state courts consistently held that a husband was legally obligated to pay such debts.

Since the 1970s, most state courts have rejected the common law rule either because it no longer comports with the realities of marriage and the status of women, or because it violates the equal rights amendments in state constitutions, or because it conflicts with the Equal Protection Clause of the Fourteenth Amendment to the Constitution, which provides that no state may "deny to any person within its jurisdiction the equal protection of the laws."

Although most state courts now agree that the rule imposing sole support obligations upon the husband is no longer applicable, there is disagreement over what the new rule should be. In 1972 New Jersey's highest court held that both husband and wife are obligated to pay the wife's bills. It enforced the right of a hospital to obtain payment from a woman whose husband had failed to pay the bills she incurred in giving birth to the couple's sixth child. Although the court held that the husband was responsible for the debt, it concluded that he did not have exclusive liability. Thus the hospital was legally entitled to collect from the wife because she too was liable.[7] In contrast, Maryland's highest court held in 1981 that neither spouse is obligated to support the other. When a hospital in that state sought payment from a wife for bills incurred by her husband, both the lower court and the state's highest court rejected the doctrine imposing sole support obligations upon the husband, as the New Jersey court had done. The lower court had held that the wife was liable for her husband's debts. The state's highest court agreed that the state's equal rights amendment nullified the common law rule, but it rejected the lower court's extension of the support obligation to the wife.[8] It concluded that the state's equal rights amendment would permit either extension of liability to wives or elimination of the necessaries doctrine altogether. It chose the latter and left it to the legislature to make another choice.

CRIMINAL LAW

For the most part, marital status is now irrelevant in criminal law. In the past, most jurisdictions adhered to the outmoded common law doctrine of presumed coercion, under which a married woman could not be held criminally liable for a misdemeanor committed in the presence of her husband; it was presumed that she acted as a result of his coercion. Coverture exempted married couples from conspiracy charges. Because it takes at least two to conspire and because coverture recognized only the unity of marital partners, not their individuality, husband and wife could not be charged with conspiracy to commit a crime. Neither of these common law exemptions is likely to be upheld by courts in the 1990s. There are, however, circumstances under which marital status may be decisive; it may determine whether a witness can testify or whether a crime has been committed.

Under the old (now obsolete) common law a wife could testify neither for nor against her husband. But as modified by both common law and statutory law, this spousal testimony rule permits neither spouse to testify against the other in a criminal proceeding involving third parties if the defendant-spouse objects. If, for example, a husband kills his wife's lover, she is not permitted to testify against him. About half of the states continue to adhere to some form of this adverse spousal testimony rule.

Some of the other states confer the right to refuse to testify on the witness-spouse alone; the rest have abolished the rule altogether.

Not until 1980 did the Supreme Court throw out the rule in criminal cases in federal courts.[9] The old rule that a wife could testify neither for nor against her husband was rooted, said the Court, in two outmoded canons of medieval law: that the accused could not testify in his own behalf and that the husband and wife were one. The modern justification for the rule against adverse spousal testimony was to protect the harmony of marriage, but the Court concluded that this reason was no more convincing than the old one; if one spouse is willing to testify against the other, marital harmony has already broken down. The new rule in federal courts is that the witness-spouse alone may invoke the privilege. Thus, in federal courts, as in many state courts, a defendant can no longer prevent a spouse from testifying against him or her. Nor, however, can the government compel either spouse to testify against the other.

Traditionally, a husband was immune from prosecution for raping his wife. One justification for this exemption stems from the pronouncement of the seventeenth-century English jurist Lord Chief Justice Matthew Hale that marriage implies consent to sexual intercourse. According to this theory, marriage is a contract, under the terms of which a husband has the absolute power to determine the time, place, and manner of sexual intercourse. The husband is authorized to enforce the contract unilaterally, by force if he deems that necessary.

In the 1970s, some states either modified the marital exemption rule or abolished it. Whereas the exemption traditionally was absolute, these states deny immunity if the parties are divorced, living apart, or legally separated; if force is used; if there is fear of bodily harm; or if physical injury is inflicted.[10] The marital exemption rule is, at the moment, still prevalent, but this situation is rapidly changing; each year witnesses another state's elimination of the rule by legislation or judicial interpretation.

SOCIAL SECURITY BENEFITS

The social security retirement benefits received by women, on average, are lower than those received by men. The disparities are both long-term and contemporary.[11] In part, the reason is simply that women earn less than men; for every dollar a man earns, a woman earns between 58 cents and 74 cents: in the 1930s, women's earnings were 58 percent of men's; in the 1970s, this proportion was 59 percent; in the 1980s, it increased to 64 percent; and in the early 1990s it was 74 percent, probably because of the increasing number of younger women entering higher-paying, male-dominated professions. Because benefits are related to earnings, the benefits received by working women who are now of retirement age are lower than those received by working men of retirement age. Indeed, many married retired women workers have chosen to receive spousal benefits rather than benefits on the basis of their earnings alone because the former are higher.

Many women receive retirement benefits that are lower than those received by men because they never held a paying job; their benefits are thus dependent upon their husbands' earnings. Spousal benefits, however, do not equal those of the retired wage earner. A retired wage earner receives 100 percent of the benefits to which he or she is entitled, but the dependent spouse over the age of sixty-five receives an amount equal to 50 percent of those benefits. Widows over the age of sixty-five receive the 100 percent to which their husbands would have been entitled. If widows start receiving benefits before age sixty-five, however, the amount is 71.5 percent. An older nonworking woman whose husband dies before she reaches age sixty-five frequently has little choice but to accept the lower benefit at an earlier age. Divorced older women who never worked outside the home during marriage receive retirement benefits that are equal to or less than spousal benefits. If a marriage lasted less than ten years (the requirement was less than twenty years until 1979), she receives no benefits on the basis of her husband's earnings; now she receives 50 percent if the marriage lasted more than ten years.

The Social Security system offers no protection to widowed homemakers under the age of sixty unless they are disabled or have minor children. Benefits cease when the child reaches the age of eighteen. The widow is not entitled to receive benefits again until age sixty. This "widow's gap" leaves many middle-aged dependent homemakers who lack job skills or work experience with no source of income. If the widowed homemaker is disabled, there are no benefits until she reaches age fifty.

One proposal aimed at reducing the economic insecurity of older married women who never worked outside the home is to assign a monetary value to homemaking and child rearing. To finance such a program, either homemakers would pay taxes on the assigned value of their services in the home, or paid workers would pay more taxes. Another suggestion intended to protect married women is an "earnings sharing" plan under which each person's benefits would be based on his or her earnings when single plus one-half of the total earnings of the married couple. For a one-income family, the worker's earnings on which benefits were based would be split 50-50; the earnings credits would be divided if the couple were to divorce or when one spouse reached age sixty-two.

Most of the economic disadvantages suffered by married women under the Social Security system are unrelated to specific gender-based distinctions but are rather a result of the different economic and domestic roles and pay scales of men and women. The Social Security Act was replete with such distinctions, but the most obvious ones have been changed by Congress or invalidated by the Supreme Court—although those that were invalidated by the Court discriminated primarily against men, not women. In 1975, for example, the Supreme Court invalidated a provision authorizing benefits for widows with minor children but denied benefits to similarly situated widowers.[12] In 1977 it invalidated a provision that authorized benefits for surviving widows over the age of sixty but denied benefits to similarly situated widowers unless they had received at least one-half of their support from their wives.[13]

Neither judicial nor legislative changes in the social security legislation provide economic security for women who have spent most or all of their adult lives as homemakers or in low-paying or part-time jobs. The Social Security system was not originally intended to be the sole source of retirement income; it was designed to supplement other resources, including private pension plans provided by employers. But married women fare no better under these plans for much the same reason that they suffer under the Social Security system. As a result of the efforts of such groups as the Older Women's League, the plight of older women is beginning to receive the attention of the nation's lawmakers. The proposed economic equity act, which deals with a variety of issues of interest to women (such as child care), seeks greater equity in both the Social Security system and private pension plans. Until both married and single women routinely enter the work force and earn as much as men, older women who have to rely on their own pensions are likely to continue to be economically insecure.

LAWS AND PUBLIC POLICIES GOVERNING DIVORCE

Public policy regarding divorce was traditionally based on the assumption that marriage is a lifelong arrangement. Grounds for divorce were both limited and gender-based. Almost 50 percent of all marriages now end in divorce. In the 1970s, most states moved toward acceptance of divorce on demand. In 1970, California inaugurated no-fault divorce when it adopted an "irreconcilable differences" standard. Irreconcilable differences are those which a court determines "to be substantial reasons for not continuing the marriage and which make it appear that the marriage should be dissolved." Irreparable breakdown, irreconcilable differences, and incompatibility are now grounds for divorce in a majority of states. Whatever grounds are statutorily specified, most states in effect allow unilateral divorce on demand. Although no-fault divorce was initially viewed as benefiting both men and women because it would lessen the recriminations associated with divorce, the reform may have further disadvantaged economically dependent women because they can no longer use the refusal to agree to a divorce as a bargaining chip to obtain a larger property settlement or alimony payment.[14]

A state's interest in the preservation of marriage may have dwindled, but its interest in related problems (property division, alimony, child custody, child support) certainly has not. Changes in these areas in the name of equality were precipitated by the no-fault movement. Early indications are that the newer egalitarian reforms, like the nineteenth-century Married Women's Property Acts, when superimposed on the unchanged social and economic roles of husbands and wives, will fail to bring about the equality sought by their advocates. On the basis of an in-depth ten-year study (1974-1984) of the postreform status of women and children in California, one scholar concluded that California's no-fault divorce, in combination with changed rules governing property division and spousal support, accounted for a post-divorce decline of 73 percent in the living standard of women and children and a rise of 42 percent in that of men.[15]

PROPERTY DIVISION

The basic issues to be decided in dividing property are which property is to be divided, how it is to be divided, and what factors are to be considered in making the division. Historically, in most states the title and acquisition source have been decisive in determining which property acquired during marriage is subject to division. The law itself was gender neutral; however, in a traditional marriage in which the husband worked outside the home for money and the wife worked either inside the home without monetary compensation or outside the home as well, at a lower paying job, the wife was clearly at a disadvantage.

In separate property law states, titled property (such as a house or a car) acquired by the husband with his earnings and held in his name belonged to him; it was not subject to division, even if the wife contributed financially to the acquisition of property held in his name. He could take it with him when he left the marriage. The court might order him to pay alimony, but the property remained his. The acquiring spouse—usually presumed to be the husband—also owned untitled family assets such as household goods. Further, the husband's earning capacity and his retirement benefits—frequently a family's most valuable assets—were considered his alone and thus not subject to division. Even if the wife worked in the home as well as at a low-paying job to help support the family and to put her husband through school, she traditionally would not reap any benefit from her labors if the couple divorced. The husband took his earning capacity, as well as any pension rights he earned during the marriage, with him when he left the marriage. If the wife were the innocent party, that fact might enable her to obtain some of what the law deemed to be her husband's property. Nonetheless, for traditional homemakers, termination of a long marriage could spell economic disaster.

Responding to the organized efforts of women's groups, legislatures began to reform marital property laws in the 1970s. As a result, title and monetary contribution to the acquisition of family assets in separate property law states have been of decreasing importance with regard to property division at the time of divorce. Instead, most of these state legislatures have expanded the definition of marital property subject to division to include all property acquired during the marriage regardless of title or whose income paid for such property. Property acquired by gift or inheritance is still not subject to division nor, in some states, is property that the couple agrees to exclude by prenuptial agreement.

As for the controversial question of whether retirement benefits and earning capacity are marital property subject to division, there is no single or simple answer. In more than half the states, pensions are now considered marital property subject to division. Few states, however, have accepted the notion that "career assets"—a professional or graduate degree, medical or dental practice, earning capacity—are marital property subject to division. Increasingly, dependent, nonworking, or lower paid spouses are arguing that such assets are divisible property, particularly if they made monetary contributions to the other spouse's acquisition of a professional degree. A wife thus might ask a court to place a monetary value on her husband's degree and to award a portion of that value to her. Although such suits may be instituted by either a husband or wife, most of them have been brought by women.

Most state courts in which the question has arisen (New York is a notable exception) have held that professional degrees and earning capacity are not "property" in the traditional sense because such assets lack what are normally considered the attributes of property—they are not transferable, cannot be sold on the open market or willed to heirs, and have no exchange value but are personal to, and terminate on death of, the possessor. If a degree is not "property," it cannot be marital property, and thus cannot be divided. Indeed, a court might consider a woman who put her husband through school to be ineligible for alimony because she has a demonstrated earning capacity. Nonetheless, many courts have ordered reimbursement to the wife for her contribution to the acquisition of the degree that enabled the husband to increase his earning capacity; a 1984 California statute explicitly provided for the reimbursement of educational costs in addition to any alimony that a court might award. Courts have also used the value of degrees and earning capacity in determining the ability to pay alimony.

Almost all separate property law states now provide for equitable distribution of marital property. Most states have also increased the factors to be considered in determining how property is to be divided. Most important, new emphasis is being given to the contributions made to the family by the wife in her role of homemaker. In determining what constitutes an equitable division of assets acquired during marriage, the courts consider the length of the marriage, the contributions of each partner to the family's well-being, and the age, occupation, and earning capacity of each spouse—in general, the needs, abilities, and both monetary and non-monetary contributions of each.

Statutory law usually establishes what property is to be considered marital property subject to division, the standard for division (equitable or equal), and the factors to be considered in making the division. Discretion in applying the law, however, continues to be vested in the judge. Whether the reforms can improve the disadvantaged economic position of dependent spouses at property division time thus depends in part on how judges use their vast discretion. If they realistically assess the partners' respective economic situations, earning capacity, and parental responsibilities, equal or equitable division can result in an approximate equality between the partners. If differences are not factored into the division and economic unequals are treated as economic equals, formal equality may still leave one partner in a disadvantaged economic position.

In community property law states, the judges' discretion and the unpredictability of property division are lessened somewhat. Whereas courts in separate property law states have considered all property acquired during marriage to be marital property subject to division and have divided that property evenly or equitably only since the 1970s, the general rule in community property law states has always been equal division—each partner is entitled to take from the marriage one-half of everything acquired during the marriage, though the actual distribution might depend on a variety of circumstances; for example, a custodial parent would probably retain the family home, or the spouse who is more anxious to obtain a divorce might be willing to make concessions.

Formal equality of property division, whether in a separate property law state or a community property law state, might not achieve real equality. Since few couples amass many divisible assets (the average has been estimated to be $20,000, usually a house), equal division frequently requires sale of the house and the award of one-half of the proceeds to the husband and one-half to the wife. Eminently fair on its face, such a division might be unequal in fact if one-half goes to the husband and one-half goes to the wife and the children, for whom she must provide primary care in addition to perhaps finding a low-paying job with flexible hours while she prepares to move from the family home. If she is not awarded, or cannot collect, child support, her descent into poverty is not forestalled by equal property division. For an older traditional housewife without minor children but with few job prospects, equal property division rarely permits continuation of the living standard she enjoyed during marriage because that standard was dependent on her former husband's earnings, which he takes with him.

FEDERAL RETIREMENT BENEFITS

Property division is essentially a state matter. Federal law, however, must be considered by state courts when they divide national retirement benefits. Since most individuals rely on pensions rather than on private savings for support during retirement, for dependent spouses the division of such benefits may spell the difference between having an adequate living standard and living in poverty.

Most states authorize division of retirement benefits at the time of divorce. Congress, too, has explicitly recognized the right of former spouses (as well as surviving spouses) to receive benefits from some federal retirement programs. Former spouses who were married for at least ten years (before 1979, twenty years) are entitled to receive benefits as dependents of a wage earner covered by Social Security. Civil service retirement benefits are to be paid to a former spouse in accordance with the property division laws of the state in which they are domiciled at the time of the divorce. Under foreign service retirement legislation, a former spouse is entitled to receive a pro rata share of the retirement benefits of a foreign service officer.

When Congress has not specifically made provision for such participation or division, courts must determine congressional intent. The Supreme Court has frequently denied former spouses the right to receive retirement benefits. In 1981, the Court excluded military pensions from community property as defined by California law. The benefits thus could not be divided by the state.[16] Congress overruled this decision. Legislation passed in 1982 authorized the states to deal with military retirement pay in accordance with state law if the couple had been married for ten years or more.

AWARD AND PAYMENT OF ALIMONY

Historically, payment of alimony was based on the common law duty of a husband to support his wife. In theory, this obligation continued after divorce if the husband was at fault. In fact, the award of alimony has been the exception, not the rule. From the late nineteenth century to the early 1970s, alimony was awarded in only 10 to 15 percent of all divorces.

In the 1970s, states began revising their alimony laws. Alimony statutes were made gender neutral, thus permitting awards to husbands. Short-term "rehabilitative" awards (temporary payments to permit acquisition of job skills) began to replace long-term alimony obligations. The enactment of no-fault divorce laws meant that the "guilty" party was no longer required to pay alimony to the "innocent" party. In determining whether and how much alimony is to be awarded, courts consider such factors as the dependent spouse's need (alimony is usually not awarded if the judge decides that the dependent spouse is able to work; a short-term award is made to those without job skills), the wage earner's ability to pay, the length of the marriage (an award of alimony is rare in short-term marriages), the age of the partners (alimony is usually not awarded to a young or middle-aged spouse if the judge decides that he or she is capable of self-support), and the contributions (including homemaking activities) of the dependent spouse. Whether the dependent or lower-paid spouse receives alimony or a sufficient amount depends on whether the judge makes a realistic assessment of such factors as the ability of a traditional housewife to enter or reenter the job market and to earn a living wage if she does. Frequently both are overestimated, with the result that the dependent spouse's income and living standard decline.

The anti-alimony trend of the 1970s has perhaps worked to the disadvantage of a few women; it probably has had little effect on most of the others, who, under the old, for-cause-only divorce laws, would have received little or nothing—although wives of "guilty" well-to-do men who wanted a divorce might have been able to extract alimony from them. About 15 percent of all divorced women are awarded alimony.

But the award of alimony and its payment are two different things. In 1978, only two-thirds of the women awarded alimony actually received some payment. The average amount received was only $2,850. In the 1980s, the average amount was not even $4,000—less than half the poverty level. In 1981, the figure was $3,000; in 1983, it was $3,980; and in 1985, it was $3,733. Of the 19.1 million divorced and separated women in 1985, 840,000 were entitled to alimony but 616,000 actually received payment.[17]

The infrequency of alimony awards and the small amounts that are awarded and received account for some of the poverty faced by traditional housewives who become divorced in middle age and by young custodial parents who receive little or no child support yet have responsibility for child care. The seemingly exorbitant alimony extracted from a few wealthy men grabs the public's attention, but the reality is that just as few men are rich, few women are awarded alimony and fewer still receive alimony payments above the poverty level. If the partners are economic and domestic equals (they divide responsibilities for child care and housework), elimination of a long-term alimony obligation is simply an acknowledgment of an egalitarian marriage and does not spell economic hardship. But because roles continue to differ in many marriages, many spouses who were dependent during marriage become poorer after divorce if alimony is not ordered or received.

CHILD CUSTODY AND CHILD SUPPORT

Which divorced parent is to have custody of children is usually decided by the parents and ratified by the courts. If there is a dispute, the courts decide. In either case, the mother usually gets custody. Her success in gaining custody may, however, translate into a financial burden. Many fathers are not ordered to pay child support. The Census Bureau reported in 1979 that only one-half of the divorced and separated women with children under the age of 21 were awarded child support payments in 1978. If the father is ordered to make payments, mothers frequently are unable to collect what they have been awarded. If the custodial parent finds the time and money to take the delinquent parent to court, the latter may find that noncompliance pays; judges frequently not only excuse back payment but excuse or reduce future payments because of changed circumstances such as job loss or decreased income, with little concern for how the needs of the child are to be met. The Census Bureau found that in 1978, only half of the women awarded child support payments received full payment —an average of about $1,800 a year.

Subsequent Census Bureau surveys revealed no dramatic change. Although 60 percent of the custodial parents were awarded child support and 50 percent of them actually received payments in 1981, only half of those receiving payments received the full amount awarded; the average amount received was $2,100. In 1983 more than half (53 percent) of the custodial parents were awarded child support, and 76 percent of them actually received it; the average payment was $2,340. In 1991, 51.4 percent of the five million custodial parents who were awarded child support by the courts received the full amount ordered, 23.8 percent received a part of what was ordered, and 24.6 percent received no payment. The average award ordered was about $3,526.

A 1979 study found that within one year after a divorce, 38 percent of the fathers were in full compliance with child support court orders, 20 percent were in partial compliance, and 42 percent had made no payments at all. By the tenth year after the divorce, 13 percent were in full compliance and 79 percent were in total noncompliance.

It has been estimated that in 1983 alone, $3 billion in child support payments was never collected; the estimated figure for 1984 was closer to $4 billion.[18] Those hardest hit by uncollected child support payments are minority women with little education, who were not married to their children's fathers. Better-educated, middle-class white women who were married to their children's fathers are more likely to receive some or all of the payments awarded.

A principal cause of the "feminization" of poverty, and of the poverty of increasing numbers of children, is divorce—in combination with maternal custody rights, receipt of little or no child support or alimony, inadequate job skills or lack of time to acquire them or to find a well-paying job, and small property awards. The single largest group of welfare recipients consists of the women and their minor children who receive payments under the Aid to Families with Dependent Children (AFDC) program, many of whom receive no paternal support. The Census Bureau reported in 1979 that the poverty rate for families with a divorced, separated, never-married, or remarried woman is 27 percent, compared with a rate of 8 percent for all other families. Moreover, 40 percent of the single-parent families headed by women live in poverty. Only 13 percent of the families receiving child support payments are poor, compared with 32 percent of the families not receiving child support.

The failure of large numbers of noncustodial parents to support their children financially not only contributes to private misery but adds to the welfare rolls. The government has therefore begun to insist that parents who are able to support their children do so. Every state has agreed to enforce the child support court orders in other states; a noncustodial parent thus cannot legally escape child support obligations by moving to another state. The Internal Revenue Service deducts child support payments from a defaulting parent's income tax refund. To encourage the states to force delinquent parents to meet their support obligation, the federal government pays the bulk of enforcement costs, rewards enforcing states by giving them a substantial portion of the money they collect, and conditions its AFDC contribution on state enforcement. Under the 1984 Child Support Enforcement Act, states are required to attach the wages and state income tax refunds of a delinquent parent who is in arrears for thirty days, and to place liens on the parent's real and personal property. The act also encourages, though it does not require, states to consider other means of enforcement such as making child support payments an automatic wage deduction rather than waiting until the noncustodial parent fails to make the ordered payments. Even before the act went into effect on October 1, 1985, almost one-half of the states had enacted compliance legislation; the act required the remaining states to do so within four months of their 1985 legislative sessions. Some jurisdictions have gone beyond federal compliance requirements and suggestions and have not only authorized automatic wage assignments but arrested and jailed delinquent parents.

Nonetheless, many of these changes either are enforced only sporadically or continue to give judges discretion as to how more effective enforcement can be achieved. Whether jurists, most of whom are male, will become less sympathetic to the financial hardship pleas of noncompliant parents and more aware of the devastation that noncompliance wreaks on the financially pressed custodial parent and minor children is problematic. Further, the epidemic of pregnancy among unmarried teenagers, in combination with unknown or denied paternity, or paternity acknowledged by teenage fathers with little income, few job skills, no job, and no sense of responsibility for the children they father, intensifies the problem of poverty among women and children.

COHABITATION AND PROPERTY

When a marriage is dissolved, the law protects the right of each spouse to some of the assets acquired during the marriage. Although divisible assets may be minimal and the dependent partner's living standard may in fact plummet after divorce, the law formally recognizes that neither partner is the sole owner of property acquired during the marriage. When a "meretricious" living arrangement ends, however, there are few statutory guidelines for determining whether or how to divide assets.[19] The traditional judicial reaction to a cohabitant's request for division of assets was summed up by a California judge in the 1950s: "The law does not award compensation for living with a man as a concubine and bearing him children." [20]

In a widely publicized cohabitation case in the 1970s, the California Supreme Court expanded the property rights of dependent "meretricious spouses" in that state.[21] Michelle Triola Marvin and Lee Marvin had lived together without marriage for about six years. Lee continued to support Michelle for over a year after the arrangement ended. When he stopped doing so, she sued to acquire part of his assets, alleging that in return for her agreement to give up her career and become a full-time "companion, homemaker, housekeeper and cook," he had promised to support her for the rest of her life and to share his property with her. The trial court refused to enforce the alleged oral agreement.

The Supreme Court of California reversed that decision. Holding that express and implied contracts between cohabitants can be enforced if not based on illicit sexual services, it directed the lower court to decide if an agreement had been made. The opinion of the state supreme court was a victory for Michelle Marvin and other dependent cohabitants. Ultimately, however, Lee Marvin was victorious. When the case was returned to the lower court, that court concluded that Michelle Marvin was unable to prove that Lee Marvin had agreed, explicitly or implicitly, to support her and to share his assets in exchange for her unpaid, nonsexual services.[22]

Although the trial court nonetheless ordered a "rehabilitative" award, an appellate court reversed that order and held that no award could be ordered if no contract existed.

Since the liberalization in California, the trend of courts in other states has been to rule that a "meretricious spouse" is entitled to a property settlement if she (and it usually is a female) can prove that an agreement to share assets has in fact been made.[23] In 1979, the New Jersey Supreme Court upheld an award to Irma Kozlowski in pursuance of her express agreement with Thaddeus Kozlowski that she would perform household tasks in exchange for financial support for the rest of her life. The relationship ended after fourteen years, and the court enforced the contract.[24] Similarly, in 1982 a Hawaii circuit court held that a woman was entitled to one-half of the assets acquired during a twenty-four-year relationship; a "domestic partnership" existed and the couple had both an express contract and an implied contract by which the man agreed to share the assets held in his name in exchange for the woman's affection, companionship, housekeeping, and childrearing.[25]

Not all state appellate courts have liberalized their views on the economic rights of dependent cohabitants, however. In 1979 the Illinois Supreme Court refused to enforce an express agreement between cohabitants that the woman, in return for future financial support, would do the housework, raise the children, and support the family while the man pursued his education and career. The arrangement dissolved after fifteen years, and a lower court awarded Virginia Hewitt half of the property acquired during cohabitation. The Illinois Supreme Court reversed that decision. Concluding that the relationship was an essentially illicit sexual one, it held that enforcement would run counter to public policies designed to "preserve and strengthen traditional marriage." [26]

CONCLUSION

The common law doctrine of coverture established the legal inferiority of married women to their husbands. By the end of the nineteenth century, state legislatures had removed many of the disabilities stemming from coverture. Married women acquired the rights to own property, to sue, and to enter into contracts. Such legal changes did not bring equality, however. If a woman played the traditional role of wife and mother, she had few legally enforceable rights. If the marriage ended, the law tended to favor men in all areas other than child custody. A lower standard of living, if not poverty, awaited many divorced women. Not only did they emerge from marriage with few of the assets acquired during marriage, they either were not awarded or did not receive alimony or child support payments.

As a result of the women's movement, legislatures began to increase married women's rights. The new legislation directed judges to divide marital property equally or equitably. Both Congress and the states have concentrated their efforts on forcing the noncustodial parent to make child support payments. In many states, the female partner in a nonmarital relationship has been given the opportunity to prove that she is entitled to some of the property acquired during cohabitation.

Because many of these changes are relatively recent, their long-term effect is difficult to assess, but there is some indication that they have not improved the status of women, particularly those whose marriages end in divorce. Even no-fault divorce and equal or equitable property division, which seemed to hold so much promise, have rebounded to the disadvantage of some, especially women who receive little or no alimony or child support and have a lower earning capacity because they have been restricted to childrearing and housekeeping roles. Whether women will in fact become equal partners in a marriage as well as after its dissolution will depend in part on judicial and legislative capacity to adapt the new laws to these realities and to change the laws found wanting.

NOTES

1. Dissenting in *United States v. Yazell*, 382 U.S. 341, 361 (1966).
2. *Green v. Commissioner*, 305 N.E. 2d (Mass. 1973).
3. *Chapman v. Phoenix National Bank*, 85 N.Y. 437 (1881).
4. *People ex rel Rago v. Lipsky*, 63 N.E. 2d 642 Ill. (1945).
5. *Forbush v. Wallace*, 341 F. Supp. 217 (M.D. Ala. 1971); aff'd mem. 405 U.S. 970 (1972).
6. *Stuart v. Board of Supervisors of Elections for Howard County*, 295 A.2d 223 (Md. 1972). For a discussion of *Stuart* and the common law rule, see Priscilla Ruth MacDougall, "Married Women's Common Law Right to Their Own Surnames," *Women's Rights Law Reporter* 1 (Fall-Winter 1972-1973): 1-14.
7. *Sillery v. Fagan and Fagan*, 294 A.2d 624 (N.J. 1972).
8. *Condore v. Prince George's General Hospital*, 425 A.2d (Md. 1981).
9. *Trammel v. United States*, 445 U.S. 40 (1980).
10. See Leigh Bienen, "Rape III: National Developments in Rape Reform Legislation," *Women's Rights Law Reporter* 6 (Spring 1980): 170-213. See also Dennis Drucker, "The Common Law Does Not Support a Marital Exception for Forcible Rape," *Women's Rights Law Reporter* 5 (Winter-Spring 1979): 181-200.
11. U.S. Department of Health, Education, and Welfare, *Social Security and the Changing Roles of Men and Women*, 1979. For an overview of the variations, see U.S. Department of Commerce, Bureau of the Census, "Social Security (OASI) Retirement Benefits, by Sex: 1960 to 1981"; and U.S. Department of Commerce, Bureau of the Census, *Statistical Abstract of the United States, 1982-83* (Washing-

ton, D.C.: Government Printing Office, 1984), 328.

12. *Weinberger v. Wiesenfeld,* 420 U.S. 655 (1975).
13. *Califano v. Goldfarb,* 430 U.S. 199 (1977).
14. Lenore J. Weitzman, *The Divorce Revolution: The Unexpected Social and Economic Consequences for Women and Children in America* (New York: Free Press, 1985).
15. Ibid., 323. Although few dispute that the economic status of most divorced women has declined, not everyone attributes that decline to no-fault divorce. See, for example, Annamay T. Sheppard, "Women, Families, and Equality," *Women's Rights Law Reporter* 12 (Fall 1990): 143-152.
16. *McCarty v. McCarty,* 449 U.S. 210 (1981).
17. Stuart S. Nagel and Lenore J. Weitzman, "Women as Litigants," *Hastings Law Journal* 23 (November 1971): 171-198. See also U.S. Department of Commerce, Bureau of the Census, *Divorce, Child Custody, and Child Support* (Washington, D.C.: Government Printing Office, 1979); *Child Support and Alimony: 1981* (1983), *Child Support and Alimony: 1983* (1986), and *Child Support and Alimony: 1985* (1987); Weitzman, *The Divorce Revolution;* Citizens Advisory Council on the Status of Women, *The ERA and Alimony and Child Support Laws,* CACSQ 23-N-1972 (Washington, D.C.: Department of Labor, 1972); Andrea H. Beller, "Trends in Child Support Payments," *Proceedings, First Annual Women's Policy Research Conference,* Washington, D.C., May 19, 1989, 52-57; Demie Kurz, "Divorce and Inequality: The Case of Child Support," *Proceedings, Second Annual Women's Policy Research Conference,* Washington, D.C., June 1-2, 1990, 32-39; and Mimi Hall, "Child Support: States Pay If Parents Don't," *USA Today,* March 28, 1994, 10A.
18. For figures on child support, see sources cited in note 17, supra.
19. There is no agreement on what to call partners in a nonmarital sexual relationship. The term "meretricious spouse" appears in the case law. ("Meretricious" is derived from the Latin *meretrix,* meaning prostitute.) The Census Bureau uses POSSLQ—persons of the opposite sex sharing living quarters. One Washington State court suggested CUPOS—cohabiting unmarried persons of the opposite sex. Other terms that have been used include de facto spouse, informal spouse, and cohabitant.
20. *Hill v. Estate of Westbrook,* 247 P.2d 19 (1952), quoted in *Marvin v. Marvin,* 557 P.2d 106, 114 (Calif. 1976).
21. *Marvin v. Marvin* 557 P.2d 106 (Calif. 1976). For an analysis of *Marvin* and of possible remedies suggested by the trial court, see Nancy A. Rochford, "Case Development: Property Agreements between Cohabiting Persons," *Women's Rights Law Reporter* 4 (Fall 1977): 33-42.
22. *Marvin v. Marvin, Family Law Reporter* 5 (1982): 3077.
23. For an examination of some post-*Marvin* decisions of courts in other states, see Nancy A. Rochford, "Updates: Cohabitation after *Marvin v. Marvin,*" *Women's Rights Law Reporter* 8 (Fall-Winter 1978-1980).
24. *Kozlowski v. Kozlowski,* 403 A.2d 902 (N.J. 1979).
25. *Artiss v. Artiss, Family Law Reporter* 8 (1982): 2313.
26. *Hewitt v. Hewitt,* 394 N.E. 2d 1204 (Ill. 1979).

CHRONOLOGY

1881 *Chapman v. Phoenix National Bank:* A New York state court interprets common law as requiring a married woman to adopt her husband's surname as her own.

1945 *People ex rel. Rago v. Lipsky:* An Illinois state court rules that under common law, a married woman's legal surname is that of her husband.

1952 *Hill v. Estate of Westbrook:* A California court dismisses a dependent cohabitant's attempt to obtain a share of the estate of her deceased partner on the grounds that a nonmarital sexual union confers no rights on the dependent partner.

1966 *United States v. Yazell:* The Supreme Court recognizes the power of a state to restrict the right of married women to enter into contracts regarding their separate property.

1971, 1972 *Forbush v. Wallace:* A federal district court holds that Alabama can constitutionally require a married woman to adopt her husband's surname as her legal name. The Supreme Court affirms that holding.

1972 *Stuart v. Board of Supervisors of Elections for Howard County:* Maryland's highest court holds that the common law rule that individuals have the right to choose their own legal name applies to married women; thus a married woman has the legal right to be known by her maiden name rather than the surname of her husband.

1972 *Sillery v. Fagan and Fagan:* New Jersey's highest court throws out the common law rule that a husband is legally obligated to support his wife on the grounds that it is an unconstitutional gender distinction and holds that both the wife and the husband are legally liable for debts incurred by the wife.

1973 *Green v. Commissioner:* A Massachusetts state court holds that the old common law rule that a wife's domicile follows that of her husband is outmoded and therefore will no longer be enforced.

1975 *Weinberger v. Wiesenfeld:* The Supreme Court invalidates a provision of the Social Security Act that provides benefits for widows, but not widowers, with minor children.

1976 *Marvin v. Marvin:* The California Supreme Court holds that property division agreements between cohabitants are judicially enforceable.

1977 *Califano v. Goldfarb:* The Supreme Court invalidates a provision in the Social Security Act that authorizes retirement benefits for surviving widows, but not widowers.

1979 *Kozlowski v. Kozlowski:* The New Jersey Supreme Court upholds a lower court's enforcement of an agreement between cohabitants concerning financial support when the relationship ends.

1979 *Hewitt v. Hewitt:* Illinois's highest court refuses to permit judicial enforcement of property division agreements between cohabitants.

1980 *Trammel v. United States:* The Supreme Court abandons the traditional rule in federal courts that a person cannot testify against his or her spouse without the consent of the defendant spouse.

1981 *Condore v. Prince George's General Hospital:* Maryland's highest court holds that the common law rule requiring a husband to support his wife violates the state's Equal Rights Amendment.

1981 *McCarty v. McCarty:* The Supreme Court holds that military pensions are not community property subject to division at the time of divorce. Congress rejects this interpretation and enacts legislation permitting states to consider such retirement benefits to be divisible at the time of divorce.

1982 *Artiss v. Artiss:* A Hawaii court awards a dependent cohabitant a share of property acquired during cohabitation.

SUGGESTIONS FOR FURTHER READING

Basch, Norma. *In the Eyes of the Law: Women, Marriage, and Property in the Nineteenth Century,* Ithaca, N.Y.: Cornell University Press, 1982.

Chused, Richard. "Married Women's Property Acts, 1830-1865." *Georgetown Law Review* 71 (June 1983): 1359-1425.

Diamond, Irene, ed. *Families, Politics, and Public Policy: A Feminist Dialogue on Women and the State.* New York: Longman, 1983.

Fineman, Martha L. *The Illusion of Equality: The Rhetoric and Reality of Divorce Reform.* Chicago: University of Chicago Press, 1991.

Glendon, Mary Ann. *State, Law and Family: Family Law in Transition in the United States and Western Europe.* Amsterdam: North Holland, 1977.

Women and Child Care

During the second week of the Clinton administration, Congress passed and the president signed into law the Family and Medical Leave Act of 1993. The signing of this legislation and two related events that came to be referred to as "Nannygate"—Zoë Baird's withdrawal of her nomination to the cabinet post of attorney general of the United States and Kimba Wood's withdrawal from consideration for the same post—are indicative of a dilemma faced today by women, men, and society as a whole. The appointments of both women (who had established successful legal careers in either the public sector or the private sector) were undermined by decisions each had made regarding the care of her children.

These events brought the issue of child care to the public's attention and also redirected the focus of the debate. Passage of the Family and Medical Leave Act was viewed as providing some relief for women who had to work but were also expected to care for children or parents. The act granted up to twelve weeks of unpaid leave for men as well as women, thus challenging the notion that "caring" is solely or even primarily a woman's responsibility. But the fact that Zoë Baird and Kimba Wood had to withdraw their names from consideration for the post of attorney general because of questions about their child care arrangements demonstrated the (potentially destructive) effect the issue can have on women's careers and career opportunities.

The problem of providing care is complex because it relates to different aspects of a traditional concern of American society. Responsibility for the care of children and of aging parents has traditionally been located with women. This role has become part of the culture and is reflected in society's institutional arrangements. The literature and public discussion have focused primarily on child care issues, however; the issue of the care of aging parents has received limited attention only recently. Many authors now speak of the "sandwich" generation of women who work and may be caught between the needs of their children and those of their own aging parents.[1] More healthful habits and early retirement mean that many men and women now live longer, more productive lives. Although many parents would prefer to live away from their children (so that all concerned can lead their own lives), changes in health and in financial circumstances instead often force aging parents to move in with their children.

Generally, it has been the daughter who has then assumed primary responsibility for parental care. This traditional role might be challenged on grounds of role equity, but economic factors have also conspired to challenge it, as well as the institutional arrangements to which it has given rise. The entry of large numbers of women into the work force has generated a widespread demand that legislation be enacted that addresses the questions women ask about the availability, quality, and affordability of day care.

Questions are being raised about the affordability of day care and its impact on the emotional and psychological needs of children; Americans, particularly working mothers, are increasingly discovering that the needs of children and working women are intimately related. Many women no longer have the luxury of deciding whether to work for wages. Women who must work often find themselves in an uncomfortable double bind: quality child care is hard to find and exceeds the budget of most single-parent and working-class families. Since most women earn less than men, it is usually more cost effective for the mother to stay home than to pursue a career. Child care is often provided by young women who do not receive adequate compensation or medical or retirement benefits. Such circumstances often pit women of the upper and upper middle classes against working-class and poor women. As a consequence of the difficulty of finding adequate, affordable child care, and the lower salaries earned by women, many of them are unable to take full advantage of the increasing opportunities for women in the workplace.

This chapter explores the relationship between the needs of children and the needs of women, focusing on two issues of importance to women: day care policies and family leave policies. A discussion of the difficulties that women face in attempting to meet both their own needs and those of their children is followed by an analysis of the societal dynamics that make child care such an important problem: the increasing number of women entering the work force, the economic necessity that forces them to do so, and the inadequacies of day care in the United States. After a review of the history of day care and family leave issues, the chapter concludes with some thoughts concerning public awareness of the problems of child care and family leave.

CAN THE NEEDS OF WOMEN
AND CHILDREN BE SEPARATED?

Many feminist organizations have been less than enthusiastic about current public policies in the areas of child care and family leave. Concerned that their association with these issues might shape public perceptions about women, women's role in contemporary society, and the women's movement itself, many feminists argue that the issues of family leave and child care should be associated with the needs of children (and should recognize the differences between the needs of working and middle-class women) rather than with the needs of women in general.

Sheila B. Kamerman points out that although many women identify child care as one of their major areas of concern, child care policy, in itself, has not generally been regarded as a "women's issue." She argues that activists concerned about child care policy have come from the ranks of child advocacy professionals (social workers, child development psychologists, and specialists in early childhood education), day care providers, and women's organizations such as the Association of Junior Leagues and the National Council of Jewish Women.[2] Absent from much of the child care debate have been some feminist organizations that, although they support initiatives in the area of child care, have been far more active in policy areas related to women's reproductive rights, rights in the work place, and political rights. Kamerman argues that many women have been convinced that any identification of child care with the women's movement would reinforce the traditional societal perception of woman as homemaker and caregiver.[3] The movement has attempted, through its consciousness-raising program, to make society aware of such preconceived notions; it has also concentrated its efforts on expanding the range of life choices and career alternatives available to women. A woman should not have to sacrifice her career opportunities in order to care for the children; the raising of children, feminists argue, is the responsibility of both parents. Compounding the feminists' problem has been the success of the conservative movement in co-opting the phrase "family values" and attaching the "pro-family" label to many aspects of its social agenda. Even when child care began to be recognized as an issue, Kamerman argues, feminist organizations tended either to view it as an issue important to working women only for a short time or to advocate policies and initiatives (such as employer-sponsored day care facilities and tax incentives) that would provide assistance for middle-class, professional women while ignoring the child care needs of women with low incomes.[4] The child care issue thus had the potential to divide the women's movement along class lines.

Kamerman argues that these issues really transcend the differences between working-class and professional women, for costs have increased and dependability of caregivers has decreased; questions are increasingly being raised about the impact of such care on children.[5] Furthermore, many contemporary solutions to the child care dilemma (out-of-home care and professional day care) promote the exploitation of women. Out-of-home caregivers are part of the "informal" economy and do not receive the benefits of "formal" employment (health insurance, paid vacation, pension plans). Moreover, the young women who work in professional day care centers are often paid low wages in order to keep down costs in this "labor-intensive" industry.[6] Indeed, if current initiatives to keep the child-to-caregiver ratio low succeed, the only way that day care can be made affordable is to continue, and even increase, the exploitation of women, especially low-paid young women with few skills.[7]

Recently there has been a change in perspective; child care has been recognized as a political issue with a broad impact on men, families, and the nation, as well as on women and children. Child care issues affect men's careers and their relationships with their children. Fathers whose career demands might require them to miss a large part of the parent-child experience are finding that taking an extended paternity leave allows them to develop stronger ties with their children. For families, child care issues raise a number of questions, ranging from the roles within a marriage relationship (whether the woman should be the primary caregiver) to economic considerations (whether two incomes are necessary to maintain the idealized middle-class lifestyle). Finally, child care issues not only affect those who are the nation's future adults but determine the perpetuation of the family unit. It has been argued that quality child care, by providing a positive nurturing environment, encourages the development of well-adjusted, capable adults. To paraphrase President Clinton, quality child care can be viewed as an investment in the nation's future. Although the problem of child care has been presented thus far in this discussion as largely a women's issue, it can also be viewed from a broader sociological perspective.

CULTURAL CONTEXT OF THE CHILD CARE PROBLEM

Since the early 1980s, Americans have become more concerned about family issues—the desirability of family leave and the availability and quality of child care. Some argue that these issues have increased in importance as a result of structural changes in the economy and consequent changes in the role of the family. Still others argue that changes in the societal roles of women and changes in the economic opportunities available to them have led to increased concern about these issues. The debates that focus on these issues are of importance to women because their outcome has the potential to challenge some of the successes women have achieved in the areas of equality of employment opportunities and the elimination of gender-role stereotypes. From what perspective should we analyze the relationship between women and child care?

In analyzing the relationship between women and child care, Judith Auerbach identifies three alternative perspectives. First, "child care can be seen as a role or a set of tasks someone—usually the mother—performs."[8] Traditionally, this role has been assigned to women for reasons based on the functionalist argument that since a woman has the biological capacity to give birth and to nurse a child, she is the logical one to perform this task within the family. The result of this role allocation, of course, has been that women have been encouraged (if not required) to stay home and take care of the children. Many women thus have entered the work force later than have their male counterparts. To the extent that society pressures women to adopt this pattern of behavior, their job prospects and their career possibilities will suffer. It is difficult for most women to make up for their later entry into the work force.

The second perspective is to view the relationship between women and child care as a qualitative relationship between the child and the caregiver—again, usually the mother.[9] Although the available evidence does not support any conclusions in this regard, many believe that maternal, at-home care is superior to care provided either in another setting or by another person. Is this a result of some physiological or innate capacity that women possess and men do not? Or is it rather a reflection of cultural (sociological and psychological) forces that have burdened women with the responsibility for the care of children? Nancy Chodorow argues that the cultural forces at work during the childrearing process largely create and perpetuate this responsibility.[10] It is the differences in the way women and men are raised that direct women toward, and men away from, caring and nurturing. Could both men's and women's relationships with their children (and perhaps with each other) be improved if men were more actively involved in the parenting process? Chodorow thinks so.[11]

The third perspective, and the one most relevant to the policy process, is to view the relationship between women and child care as an institutional arrangement of society. The basic questions that arise concern the effect that societal considerations (especially family composition and economic and social class) have on women and child care.[12] Changes in work patterns, the increasing instability of families, the workings of a capitalist economic system, and the lack of organized governmental response to child care issues are the key to understanding the child care dilemma in the United States. How will the government respond to changing circumstances in the future? To answer these questions we must examine how the issue of child care has become part of the public agenda.

THE INCREASING IMPORTANCE OF CHILD CARE ISSUES

In the literature on public policy, some questions that frequently arise are: How does an issue get on the public agenda? Does some action or event propel an issue to the center of public attention? Does a problem become so intolerable that the public demands prompt action? The attention that has recently been focused on the problem of child care—by newspaper and magazine articles, television documentaries, national conferences, and congressional hearings— might create the impression that problems related to child care are new. As will be discussed later in this chapter, calls for a federal policy on the subject of child care have been sounded for decades.

In large measure, the issues of family leave and day care have been brought to the forefront by women's victories with regard to increased career opportunities; by changes in the economy; and by changing expectations about women's traditional role as nurturers of children. Whether because of economic necessity or career objectives, women have been entering the work force in increasing numbers since the end of World War II. The number of women in the work force increased by 173 percent from 1947 to 1980; the comparable percentage for men was only 43 percent.[13] Women have also been starting their careers at earlier ages; often they postpone marriage and childbearing until they are established in their careers. Past assumptions that women would get married, have children, and perhaps enter the labor force after their children were grown are no longer valid. Currently, approximately 65 percent of the American women of childbearing age (18-44) are part of the work force.[14] In 1987 an article in *Time*, on the subject of child care and the changing nature of the American family, included the comment that "Beaver's family, with Ward Cleaver off to work in his suit and June in her apron in the kitchen, is a vanishing breed. Less than a fifth of American families now fit that model, down from a third 15 years ago."[15] It is likely today that June is also off to work. If she has just had a child, she is probably planning to reenter the labor force within a year. If the child (or children) is (are) older, June is probably trying to find some form of day care that she can both afford and trust. She often has to worry about (1) the availability of child care (if she employs a sitter, what happens if the sitter gets sick?), (2) the cost of day care (a legally employed in-home caregiver is more than June and Ward can afford), and (3) the quality of the day care (the day care center close to home is affordable, but it has a large number of children and they are cared for by untrained personnel).

Until recently, only a few women were lucky enough to have benefits packages that covered maternity costs, and only some women had employers who would keep their jobs for them until their return. Such benefits packages were generally made available only by the largest corporations. Therefore, large numbers of women working in small enterprises that offered few or no benefits were put in an unenviable position: either they had to give up their careers so they could stay home and care for their newborn infants, or they had to return to work almost immediately and face uncertainty regarding the adequacy of the day care that was provided.

Whether because of economic necessity, career dedication, or the fear that an extended absence might jeopardize their careers, more than one-half of all women return to work before their child's first birthday.[16] The proportion of children under six years of age belonging to two-parent families with a mother in the work force increased from 40.4 percent to 50.3 percent between 1970 and 1984.[17] The proportion of children between the ages of six and seventeen belonging to two-parent families with a mother in the work force increased from 57.2 percent to 68.7 percent between 1970 and 1984. The proportions are, of course, even higher for children of single mothers: for children under age six, the proportion increased from 27.6 percent in 1979 to 50.6 percent in 1985; for children between the ages of six and seventeen, the proportion increased from 41.8 percent to 62.4 percent during the same years.[18] Not only are more women with children entering the labor force but they are also coming back to work sooner after childbirth. The percentage of women between the ages of eighteen and forty-four who were back in the work force after having had a child within the previous twelve months increased from 31 percent in 1978 to 48.4 percent in 1985.

When they do re-enter the work force, women often find that much of their time is spent trying to find adequate care for their child or children. In both single-parent households and households in which both parents work, the need to return to the workplace often requires that parents quickly find some suitable arrangement. If there is no close relative or trusted friend, they face the difficult problem of finding individuals who are qualified, competent, caring, and trustworthy—and who meet the child's physical and emotional needs. For many of these parents, the situation is far from comforting.

In general, three types of child care are available to working parents in the United States: out-of-home care, in-home care, and professional day care. Out-of-home child care is usually provided in the home of another woman. Working parents typically transport their child to the home of a woman who is caring for her own children. Approximately 40 percent of the preschool-age children of working mothers receive this type of care.[19]

This type of child care may be the most affordable option for many working parents, but it is often undependable. Women who depend on other mothers to provide care often find that the care may be withdrawn totally (the caregiver decides not to provide the service) or temporarily (the caregiver goes on vacation, her children are sick). Moreover, the quality of care is sometimes questionable, since the women providing the service are seldom trained in areas of child care such as nutrition, creative play, and child development. Whereas older women may have already had the experience of raising children, those providing the service are frequently new or recent mothers themselves.

In-home care is care provided to the child by a nonparent individual—usually either a relative, a babysitter, a friend, a nanny, or an au pair. Normally found in more affluent homes, the nanny or au pair is generally a live-in caregiver whose primary responsibility is the care of the child, although other services may also be performed. Many au pairs are young European women who seldom work for more than a year and frequently do not have the necessary legal papers. Neither au pairs nor nannies tend to have any formal training, although nanny-training programs have been started recently in some areas. In Ohio, there are four such programs that emphasize nutrition, health, music, communications skills, safety, and creative play.[20] They are, of course, still the exception rather than the rule. The qualifications and dependability of an au pair or a nanny are uncertain, and the costs of employing them are generally prohibitive for most working mothers. Parents who choose this option may also risk incurring fines for violating laws governing the hiring of undocumented workers (as did Zoë Baird) or for failing to pay social security taxes. It should be noted that parents who choose other types of out-of-home and in-home child care also risk violating these laws.

The third type of care, and the most rapidly growing option for many women, is the professional day care center. These centers vary widely both in the type and quality of care given and in the fees charged. They range from day care facilities associated with universities and staffed by well-trained professionals to for-profit business ventures operated by persons with little or no training that, as discussed in the previous section, are frequently exploitive of young women. Recent horror stories about degrading treatment (children put in boxes or cages) and child molestation that exists in some facilities have aroused fear among working parents regarding the safety, both physical and emotional, of their children.

All three types of day care situations raise general questions for women having to place their children in them: What are the qualifications of the persons providing the care? How much individual attention will my child receive? What will the impact of this experience be on my child? These questions are equally relevant for fathers, but the cultural expectation is that women are primarily responsible for child care.

An analysis of day care regulations in different states reveals that "the overall regulations for staff qualifications for all three types of day care are so minimal that the possibility of having a qualified staff is virtually non-existent." [21] The amount of individual attention depends on the number of children in the day care situation (and there is little agreement concerning appropriate staff-child ratios); in this study, 40 percent of the states were found to have staff-child ratios in excess of one staff member for eight children, and 16 percent of the states had no staff-ratio requirements for children under two years of age.[22] Studies of the effects of child care on children are inconclusive; some have emphasized dangers and possible emotional damage, whereas others have not found consequences of any type.[23]

Many women find that society is not necessarily supportive of working mothers but perpetuates the idealized version of the nuclear family with the mother home taking care of the children. As T. Berry Brazelton suggests, contemporary reality puts a heavy burden on new parents:

> As each sex begins to face squarely the unforeseen anxieties of dividing the self into two important roles—one geared toward the family, the other toward the world—the pressures on men and women are enormous and largely uncharted by past generations. It is no wonder that many new parents are anxiously overwhelmed by these issues as they take on the important new responsibility of creating and maintaining a stable world for their baby." [24]

The effects of these concerns on parents in general and women in particular are frequently dramatic. Mothers who must return to work early and leave their child in the care of another person often suffer feelings of guilt, loss, grief, loneliness, and depression and develop defense mechanisms for coping with the situation such as denial, projection, and detachment.[25] Another source of stress for many parents is the knowledge that the findings of studies on the effect on children of parent-child separation during infancy are inconclusive.[26]

In sum, many factors influence the current debate over child care and family leave. They range from changes in the economy (the increasing number of women who are entering the work force and entering it earlier in life and sooner after childbirth) to changes in society (the increase in the number of single mothers and the change in societal attitudes toward women who work). Underlying this debate is the conflict between changing expectations concerning the role of modern woman and the traditional view of woman's proper role as nurturer—a conflict that takes place both within society and within the individual. The debate centers on questions such as the following: When women decide to pursue careers, must they ignore their children and forsake family life? If they try to balance career and family obligations, will they be plagued by feelings that their children might be suffering because of the absence of their mother? Will traditional stereotypes eventually be eliminated as a result of the new emphasis on family leave for both the mother and the father? Will new approaches to the provision of child care facilities by employers result in a broader discussion of the responsibilities of employers with regard to employees? Such questions surround the issues of child care and family leave and suggest that the debate concerning them will have wide ramifications—not only for women but for society as a whole.

HISTORICAL BACKGROUND OF CHILD CARE AND FAMILY LEAVE ISSUES

Although child care and family leave are often thought of as "new" issues, they have their roots in policies and societal dynamics that can be traced back to the beginning of industrial society. Changes in the nature of such care have often reflected changing societal ideas about the proper role of women in the family and in society, as well as economic necessity (women were needed in the work force during World War II).

CHILD CARE

Child care in the United States has been influenced by the interplay of economic, social, and educational forces. According to John P. Fernandez, industrialization, urbanization, and mandatory public schooling all had a tremendous impact on the development of child care.[27] The industrial revolution changed familial relationships because it eliminated the necessity that all family members contribute to the provision of basic family needs. Previously, all family members had to work to earn a subsistence living. The industrial revolution enabled one person (normally the father) to become the "provider" for the entire family unit. Fernandez argues that this freedom from obligation to work allowed children (particularly boys) "to prepare themselves for the new industrial jobs which would allow them, in turn, to support their own families." [28] As people moved closer to their places of employment, urban centers were created, and there was a need for service industries near the manufacturing industries; women increasingly filled the demand for labor in the new service industries.

These economic and social changes were accompanied by a development in the field of education that would have an effect on child care—the establishment of nurseries and kindergartens. Nurseries were originally philanthropic institutions designed to provide care and protection for the needy children of Civil War widows and working women (particularly immigrants). Kindergartens, often located in the settlement houses that served the needy, stressed children's education and development.[29] The nursery school and the kindergarten represented the two competing perspectives concerning child care—custodial and developmental. Those who emphasized the developmental perspective (which was influenced by Enlightenment philosophy) claimed that nurseries should contribute to the development of happy, educated, well-adjusted children. According to Lawrence Lynn, the earliest day nurseries in the United States reflected the optimism of European social reformers.[30] By the middle of the nineteenth century, however, influenced by developments in the field of medicine and the increase in the number of working women, supporters of the nursery movement began to favor the custodial perspective: nurseries should attend to the physical needs of the children of women who had to work because of the changes wrought by industrialization. By the end of the nineteenth century, the number of child care centers had greatly increased. But critics argued that such facilities "encouraged mothers to work, loosened family ties, and minimized the parents' sense of responsibility toward their children."[31] They also charged that there were few standards governing the type of child care provided. Scandals that emerged during World War I solidified in peoples' minds the idea, expressed at the first White House Conference on the Care of Dependent Children (1909) and at the White House Conference on Standards of Child Welfare (1919), that nurseries were nothing more than a temporary expedient and that the best care was home care.[32] Contributing to this idea was the unsympathetic approach to day care on the part of social workers. Lynn explains that the philanthropic view of working women as victims of industrialization was replaced by an emphasis on therapeutic intervention by social workers to help families whom they viewed as maladjusted or cared for by incompetent mothers.[33] Thus, the day care movement foundered. Facilities (such as Montessori schools) that emphasized the Enlightenment perspective of providing the child with enriching experiences were still available to more affluent families, but for the vast majority, the child care provided was custodial and available only to "problem" families.

It was during the Depression that federal funds were first used to finance nursery schools as part of a program under the Works Progress Administration. Fernandez points out that although the primary aim of the program was not child care but the provision of jobs for the unemployed, the result was both the creation of an excellent child care program and the setting of a precedent for the public funding of child care.[34] In 1941, Congress passed the Lanham Act, which provided federal grants to states to establish child care facilities for women working in defense plants during World War II. Fernandez argues that the commitment of the federal government was less than total because it feared that such a program might communicate the wrong message about working women.[35] The demands of the war effort were paramount, however, and by 1945 more than $50 million had been spent on the construction and operation of day care facilities, and more than 1.6 million children were enrolled in federally assisted child care centers and nurseries.[36]

After the war, funding for child care centers was withdrawn and 95 percent of them had to close for lack of funds.[37] Servicemen returned to their jobs and women were expected to return to the home. Although the 1950s and early 1960s are generally viewed as a period of rapid economic expansion and population increase (the baby boom that resulted when veterans started families), in fact the percentage of working mothers increased steadily from 1940 (when one in eight mothers worked) to the end of the 1960s (when two in five mothers worked).[38] From the end of the war to the 1950s, the only government policy related to child care was a tax allowance for the deduction of some employment-related child care expenses. In the 1960s, the federal government again launched some programs, primarily of a remedial nature, for economically disadvantaged children. The most notable of these was Project Head Start, created under the Economic Opportunity Act of 1965 and intended as a preschool program to help prepare such children for school. As in the past, these programs were designed to assist economically disadvantaged families, not working mothers.

During the late 1960s, child care advocates began to lobby for a more general federal policy toward child care. The result was the proposed Comprehensive Development Act of 1971, which would have provided services for welfare recipients (with an increase in expenditures for new programs under Head Start), increased tax deductions for child care expenses for working families, and allocated funds for the construction of new facilities and for planning and technical assistance.[39] The monetary commitment would have been substantial, and although the proposed legislation appeared to have strong support and passed both houses of Congress, it was vetoed by President Nixon largely as a result of pressure by conservative groups such as the Moral Majority, which argued that such legislation was antifamily and would encourage women to leave the home for the work place.[40]

Since the veto of the Comprehensive Development Act, the effort to establish a child care policy has succeeded only in the area of tax policy. In 1978, Congress replaced the proposed tax deduction with a tax credit for child care costs irrespective of income or marital status. Maximum deduction ceilings have been increased since then. Congress has also encouraged employers to provide child care assistance by allowing tax benefits for employers who do so. During the 1980s, there was a general recognition of the problem of child care, as evidenced by the proposal of hundreds of bills intended to resolve it.[41] The Act for Better Child Care, proposed in 1988, included provisions for federal grants to the states and the establishment of federal standards for child care. Conservative forces, led by President Bush, suggested that tax incentives rather than federal subsidies should be the key ingredients of child care policy. Some feminists also supported this approach, arguing that because tax credits could be utilized by both homemakers and working mothers, child care would be seen as an issue for all women, not just working women. Some groups argued the reverse position, that providing tax incentives for nonworking women would reinforce the notion that women should stay at home and raise the children by giving them an inducement to do so. As a result of the conflict between these opposing views, there have been no federal initiatives, and although some states have sought solutions to the child care problem, the attempt to reduce the budget deficit by cutting federal funds for state block grant programs has seriously hindered the states' efforts to increase their involvement in child care. As in the past, it is economic conditions that determine the policies and the debate with regard to child care.

FAMILY LEAVE

The origins of current federal policies concerning family leave can be traced to state protective legislation of the nineteenth century that restricted the number of hours that women could work. Such restrictions were justified by medical testimony suggesting that certain types of work, as well as long periods of work, would have detrimental effects on the childbearing capabilities of women.[42] In its decision in *Muller v. Oregon* (1908), the Supreme Court prohibited regulations setting maximum hours of work for men but argued that such regulations for women were necessary to protect offspring.[43] This legislation reflected prevailing attitudes concerning the health of women (see Chapter 3) and the "proper" role of women as childbearers and nurturers.

In the 1920s and 1930s, women were still treated as "temporary workers," assumed to be present in the workplace only until they got married and began to raise children. Many employers refused to hire married women and dismissed single women after they became married. In businesses where married women were allowed to work, they were often forced to resign or were fired after they became pregnant.

World War II brought about some fundamental changes for women in the work force. The labor shortage created by the military draft necessitated the increased employment of women in key industries that supported the war effort. With women now playing an essential role, federal agencies had to establish standards for their protection, which included the recommendation of a six-week prenatal leave and a two-month post-natal leave. Many employers, however, cited "aesthetic and moral" reasons for not wanting women in the work place, such as the "bad effect" that the sight of a pregnant woman had on male workers.[44]

Public policy with regard to pregnant women changed after passage of the Civil Rights Act of 1964. Although Title VII of the act prohibits discrimination in private and public employment on the basis of gender, initial rulings by the Equal Employment Opportunity Commission held that "the denial of benefits to pregnant employees comparable to those provided to male and nonpregnant employees did not constitute sex discrimination."[45] In 1972, however, the guidelines were changed to define disabilities resulting from pregnancy (such as miscarriage, abortion, or childbirth) as "temporary disabilities" and to award those having such temporary disabilities all of the usual benefits associated with a temporary disability.[46] This ruling was the policy governing the treatment of pregnant women in the workplace until 1976-1977, when the guidelines were challenged in two cases decided by the Supreme Court.

In *General Electric Company v. Gilbert* (1976), the Court ruled that a company plan that failed to cover pregnancy-related disabilities did not discriminate on the basis of gender since the plan did not discriminate between men and women but between pregnant and nonpregnant persons.[47] In a related case, *Nashville Gas v. Satty* (1977), the Court ruled that sick pay could be refused to women who were unable to work because of pregnancy or childbirth.[48] Both cases suggested that the Court did not find that discrimination against pregnant women necessarily violated Title VII's prohibitions against gender discrimination. The task of establishing prohibitions against discrimination toward pregnant women was left to Congress.

In 1978 Congress responded by passing the Pregnancy Discrimination Act, which amended Title VII and prohibited discrimination against pregnant women. The act generally required employers who offer health insurance or disability plans (or both) to provide coverage to pregnant women for all conditions related to pregnancy and childbirth. In the area of abortion the act is less clear, since it does not require coverage for abortion unless the health of the mother is at stake. Abortions are not precluded from coverage, however. The Pregnancy Discrimination Act established the following: (1) discrimination on the basis of pregnancy or conditions related to childbirth is a form of gender discrimination; (2) such conditions must be treated the same as other forms of temporary disability; (3) abortions, except when the life of the mother is at stake, need not be covered by an employer plan although they may be, at the discretion of the employer; (4) an employer may not discriminate in the hiring, firing, or promotion of a pregnant woman; (5) an employer may not establish a mandatory leave policy for a pregnant woman that is not based on her inability to work; and (6) all reinstatement privileges and benefits provided to those who are temporarily disabled must be available to pregnant women.[49] Unfortunately, most women do not have jobs that provide them with disability benefits; thus, many women are not covered by the act.

Title VII and its amendment were federal actions that expanded the rights of pregnant women in the workplace; policies concerning maternity and family leave were generally left up to the private sector, with the assumption that they would be included in the fringe benefits packages negotiated between employers and unions. Unions historically have concentrated on increasing the basic wage rates for workers; however, fringe benefits packages have increasingly been a subject of collective bargaining between unions and employers. The most generally available maternity-related benefit is job-protected leave; the benefits provided tend to be proportional to the size of the firm, that is, the larger the firm, the more benefits are normally available to each woman.[50]

Business interests resisted inclusion of such benefits in their bargaining agreements. Dramatic increases in the cost of fringe benefit packages were often cited as a reason for opposition to family leave legislation. Opponents of leave policies frequently pointed to their destructive effects on the ability of U.S. business to compete abroad, but they were often confronted by the fact that virtually all the western industrialized nations have already adopted such policies, and most of them include some form of guaranteed leave and protection of wages; some (most notably those of Germany) include similar benefits for the male parent.

If the primary responsibility for providing family leave is assumed to be that of the business community, the evidence does not suggest that the burden would be too heavy. Judith Lichtman argues that statistics for 1987 presented by the United States Chamber of Commerce refute the argument that the costs of providing family leave are too high: (1) Chamber of Commerce estimates of the costs dropped from $16 billion per year to less than $3 billion per year; and (2) half of the firms surveyed by the Chamber of Commerce cited the benefits such programs provided them in the hiring and retaining of good employees.[51]

Some may question whether it is the government's responsibility to provide family leave. If the answer is yes, a related question would be, What level of government should be responsible? Lichtman argues that a guaranteed job leave is not a benefit but a minimum standard, similar to those in the area of safety conditions, hiring practices, and working hours.[52] Since government regulates these areas, why should it not regulate family leave? Edward F. Zigler, director of the Yale Bush Center in Child Development and Social Policy, and Rita E. Watson argue that child care should be a state responsibility similar to the state's responsibility for education.[53]

Some states have provided some form of maternity leave, and this was viewed as an important success for women. The issue demonstrated that women's organizations were not monolithic in their opposition to it, as would be suggested by their concern that the association of the child care issue with women's issues would have a detrimental impact on the gains women had made in the workplace. Some feminist organizations argued that maternity benefits generally "boomerang" against women because they single them out for special privilege, which encourages the belief that women are different and should be treated differently.[54] Furthermore, creating this special privilege for women was likely to reinforce society's notion that women's proper roles were childbearing and nurturing, thus encouraging support for the argument that policies should not be created that encourage women to abandon their traditional roles. Feminists also argued that such special treatment, if mandated, could make employers reluctant to hire women of childbearing age.[55] Their reluctance was generally encouraged by the U.S. Chamber of Commerce, which argued that mandatory leave would certainly harm small businesses that could not absorb the costs of finding and training temporary help to replace on-leave employees. Feminist organizations asserted that maternity leave merely neutralizes the effect of childbearing on career advancement and emphasizes the growing need for a system of family support in the United States.[56]

This debate, between what were often referred to as the "equal treatment" feminists and advocates of "special treatment" for women, was intensified in January 1987 by what was known as the Garland case (*California Federal Savings and Loan Association et al. v. Guerra*). After giving birth, Lillian Garland, an employee of the California Federal Savings and Loan Association, was told that her position had been filled; she was not offered another position. This violated the 1987 California Fair Employment and Housing Act, which required that employers of fifteen or more workers offer pregnant women four months of unpaid leave and the guarantee of a comparable job upon their return to work. When the case was decided by the Supreme Court, the National Organization for Women, the American Civil Liberties Union, the League of Women Voters, and the National Women's Political Caucus all filed amicus curiae briefs in which they argued against preferential treatment for women and in favor of unpaid leaves of absence for all disabled workers—both male and female. These groups viewed protectionist laws as reinforcing the traditional childbearing role of women and engendering a notion among employers that female workers are both more expensive and less reliable than male workers. The Court, however, decided that a state was indeed permitted to require an employer to provide special job protection for workers temporarily disabled by pregnancy.[57]

Groups in several states met with some success in their attempts to pass family leave laws, but they were not successful at the national level. Although both houses of Congress passed family leave legislation, President Bush vetoed such bills in both 1990 and 1992. Interestingly, family leave became an issue in the 1992 campaign, and family leave legislation was a primary focus during the first two weeks of the new Clinton administration. The first bill up for a vote in the new Congress, and the first bill signed into law by President Clinton in 1993, was the Family and Medical Leave Act (which had originally been proposed by Rep. Patricia Schroeder in 1985). The speed with which the act was passed demonstrates that the family leave issue had finally permeated the conscience of Congress and the voters. The act grants up to twelve weeks of unpaid leave for workers (both male and female) so that they can care for a newborn or adopted child or a critically ill family member. The act's restrictions (the company must have at least fifty employees, the worker must have been employed for at least one year, and employees in the top 10 percent of the company's pay scale are excluded) mean that many women in small enterprises, women whose families cannot afford to miss twelve weeks of income, and women at the top of the organization chart will not be able to take family leave. Nevertheless, the significance of the legislation should not be underestimated. For thousands of workers, especially women, the decision of whether to have a child, or whether to take time to care for a sick child or parent, has become less difficult.

THE PROBLEMS OF CHILD CARE AND FAMILY LEAVE: A NEED FOR PUBLIC AWARENESS

Public policy with regard to child care and family leave, perhaps more than in any other area, reflects the attitudinal changes that have taken place in recent decades concerning the roles of women in the family and the workplace. The family as glorified in "Leave It to Beaver" and "Ozzie and Harriet" in the 1950s and 1960s does not exist. For reasons of personal career objectives or economic necessity, tens of millions of women go to work every day. Because of the virtually nonexistent or at best haphazard system of child care, many of them worry constantly about the type of care their children are receiving and whether that care will be there tomorrow.

Unfortunately for these working women, government and society have not been particularly sympathetic to their cause—in part because of the traditional notion that upper- and middle-class women should stay home while their husbands work or that they can work while their children are being cared for by working-class young women for wages low enough to make child care affordable. Thus the issue still has its class aspects. Working-class women who need to work must generally make other, more complex arrangements because they cannot afford professional child care; the alternative is to move out of the job market periodically and care for their children themselves. The fact that women's groups have found the child care and family leave issues so difficult to deal with demonstrates their complexity. Can some women enjoy the opportunities or gains resulting from the new role of women as members of the work force only at the expense of other women?

Government, for its part, has shown an unwillingness to become involved. Conservative forces will no doubt continue to fight government-supported day care options. By using adjectives such as profamily and antifamily to describe various proposals for reform, they endorse the traditional view of the family—the idealized version of Americans' recent past. Conservative forces will also continue to argue that government policies that regulate are an unnecessary governmental intrusion in people's lives. Many will also argue that at a time of scarce financial resources and a huge budget deficit, it is impossible to expand government programs.

Several developments have recently brought to the public's attention various issues related to the needs of children. The discussion of children's issues during the 1992 presidential campaign, the perceived debt that the Clinton administration owes to women, and the Nannygate controversy involving Zoë Baird and Kimba Wood have definitely raised the consciousness of Americans regarding the problems associated with work and family. The successful resolution of the problems of child care and family leave is of primary importance for women, for children, and for the future of society.

NOTES

1. For further discussion of this subject, see Jane Aronson, "Women's Sense of Responsibility for the Care of Old People: 'But Who Else Is Going to Do It?' *Gender and Society* 6, no. 1 (March 1992): 8-29; Morton H. Kleban, "Family Help to the Elderly: Perceptions of Sons-in-Law Regarding Parent Care," *Journal of Marriage and the Family* 51, no. 1 (May 1989): 303-312; and Elaine M. Brody, "Caregiving Daughters and Their Local Siblings: Perceptions, Strains, and Interactions," *Gerontologist* 29, no. 4 (August 1989): 529-538.

2. The discussion in this paragraph and the next is drawn largely from Sheila B. Kamerman, "Child Care Services: An Issue of Gender Equity and Women's Solidarity," *Child Welfare* 64 (May-June 1985): 260, 268-269.
3. Ibid., 260.
4. Ibid.
5. Ibid., 268.
6. Ibid., 269.
7. Ibid.
8. Judith D. Auerbach, *In the Business of Child Care* (New York: Praeger, 1988), 3.
9. Ibid., 6.
10. Ibid., 7.
11. Ibid.
12. Ibid., 8.
13. Leslie W. Gladstone, Jenifer D. Williams, and Richard S. Belous, "Maternity and Parental Leave Policies: A Comparative Perspective," Report no. 85-148 GOV., Congressional Reference Service, July 16, 1985, 1.
14. Ibid., 1-2.
15. "The Child Care Dilemma," *Time*, June 22, 1987, 54.
16. Ibid.
17. Data in this paragraph are from Sara E. Rix, ed., "The American Woman Today: A Statistical Portrait," *The American Woman, 1987-1988* (New York: Norton, 1987), 306, 307.
18. Ibid., 306.
19. "The Child Care Dilemma," 58.
20. "Need for Nannies Tops Supply, Mothers Find," *Dayton Daily News*, April 3, 1988, 1-G.
21. Kathryn T. Young and Edward Zeigler, "Infant and Toddler Day Care: Regulations and Policy Implications," *American Journal of Orthopsychiatry* 56, no. 1 (January 1986): 52.
22. Ibid., 47.
23. T. Berry Brazelton, "Issues for Working Parents," *American Journal of Orthopsychiatry* 56, no. 1 (January 1986): 23.
24. Ibid., 14.
25. Ibid., 22.
26. See, for example, Thomas J. Gamble and Edward Zeigler, "Effects of Infant Day Care: Another Look at the Evidence," *American Journal of Orthopsychiatry* 56, no. 1 (January 1986): 26-42.
27. John P. Fernandez, *Child Care and Corporate Productivity* (Lexington, Mass.: Lexington Books, 1986), 17.
28. Ibid.
29. Ibid., 18.
30. Lawrence E. Lynn, *Designing Public Policy* (Santa Monica, Calif.: Goodyear, 1980), 258.
31. Ibid., 259.
32. Ibid.
33. Ibid., 260.

34. Fernandez, *Child Care and Corporate Productivity*, 18.
35. Ibid., 19.
36. Lynn, *Designing Public Policy*, 26.
37. Fernandez, *Child Care and Corporate Productivity*, 19.
38. Lynn, *Designing Public Policy*, 261.
39. Fernandez, *Child Care and Corporate Productivity*, 19.
40. Ibid.
41. For a good description of some of these proposals, see Leslie W. Gladstone, "Parental Leave Legislation in the 100th Congress," Report no. IB 86-132, Congressional Reference Service, January 26, 1988.
42. Ibid., 8-9.
43. *Muller v. Oregon*, 208 U.S. 412 (1908).
44. Gladstone, 9.
45. Ibid., 11.
46. Ibid.
47. *General Electric Company v. Gilbert*, 429 U.S. 125 (1976).
48. *Nashville Gas v. Satty*, 434 U.S. 137 (1977).
49. Gladstone, 13-14.
50. Ibid., 20.
51. Judith L. Lichtman, "Leave Policies Establish Pro-Family Work Place," *Dayton Daily News and Journal Herald*, September 7, 1987, 7A.
52. Ibid.
53. Edward F. Zigler and Rita E. Watson, "States Should Provide Solution to Day Care Problem," *Dayton Daily News and Journal Herald*, November 27, 1987, 11A.
54. Amy Wilentz, "Garland's Bouquet," *Time*, January 26, 1987, 5.
55. Gary S. Baker, "Let's Put Regulation to Work in Labor," *Business Week*, July 14, 1986, 11.
56. *Time*, January 26, 1987, 11.
57. *California Federal Savings and Loan Association et al. v. Guerra*, 479 U.S. 272 (1987). For an interesting discussion of the Garland case, see Kai Bird and Max Holland, "Capitol Letter," *The Nation* 243 (July 5-12, 1986): 8.

CHRONOLOGY

1908 In *Muller v. Oregon*, the Supreme Court prohibits regulations setting maximum number of work hours for men but rules that such regulations are necessary for women because of their maternal role.

1909 Meeting of the first White House Conference on the Care of Dependent Children.

1919 Meeting of the White House Conference on Standards of Child Welfare.

1941 Congress passes the Lanham Act, allocating federal funds to states to establish child care facilities for women working in defense plants during World War II.

1976 In *General Electric v. Gilbert*, the Supreme Court rules that a company plan that fails to cover pregnancy-related disabilities does not discriminate on the basis of gender because the plan does not discriminate between men and women but between pregnant and nonpregnant persons.

1977 In *Nashville Gas v. Satty*, the Supreme Court rules that sick pay can be refused to women who are unable to work because of pregnancy or childbirth.

1978 Congress passes the Pregnancy Discrimination Act, amending Title VII of the Civil Rights Act of 1964.

1978 Congress approves the allowance of tax credits for child care costs.

1987 In *California Federal Savings and Loan Association et al. v. Guerra,* the Supreme Court upholds a California law that requires employers of fifteen or more workers to offer pregnant women four months of unpaid leave and the promise of a comparable job when they return to work.

1988 The Act for Better Child Care is proposed in Congress, but is not passed.

1993 Congress passes the Family and Medical Leave Act, which allows employees to take up to twelve weeks of unpaid leave because of their own illness, the illness of a family member, or the birth or adoption of a child.

SUGGESTIONS FOR FURTHER READING

Abel, Emily K., and Margaret K. Nelson. *Circles of Care: Work and Identity in Women's Lives.* Albany: State University of New York Press, 1990.

Adams, Carlyn T., and Kathryn T. Winston. *Mothers at Work.* New York: Longman, 1980.

Auerbach, Judith D. *In the Business of Child Care.* New York: Praeger, 1988.

Fernandez, John P. *Child Care and Corporate Productivity.* Lexington, Mass.: Lexington Books, 1986.

Hartmann, Heidi I., and Diana M. Pearce. *High Skill and Low Pay: The Economics of Child Care Work.* Washington, D.C.: Institute for Women's Policy Research, 1989.

Kahn, Alfred J., and Sheila B. Kamerman. *Child Care: Facing the Hard Choices.* Dover, Mass.: Auburn House, 1987.

Nelson, Margaret K. "A Critical Analysis of the Act for Better Child Care Services." *Women and Politics* 12 (1992).

Norgren, Jill. "Child Care." In *Women: A Feminist Perspective,* ed. Jo Freeman. 4th ed. Mountain View, Calif.: Mayfield, 1989.

Steinfels, Margaret O'Brien. *Who's Minding the Children?* New York: Simon and Schuster, 1973.

Thorne, Barrie. "Re-Visioning Women and Social Change: Where Are the Children?" *Gender and Society* 1 (1987): 85-109.

United States Congress. House Select Committee on Children, Youth, and Families. *Improving Child Care Services: What Can Be Done.* 98th Cong., 2d sess., September 5-6, 1984.

9

Women and the
Criminal Justice System

Earlean M. McCarrick

Janet Reno was confirmed as Attorney General of the United States in March 1993. She is the first woman to serve as the nation's chief law enforcement officer. In becoming head of the Department of Justice (one of the four top cabinet positions), Reno shattered the "glass ceiling" in a profession long dominated by men. In nominating Reno for the position, President Bill Clinton broke with the recent tradition of nominating a close personal friend or legal adviser. Some accused him of reserving one high-level cabinet position specifically for a woman and pointed to the withdrawn nominations of Kimba Wood and Zoë Baird as proof of the existence of this "quota"; nevertheless, Reno has excellent qualifications for the job. She has a law degree from Harvard; was elected state attorney of Dade County, Florida, in 1980, 1984, 1988, and 1992; was honored as Woman of the Year by the Florida Council on Crime and Delinquency in 1984, and was awarded the Medal of Honor by the Florida Bar Association in 1990. Symbolic or not, the appointment of Janet Reno was an important event for women. As Helen Neuborne, executive director of NOW's Legal Defense and Education Fund, pointed out, "It is symbolic, but it goes beyond that. She cares and understands the issues important to women. Her presence in the cabinet will help build toward that critical mass that says women are as competent as men, and women can serve in any place in the administration." [1]

By July 1993, Reno had dealt with such diverse problems as the Branch Davidian complex crisis in Waco, Texas, the "Travelgate" imbroglio of the Clinton administration, and the firing of FBI Director William Sessions. In each of these instances, Reno was generally praised for her decisiveness and willingness to take responsibility for the outcome of her decisions. Many also expected her to improve the morale of the Justice Department. Some political pundits even suggested that she was one of the best appointments made by President Clinton.

The criminal justice system that Janet Reno oversees is still predominantly male. Men make, break, enforce, and adjudicate the law in significantly higher numbers than do women. Male predominance in positions of power throughout the criminal justice system is of importance to women because discretion is employed throughout the criminal justice process, with the result that individual attitudes toward gender-specific roles, rather than the letter of the law, may determine how women are actually treated. Despite the constitutional guarantee of equality, criminal law treats men and women differently. This differentiation is most obvious in gender-specific crimes such as rape and prostitution, but it is also evident in such gender-neutral crimes as assault in cases where the victim is married to or living with the assailant.

This chapter explores the role of women in the criminal justice system and the impact of the system on the lives of women. First, law in American society is analyzed as both a reflection of values and a restraint on behavior. The chapter then focuses on women as decision makers in the criminal justice system (and their promotion from entry-level positions such as police officer to positions of authority, responsibility, and power); women as criminals; the specific crimes in which women have traditionally been the victims; and the abortion controversy.

THE FUNCTIONS OF LAW IN AMERICAN SOCIETY

Laws are one of many instruments that governments can use to influence societal behavior—both collectively (tax laws encourage conservation rather than consumption) and individually (criminal laws prohibit speeding). Laws are also one of the outputs of the public policy process that are most easy to recognize, for they can affect all of us in a number of ways. They can restrict our rights as well as expand them. The government makes many decisions concerning the expansion and contraction of rights and the regulation of collective and individual behavior. It has the authority and power to enforce the laws it creates.

Laws generally reflect the historical circumstances, as well as the prevailing views, of the society at any given point in time, although a society generally changes faster than its laws do. As a reflector of cultural values and norms, the law requires that all members of society conform to the cultural norms codified in it, yet there may be a lag between changes in the law and changes in cultural values and norms. For women, this failure of laws to keep pace is significant. A society that has long had a patriarchal culture generally finds that its laws have historically treated women differently from men—denying or according them more rights solely because they are women. Under the common law doctrine of coverture (see Chapter 7), a woman's legal identity was suspended during marriage. The disabilities that stemmed from this doctrine continued to restrict women until the late nineteenth century.

The manner in which laws are enforced also has significance for women. Those who enforce the laws generally have a great deal of discretion in deciding whether a particular action falls inside the parameters of the law, and if so, whether the law should be enforced. Since law enforcers are human beings and not automatons, they frequently bring to their job the prevailing attitudes, opinions, and prejudices of that society. If the laws reflect the attitude that women are the subordinates of their husbands, or that the victim in some crimes is partly to blame, then the law enforcers' actions are likely to reflect those attitudes even if the laws no longer reflect them. Furthermore, although the laws generally apply to everyone in society, the law's enforcers are not necessarily representative of the population whose compliance is their responsibility. This is certainly the case with regard to women and the criminal justice system. As we shall see, the small, albeit growing, number of women in the criminal justice system is reflective of both societal attitudes toward women and the law in general, and the denial, in the past, of opportunities for women in this area of employment.

WOMEN AS DECISION MAKERS IN THE CRIMINAL JUSTICE SYSTEM

From the cop on the beat to the justices on the Supreme Court, men are, and traditionally have been, the decision makers. Women have been making inroads into previously male bastions since the 1970s, however. The women's movement, congressional legislation, and judicial decisions have expanded women's opportunities in the legal and judicial system in the past twenty years, and many are now ready for promotion to decision-making positions.[2]

LAWYERS, JUDGES, PROSECUTORS

In 1873, the Supreme Court upheld the authority of the state of Illinois to exclude Myra Bradwell from the bar because she was a woman.[3] In 1981, Sandra Day O'Connor was appointed to the Supreme Court—the first woman justice in the Court's history. In the century that elapsed between the Bradwell exclusion and the O'Connor inclusion, the legal profession remained largely male. But the male dominance of the work force did not continue throughout that century. The reality of increasing numbers of women in the workplace and in colleges and universities challenged the traditional assignment of women to the domestic sphere.

A breeze of change was stirred in the 1960s by the publication of Betty Friedan's *The Feminine Mystique* and of the report of President John F. Kennedy's Commission on the Status of Women. In the next three decades, there would be a noticeable movement of women into the public sphere—a movement so dramatic that the remarks of a nineteenth-century jurist about working women would seem laughably quaint. Supreme Court justice Joseph Bradley, concurring in the 1873 *Bradwell* decision, could say, without embarrassment, that "[t]he natural and proper timidity and delicacy which belongs to the female sex evidently unfits it for many of the occupations of civil life." Bradley's attitude concerning the status of women in the public sphere differed little from that revealed by John Adams's response to his wife's famous 1776 "remember the ladies" letter—"I cannot but laugh." In that letter Abigail Adams pleaded with her partner in a long and loving marriage—who, at the time, was a delegate to the Continental Congress—to include in the new "code of laws" (the Constitution) protection for women against the "tyranny" of men and said that women would "foment a rebellion" if their legal status was not improved. In view of the actual status of women at the time, Abigail's plea for change was more revolutionary than the break with England and the establishment of republican government that her husband so passionately sought. A century after *Bradwell*, the Supreme Court's assertion that "[n]o longer is the female destined solely for the home and the rearing of the family" was a measure of the distance traveled.[4]

The most significant public policy change that directly affected women and reflected their new role as decision makers in the criminal justice process occurred in 1972, when Congress passed Title IX of the Higher Education Act, which prohibits "discrimination on the basis of sex" in admissions to all graduate and professional schools receiving federal money. More women began to study law. In the years immediately preceding passage of that legislation, about 4 percent of law students were women; since the 1980s, about 40 percent have been women.[5]

The number of female law students is significant because lawyers constitute the pool from which prosecutors, public defenders, judges, and their staffs are chosen.[6] As the number of politically active women lawyers increases, the potential for the advancement of women to positions of power increases. One judicial scholar suggested in the 1970s that the number of female judges mirrors the number of female lawyers, but with a ten-year time lag.[7] In the 1950s, women constituted between 1 and 2 percent of all lawyers; in the 1960s, they constituted between 1 and 2 percent of all judges. In the 1960s, about 4 percent of all lawyers were women, and by the 1970s about 4 percent of all judges were women. If such a pattern continues, women may be more than tokens in the judiciary by the twenty-first century, as some of the 40 percent of women law students in the 1980s and 1990s earn their degrees, are admitted to the bar, become clerks for judges, and join the offices of public defenders, prosecutors, and other officials—the group from which judges are selected. More than the passage of time and an increasing number of women lawyers are necessary for women to achieve positions of power in proportion to their numbers, however. That will require greater receptivity to women on the part of the "opportunity structure"—those who participate in selecting judges and in securing for young law students and lawyers those positions which put them in line for selection as judges.[8] President Jimmy Carter demonstrated such receptivity in going outside the customary sources to find qualified women nominees for federal judgeships. Presidents traditionally have chosen judicial nominees from among the active partisans of their own party who occupy positions such as United States attorney, but Carter deviated from that pattern. Most of his female nominees did not have the usual credentials. A majority of the twenty-nine women he appointed to district courts had no prosecutorial experience; a majority of his eleven women appointees to courts of appeals had neither prosecutorial nor judicial experience.

Although there were no Supreme Court vacancies during the one-term Carter presidency, there was an unusually large number to be filled in the lower courts; in addition to the normally occurring vacancies, there were 152 new lower-court judgeships created by Congress in 1978. Of the total number of Carter district court appointees, 14.4 percent were women (compared with 1.9 percent of President Gerald Ford's appointees, 0.6 percent of President Richard Nixon's appointees, and 1.6 percent of President Lyndon Johnson's appointees). Moreover, 19.6 percent of Carter's appointees to the courts of appeals were women. Because Carter was committed to affirmative action to increase the number of women in positions of authority, he increased the proportion of women federal judges from 1 percent to nearly 7 percent.

Although President Ronald Reagan fulfilled his campaign promise to appoint the first woman Supreme Court justice, his record, and that of his successor, George Bush, fell short of that established by Carter.[9] Nonetheless, both appointed significantly more women to federal judgeships than any of their pre-Carter predecessors. Between 1980, when Reagan was elected, and 1992, when Bush was defeated for a second term, women had entered the work force, and many held governmental positions. Even though fewer women were appointed to the federal bench during the Reagan and Bush administrations than was warranted by either their numbers or their credentials, and women judges are still a distinct minority (about 10 percent) in both federal and state courts, women are already in state and federal tracks that qualify them for policy positions in the legal and judicial systems.

President Clinton's emphasis on "diversity" in selecting cabinet nominees and his appointment of Ruth Bader Ginsburg to the Supreme Court (and of Janet Reno to head the Justice Department) suggest that he will be inclined to follow the Carter precedent. If so, the number of women judges at the federal level will probably increase significantly.

POLICE OFFICERS, CORRECTIONS OFFICERS, AND JURORS

Women have served as both police officers and corrections officers since the nineteenth century, but their numbers have been small, and they have been virtually invisible. The few women who served on police forces (approximately 1 percent of the total until the 1970s) performed clerical tasks or worked in the women's bureaus. Since the 1970s, women have been integrated into the police forces; they now perform the same tasks as men and compete with them on an equal basis for promotion. Application of Title VII of the 1964 Civil Rights Act (which prohibits sex discrimination in employment) to government employees in 1972, together with the threatened cutoff of federal funds to law enforcement agencies that discriminate on the basis of gender, made it easier for women to enter police work. The number of women police officers in the United States has risen to between 10 percent and 12 percent.[10]

The number of women in correctional work is larger than the number serving on police forces because women have served in women's prisons since the nineteenth century. The number of such institutions and the number of women prisoners, however, are both small. Unless women are permitted to work in integrated institutions and in male prisons, their numbers will continue to be small; 17.4 percent of all corrections officers are women.[11]

Only in the area of jury service have women achieved parity with men in the criminal justice system. When women won the right to vote, their service on juries became a more common occurrence because jurors are frequently selected from voter registration rolls. As recently as the 1960s, however, a few states still excluded women from juries and in most states the rules that applied to women were such that few were on jury lists.

In 1961, in *Hoyt v. Florida*, the Supreme Court upheld the authority of a state to exempt women automatically from jury service unless they had volunteered. The Court held that Florida's exemption of women in forming a jury pool was constitutional because it was reasonable for a state to recognize women as the center of the home and therefore to exempt all women from jury duty.[12] About fifteen years later, the Court ruled in *Tay-*

lor v. Louisiana that Louisiana's exemption of women was unconstitutional. It no longer seemed reasonable to the Court in 1975 for the state to assume that home duties so preoccupied most women that they were unable to assume this obligation of citizenship.[13]

The rules governing jury selection are now much the same for men and women. In some jurisdictions, however, fewer women than men actually serve. Some of the discrepancy may be due to the availability of gender-neutral criteria for exemption, such as child care. But it may also be the result of unsubstantiated sexual stereotyping; many attorneys exclude women because of their belief that women jurors are harder on women defendants.[14] The question of whether the presence of women on juries (or in other positions) makes any difference to the women who are the victims or alleged perpetrators of crime has been studied more systematically with reference to juries, perhaps because there are so few women in positions of authority in the system. The results of these studies are inconclusive.[15] There is, however, some support for the hypothesis that likes attract; that is, that female jurors favor female defendants and male jurors favor male defendants. Further, there is some indication that women serving on juries in rape cases are somewhat less inclined to be influenced by the victim's prior sexual history and by her socioeconomic status. If these theories are true, then the underrepresentation of women on juries, and perhaps in positions of authority, works to the disadvantage of women.

WOMEN AS CRIMINALS

Women constitute a small percentage of the criminal population. Explanations for their low rates of arrest, conviction, and imprisonment vary.[16] A nineteenth-century scientist insisted that few women commit crimes because of the biologically determined lower intelligence of normal women and the aberrational masculinity of women criminals.[17] In contrast, the author of a 1950 analysis concluded that few women are labeled criminals, not because they commit fewer crimes but because the kinds of crimes they tend to commit (shoplifting, for example) frequently go undetected or unreported; if detected and reported, women are less likely to be arrested and convicted because the attitudes of victims, police, and courts toward them are more favorable and less fearful.[18] Both a 1967 report and a 1975 study emphasized the "chivalry" factor; a women's victim is inclined to overlook her transgressions, as are the police and the courts.[19] But a scholar who disputed this chivalry or paternalism hypothesis concluded from his analysis of national victimization data that arrest statistics are reasonably accurate indicators of the relative relationship between male and female commission of crimes.[20] If this is correct, fewer women than men are arrested for committing crimes for the simple reason that they commit fewer crimes and fewer serious crimes.

Whatever the reason, fewer women than men are arrested.[21] Although women consistently constitute about 50 percent of the population, they have never constituted more than 10 to 20 percent of those arrested. However, the number of women arrested, as a proportion of the total number of persons arrested, increased from about 10 percent in the 1950s and 1960s to about 15 percent to 20 percent in the 1970s, 1980s, and 1990s. The increase between the 1960s and the late 1970s in particular drew attention both because of its rapidity and because it occurred in tandem with the rise of the women's movement, thus seemingly portending the possibility of gender equality in the world of crime. Percentage increases are frequently misleading, however; because the number of women arrested is small, any increase is magnified when calculated as a percentage. Raw figures are perhaps better indicators when comparing the relatively small female criminal population with the male criminal population. In 1960, for example, 304,165 adult women were arrested, compared with 2,655,044 adult men; in 1977, at the height of the public concern over the increase of crime among women, the number of adult women arrested was to 536,132, compared with 2,930,027 adult men. This increase of 231,967 women arrested represented a 75 percent increase, but adult women constituted only about 15 percent of the total number of persons arrested in 1977. Though total arrests soared in the 1980s and early 1990s, and the number of women arrested increased from the thousands to the millions, the male-to-female ratio did not change dramatically; twenty years after the 1970s surge in adult female arrest rates, adult males still constitute about 80 percent of all persons arrested. According to the FBI's *Uniform Crime Reports for the United States* for 1991, the total number of persons arrested was 14.2 million; 81 percent were male and 19 percent were female.

The reasons advanced for the increase in arrest rates are many and varied. They include the changing roles of women; better reporting, recordkeeping, and law enforcement; greater inclination of victims to demand arrest; decline of the chivalry factor in the wake of the women's movement; and various other changes in society that have affected women. The largest increases in female arrests, other than for prostitution and drug-related crimes, have been for property crimes—the kinds of crimes that women tend to commit: shoplifting, welfare cheating, passing bad checks, and credit card fraud. Social and economic changes that began in the 1960s have opened up new opportunities for practicing these vices. The expansion of the welfare state increased the opportunities for welfare fraud, particularly for women. The clientele of one of the largest of these programs, Aid to Families with Dependent Children, consists largely of female-headed families. The food stamp program also has a largely female clientele. The increase in the number of women in the work force has opened up new opportunities for work-related crimes—fraud, embezzlement, and employee theft. Although women have been committing an increasing number of violent crimes, the percentage of women arrested for violent crimes has tended to remain stable over time—about 10 percent. Nor has there been any change in the prime targets of women's violence—their abusive spouses and lovers—or in the percentage of women arrested for drunkenness, disorderly conduct, and prostitution—nonproperty offenses for which women have long been arrested.

PROSTITUTION

Prostitution is the quintessential female crime, the only offense for which women are arrested in greater numbers than men. Prostitution accounts for 30 percent to 50 percent of the women in jail at any given time.[22] Though few would argue that prostitution is a positive good for society as a whole, for women in general, or for those women who so earn their living, the increasing prominence of the women's movement in the 1970s led to renewed scrutiny of the criminalization of sex for sale.[23]

Laws criminalizing prostitution have been criticized as sexually discriminatory because neither the male prostitute nor the male customer is likely to be arrested and charged with a crime. They have also been criticized because enforcement may lead to harassment. The police may arrest prostitutes even if there is insufficient evidence to warrant arrest or prosecution. Prostitutes are frequently not prosecuted because their crime is difficult to prove; although street prostitutes must display their wares conspicuously to attract customers, they are frequently discreet in their verbal offers to sell. Not until they solicit for or engage in sexual activity for hire are they considered to have committed a crime. Lacking evidence to prove commission of a crime but pressured by public demand to clear the streets of prostitutes, the police may resort to tactics that, critics charge, border on harassment or entrapment. For the most part, however, such objections have not been persuasive in either the political or the judicial arenas. With the exception of a few counties in Nevada, prostitution is illegal in every jurisdiction.

CONVICTIONS AND SENTENCING

Since the 1970s, women have constituted from 10 percent to 20 percent of those arrested, but they have constituted a relatively stable 5 percent to 6 percent of the population of state and federal prisons. Whether women are sentenced to prison at a significantly lower rate than men because they are women or for some non-gender-based reason (such as first-time offender, accessory rather than principal, sole support of minor children, or less serious offenses) is not entirely clear. There is some indication that courts favor women. The authors of a 1971 study concluded that judges tended to be paternalistic and therefore more lenient with women.[24] Their finding agreed with that of a 1975 study of the judicial treatment of 1,255 arrested persons (1,124 men and 131 women) tried in Alabama's criminal courts: the traditional attitudes of judges toward women are reflected in their sentencing practices and might account for the fact that of Alabama's 4,000 inmates, only 120 were women.[25] An analysis of data on sentences in California and Ohio criminal courts also revealed that women tend to fare somewhat better than men in the courts.[26] A study of twelve California counties in the same year showed, however, that women fare only slightly better than men when such factors as the nature of the offense, prior record, and criminal status are taken into account.[27] The tentative conclusion of a 1985 study of sentencing in 50,000 felony cases in a northeastern "Metro City" was that failure to control for race might distort studies of the respective treatment of men and women; little difference was found in the sentences imposed on white women, white men, and black women, but black men received significantly harsher treatment.[28] In view of the increase in drug-related offenses by women in the 1980s and early 1990s, combined with governmental determination to crack down on the illegal sale of drugs, as well as mandatory minimum sentences in drug cases, there seems little reason to believe that gender is a decisive factor. The percentage of women in local jails, a large proportion of whom were there for drug-related offenses, had soared to almost 10 percent of the local jail population by the early 1990s.[29]

JAILS AND PRISONS

In some ways, women prisoners are accorded better treatment than men, but in other ways are treated less favorably. Women's prisons tend to be smaller, with rooms rather than cells; inmates may be permitted to wear their own clothes and to decorate their rooms with personal effects. Frequently located in rural areas, these buildings may not be surrounded by walls or barbed wire. The fact that there are fewer prisoners and fewer and smaller prisons, however, may work to the detriment of women. Women's prisons are more likely to be located some distance from an inmate's home, thus loosening family ties and intensifying her anxiety about child care. Smaller women's prisons tend to have less adequate vocational training programs, library facilities, and medical care. Women who are placed in larger facilities with men may be isolated from the recreational and vocational training opportunities provided for the men.[30] Women confined to jails rather than to prisons may find harsher conditions in these institutions, which are designed for men. In small towns or rural areas, there may be only a handful of women in a jail at a time, and for them the time spent there may turn out to be solitary confinement. In the larger jails, overcrowding rather than isolation may make jail a harsher experience than that resulting from a longer prison sentence.

WOMEN AS CRIME VICTIMS

RAPE AND STATUTORY RAPE

The common law defined rape as unlawful carnal knowledge of a female against her will and without her consent. Though the crime was considered so heinous that death or life imprisonment was the traditionally authorized penalty, few rapists were arrested and convicted. This contradiction reflected society's ambivalence toward the crime, the victim, and the perpetrator.

Rape is a distinctive crime in several respects. First, it is the most underreported and rapidly increasing violent crime, affecting perhaps 40 percent of American women at some time during their lives.[31] Second, it is a gender-specific crime, committed primarily by males against females. Third, rape victims are treated harshly by the criminal justice system, reflecting attitudes suggested by the term "despoiled" used in earlier laws.

Until the enactment of rape reform legislation beginning in the 1970s and the concomitant demand for change, the usual reaction of the police (a group that was uniformly male until the 1970s) to a rape report was disbelief unless the victim was attacked by a stranger, reported the crime immediately, and was bloody, bruised, and hysterical. If the police investigated the rape and arrested a suspect, the victim frequently encountered further skepticism on the part of the prosecuting attorney. Even if the prosecutor was convinced that a crime had been committed, that the arrested man was the culprit, and that the evidence was sufficient to obtain a conviction, he was more likely to opt for plea bargaining to a lesser charge such as assault because rape cases are difficult to win. A rape case frequently was not brought to trial unless there was evidence of extrinsic violence or other evidence corroborating the victim's testimony. If a prosecutor decided to prosecute, the stage was set for the public humiliation of the victim.

Rape was more difficult to prove than other crimes, and such a trial was more degrading for the victim than for victims of other crimes for several reasons. The law imposed more stringent protection of the accused than laws aimed at protecting persons accused of other crimes. Equally important perhaps was that the law reflected certain attitudes toward women: women falsely accuse men of rape, respectable women are not raped, and women who charge rape have precipitated the crime by engaging in conduct unbecoming a lady.

The common law concept of sexual intercourse "without consent" was interpreted by the courts to mean sexual intercourse "by force." To prove that it occurred "without consent," the prosecutor had to prove that the victim had physically resisted—in some instances, proof of "utmost resistance" was required. In 1979, a Maryland court decided that a victim who was "lightly choked" had "consented."[32] A few years earlier, a Washington, D.C., jury had acquitted an admitted rapist (the confession was not admissible), despite the requisite bruises and screams, because the victim did not resist to the extent the jury thought warranted.[33] Such concepts of consent led one scholar to conclude that "consent to rape came to mean that a woman could consent to sexual intercourse with strangers and acquaintances under circumstances of force, brutality, humiliation, and degradation."[34]

To prove consent, defendants have traditionally been permitted to inject testimony regarding the victim's sexual history. Such evidence was considered relevant not only to the central issue of the victim's propensity to consent but to her credibility. The prejudicial impact of such evidence is devastating to the rape victim. Juries tend to acquit accused rapists if they perceive the victim to be sexually promiscuous (as evidenced by illegitimate children or living with a man without benefit of marriage, for example), to have contributed to or precipitated the rape or at least consciously risked incurring rape (by hitchhiking or being out alone at night), or to have been sexually provocative (as evidenced by her attire). Testimony regarding the victim's sexual activities further predisposes a jury to acquit the defendant and reinforces the victim's feeling that she is the accused.[35]

Another obstacle unique to the rape cases tried in some jurisdictions was the judge's issuance of cautionary instructions to the jury that invited skepticism of a rape victim's testimony. Thus, a judge might tell the jury, "A charge such as that made against the defendant is one that is easily made, and once made is difficult to defend against, even if the person accused is innocent. Therefore, the law requires that you examine the testimony of the female person named in the Information with caution." Such instructions tended to reinforce the jurors' view that women who bring such charges are inclined to lie.

The now-rejected corroboration requirement was another legal barrier unique to rape cases. Imposed in a minority of states, this evidentiary rule required the testimony of a rape victim to be supported by extrinsic evidence or by the testimony of others. A defendant could not be convicted on the basis of the victim's testimony alone, regardless of how credible and convincing that testimony might be.[36] Even without a formal corroboration requirement, it is difficult to obtain a conviction on the basis of the unsupported testimony of the victim, partly because of the "she asked for it" syndrome and the continuing skepticism about nonconsent, both of which reflect attitudes, not legal dictates.

Beginning in the 1970s, all states reexamined their rape laws. Most states made some changes, ranging from minor and cosmetic to substantial. All reform statutes preclude the defense of consent under certain circumstances. For example, a defendant cannot argue that his victim consented if he used a weapon or if the attack was committed in connection with another crime such as kidnapping. Some states have eliminated the concept of consent and now define sexual assault in detail. For example, rape might be defined as any intrusion into the openings of the victim's body by force or threat of force. Many states define various degrees of sexual assault, with punishment dependent upon aggravating circumstances. First-degree sexual assault thus might include sexual penetration accompanied by great bodily harm (such as a knife wound), serious personal injury (such as bruises), or great mental anguish (such as emotional damage requiring psychiatric care). The penalties are greater than for second-degree sexual assault, which might be defined as sexual penetration accompanied by the threat of force. Lesser penalties are prescribed for the crime of sexual contact (intentional touching of the victim's clothing that covers sexual parts). Many states have reduced the penalties for all sexual assaults in the hope that juries would be less reluctant to convict if punishment were tailored to fit the prescribed circumstances of the crime. Some states specifically prohibit the "utmost resistance" rule.

Forty-one states enacted rape shield laws, which limit testimony regarding a victim's history of sexual involvement with third parties. Rape shield laws vary from virtual exclusion of such testimony to its admission only under prescribed circumstances and for limited purposes. Some states exclude such evidence for purposes of proving consent but admit it for purposes of attacking the victim's credibility. Others permit it to prove consent but exclude it for other purposes. Some states prohibit testimony regarding prior sexual conduct unless the judge specifically finds it relevant and concludes that the defendant's need for such evidence outweighs its prejudicial impact. The cautionary jury charge and the corroboration requirement are now relics of the past.[37]

Whether such changes will achieve their proponents' goals is problematic. The changes vary among states. The victim's new rights are tenuous. A judge's discretion is broad. Any real change that is achieved may, therefore, be less than the law seems to require. Many problems stem not from the letter of the law but from the public's attitudes as well as those of the police, prosecuting attorneys, judges, and jurors. Whether the attitude of skepticism toward rape victims that gave rise to such requirements as corroboration and cautionary jury instructions will change with the law is not clear. If it does not, the elimination of such requirements is likely to have little impact.

The Big Dan's rape case, the most highly publicized such case of the postreform period, was reminiscent of the prereform period. So called because the gang rape was committed on a pool table in the bar of that name in New Bedford, Massachusetts, the case received extensive coverage by both electronic and print journalists (most notably by some cable television stations, which broadcast the trial in its entirety, and by the *Boston Globe*) from March 9, 1983, when the crime was committed, until the trial's conclusion on March 24, 1984. The trial featured the time-honored consent defense, complete with a portrayal of the victim as a drinking, flirting, unwed mother with a live-in boyfriend who had entered the bar alone. When four of the six defendants were convicted and given sentences ranging from six to twelve years, local residents marched in support of the rapists and in protest of their convictions. The victim left town.

Although the rape reform law of Massachusetts is one of the nation's most stringent and Massachusetts citizens are among the nation's most liberal, this trial was less than reassuring to rape victims trying to decide whether to report the crime committed against them and to risk having to undergo the kind of searing cross-examination to which the Big Dan's victim was subjected.

The refusal of a Texas grand jury in October 1992 to indict the "condom rapist" on the grounds, according to one juror, that the victim's request that the man use a condom implied consent, is a reminder that ordinary citizens continue to be suspicious of women who charge rape. The reaction of the community, however, is an indication of how far women have come since the women's movement began. The grand jury's refusal to indict so enraged women's groups that the prosecutor brought the case before a new grand jury. The accused was indicted, tried, and convicted, and in May 1993 was sentenced to forty years in prison. But local residents did not march in support of the rapist.[38]

Equally encouraging (or perhaps discouraging in view of the record that led to its proposal) is the pending Violence against Women Act, introduced in 1993 by the Senate Judiciary Committee to assist the states in protecting women against rape. The legislation is based on the committee's findings that half of all rape cases are dismissed before trial and that almost half of all convicted rapists serve less than a year.

Statutory rape has traditionally been defined as carnal knowledge of a female (not the wife of the perpetrator) who has not reached the statutory age of consent, usually between 12 and 18. Laws concerning statutory rape are designed to protect young girls from sexual abuse by males and thus are usually gender specific. They assume that girls under a certain age are unable fully to comprehend the potentially devastating consequences of sexual intercourse, incapable of giving informed consent, and likely to suffer more grievously. As recently as 1981, the Supreme Court authorized this gender differentiation; it upheld the statutory rape conviction of a boy who had struck a sixteen-year-old girl in the face, after which she submitted to sexual intercourse.[39] Michael M. asked the Court to reverse his conviction because the gender-specific law discriminated against males; it refused to do so.

WIFE BATTERING

Wife abuse, like rape, is widespread and underreported. Estimates range from over one million to two million such incidents a year; abuse is thought to occur in one of every two or three marriages.[40] A violent attack by one person on another is, of course, a crime in every jurisdiction. When the assailant is married to or living with his victim, however, the relationship between the two, rather than the nature of the act, has frequently conditioned the authorities' response.[41] The traditional pattern has been police reluctance to arrest the assailant, district attorneys' reluctance to prosecute, and judges' proclivity to suspend sentences, put the criminal on probation, or dismiss the charges.[42]

Until women's groups forced the issue in the 1970s, wife abuse was not even on the public policy agenda. It was considered a private matter, not public business. Even if a woman was seriously injured and actively sought help, she was ignored by law enforcement officials. Not until the violence escalated to murder (committed in most cases by the husband rather than the wife) did they take the matter seriously. If a battered woman turned on her tormentor after years of abuse, judges and jurors were unlikely to view her plight sympathetically. A substantial proportion of women in prison for violent crimes were those who, having found all other avenues of escape closed to them, killed their abusive mates.

By the 1970s, women's groups were vocal and visible enough to bring into the open what had for centuries been a private shame for women and a presumed prerogative of brutal men. Since the early 1970s, forty-eight states have enacted some form of legislation to protect women from spousal abuse.[43] More than half of the states have expanded police authority to arrest the assailant; indeed, a few jurisdictions now require his arrest. Experimentation with mandatory arrest and prosecution suggests that arrest may be the most effective means of breaking the cycle of violence that frequently escalates until the woman is killed. In Minneapolis, for example, the police department calculated that in a sixteen-month trial period in 1982-1983, 10 percent of the men arrested repeated the offense, compared with 17 percent of those agreeing to mediation and 24 percent of those evicted from the home.[44] In part as a result of the widely known Minneapolis experiment, police departments in other cities began to opt for arrest.[45]

More than half of the states now impose some obligation on the police to aid the victim: to respond to a call for help and, if necessary, to take the victim to the hospital or to a public or private shelter for women and their children. The continued lack of police protection in some jurisdictions, however, has led to litigation to require police to enforce the law.[46] As a result, some police departments have agreed to abide by consent decrees requiring them to consider each abuse case on its merits without regard to the relationship between assailant and victim.

If the police fail to protect her, an injured woman may seek monetary damages. In the first such suit filed in a federal court, the jury in a 1985 case tried in a federal district court in Connecticut awarded $2.6 million (later reduced to $1.9 million in an out-of-court settlement) to a Torrington woman who had been permanently paralyzed as a result of thirteen stab wounds inflicted by her estranged husband. She alleged that the police had ignored her repeated pleas for protection. Three years after the 1983 attack, Connecticut became the seventh state to require the arrest of wife abusers.[47] Despite the new state law, the Torrington police apparently did not opt for arrest; in 1988 an abused woman sued the town for police refusal to protect her despite repeated requests, even after her husband ran over her with his car and four days later bashed her in the face and knocked her against a wall. Since 1988, thirty other women have brought similar charges against the Torrington police.[48] After a New York City woman won a $2 million award in 1986 for police failure to respond to her requests for protection from her knife-wielding spouse, the city police department adopted an arrest policy.[49]

None of these changes will afford protection unless judges view a husband's assault on a wife as a crime. If, in exercising their discretion, they continue to excuse the assailant, formal changes in the law or in police department policies will effect little real change.[50] Indeed, achievement of deep-rooted change may necessitate a change in the power relationship between husbands and wives, including the economic independence that comes with an adequate paycheck.

ABORTION: FROM CRIME TO CONSTITUTIONAL RIGHT

Until January 22, 1973, abortion under most circumstances was still a crime in a majority of states. Abortion is no longer a crime. Abortion reform is virtually unique among the changes in criminal law affecting women that have been made since the 1970s because it has brought genuine change; it demanded immediate compliance, with no opportunity for the public, police, prosecutors, judges, jurors, or legislators to deny in fact a right conferred by law. Some states had already liberalized their laws in the late 1960s in response to growing public acceptance of abortion. Most liberalizations, however, imposed so many restrictions (abortion was allowed only if the pregnancy was a result of rape or incest, endangered the life or health of the woman, or would result in a mentally or physically impaired child, for example) or procedural requirements (such as certification of necessity by a panel of physicians) that abortion was associated more with crime than with medicine, considered a privilege rather than a right. It may well be that, in time, liberalization would have spread and laws criminalizing abortion would have been repealed in most states without judicial intervention. Be that as it may, the decisive change, making abortion not a crime but a right, was wrought by the Supreme Court's holding in *Roe v. Wade*, that the fundamental constitutional right to privacy is broad enough to embrace the right to an abortion.[51]

Hostility was immediate. Citizens galvanized by the Court's decision sought congressional and state legislative action. Neither the states nor Congress, of course, can overrule a constitutional interpretation by the Supreme Court. Together, however, they can override such opinions by constitutional amendment. Though proposals to overrule *Roe v. Wade* have been introduced in virtually every Congress since the decision, none has passed. Those opposed to abortion had some success in pressuring state and local legislative bodies, which sought to test the outer limits of *Roe* by placing restrictions on abortions. But most of these early efforts were invalidated when challenged in the Supreme Court, with the major exception of legislation denying public funds for abortions for the indigent.[52]

Hopes for the continued vitality of *Roe* were dampened in the 1980s. Both Ronald Reagan and George Bush were elected to the presidency on anti-abortion platforms. Abortion became an issue to consider in the appointment of Supreme Court justices. The Department of Justice began to intervene in abortion cases and asked the Court to overrule *Roe*. A badly splintered Court reaffirmed *Roe* in both the much-awaited *Webster* decision (1989) and the *Casey* decision (1992).[53] Nonetheless, in both of these cases, the Court upheld the kind of restrictions (such as a twenty-four-hour waiting period, mandatory viability testing at twenty weeks, and informed consent requirements) that would have been invalid under the stringent standards of *Roe* and made it easier for a state to regulate abortions by holding that only those regulations which "unduly burden" the right to an abortion are unconstitutional.

As a result of the election of Bill Clinton to the presidency on a pro-choice platform in 1992, abortion is likely to remain a constitutionally protected right; the Justice Department will not urge that *Roe* be overruled and the president's judicial nominees will presumably be more liberal on the abortion issue than those of his two predecessors. Moreover, it is likely that the Clinton administration will support congressional enactment of the proposed Freedom of Choice Act, which gives statutory protection to abortion as a right, as enunciated in *Roe*.

CONCLUSION

Until the late 1960s and the 1970s, issues affecting women received little sympathetic attention from police officers and the courts. Although women who committed crimes may have received more lenient treatment than men who committed similar crimes, the prevailing attitude reflected male dominance of the criminal justice system. Contraception was illegal in some states; abortion under most circumstances was a crime in most states. Rape laws reflected the fear of false charges rather than concern with the legal protection of women. Spousal abuse was considered a private matter rather than a crime.

In the 1970s, largely in recognition of the changing role of women and the increasing prominence of the women's movement, legislatures and the courts began to change the criminal law and its application. Women began to enter the legal profession in large numbers and to occupy positions of influence in the criminal justice system. Abortion was now defined as a constitutionally protected right rather than a crime. The plight of rape victims was recognized and wife abuse became a focus of public attention; some states revised their laws to afford more protection to victims of rape and spousal abuse.

Whether such changes will be sustained and expanded will depend on whether there is continued vigilance on the part of the activists in the women's movement, the increasing numbers of women who will occupy positions of political power in the coming decades, and nonactivist women who have come to expect, as a matter of course, many of the rights that were denied their predecessors. Reform of the written law, although difficult to achieve, is far easier to accomplish than changes in the attitudes of those having the discretion to interpret and apply that law: police, prosecutors, jurors, and (especially) judges. So strategic is the judge's equal treatment of women—as lawyers, colleagues, litigants, and victims—and so widespread is the perception of judicial discrimination that increasing numbers of states are following the lead of New York and New Jersey and establishing task forces on women in the courts. Charged with the responsibility of examining the adverse impact of gender bias on women, these task forces have, among other things, established educational programs designed to make judges aware of bias and to encourage them to change their attitudes.[54]

NOTES

1. Jeanne Cummings, "Reno's Approval Would Shift Priorities," *Atlanta Journal and Constitution*, March 9, 1993, 8A.
2. Whether a person's gender influences his or her attitudes and decisions has been the subject of much debate. See the panel discussion by scholars whose research has focused on this question in "Making a Difference: Women on the Bench," *Women's Rights Law Reporter* 12 (Winter 1991): 255-273.
3. *Bradwell v. Illinois*, 83 U.S. 130 (1873).
4. *Stanton v. Stanton*, 421 U.S. 7 (1975).
5. *Prelaw Handbook 1991-92* (Law School Admission Council, 1991), 35.
6. Lawyers constitute what has been called the "base office," from which prosecutors and public defenders are chosen. Prosecutors and public defenders, along with lawyer-legislators and lawyers in large law firms, constitute the "manifest office," from which judges are chosen. For an analysis of the progression from base office to manifest office to judgeship, see Beverly Blair Cook, "Women Judges: The End of Tokenism," in *Women in the Courts* ed. Winifred L. Hepperle and Laura L. Crites (Williamsburg, Va.: National Center for State Courts, 1978), 84-113. Cook defines the base office as "the common experience or shared mode of entry" (91). A manifest office is "a position which has been a historical source of candidates for higher office" (92).
7. Ibid., 84.
8. Beverly Blair Cook, "Women Judges in the Opportunity Structure," in *Women, the Courts, and Equality*, ed. Laura L. Crites and Winifred L. Hepperle (Newbury Park, Calif.: Sage, 1987), 143-174. According to Cook, in the 1970s approximately 5 percent of all lawyers were women. The proportion was 14.2 percent in 1980, 16 percent in 1985, and 20 percent in the early 1990s. In 1985 about 7 percent of all state judges and 7 percent of all federal judges were women; by the early 1990s, 10 percent of both state and federal judges were women.
9. In his first term, Reagan appointed 129 district judges, only 12 of whom were women. Of the 31 Reagan appointees to the courts of appeal, only one was a woman. Reagan's record improved in his second term. Overall, 8.3 percent of his district court appointees and 5.1 percent of his appointees to the courts of appeals were women, in contrast to Carter's 14.4 percent and 19.6 percent, respectively. Although Bush appointed only 7 women to the 77 judicial vacancies that occurred in his first two years, the percentage increased in the second half of his one-term presidency; overall, he appointed about 36 women, compared with Carter's 40 woman appointees. See Sheldon Goldman, "Carter's Judicial Appointments: A Lasting Legacy," *Judicature* 64 (March 1981): 344-

355; Goldman, "Reorganizing the Judiciary: The First Term Appointments," *Judicature* 68 (April-May 1985): 313-329; and Goldman, "Reagan's Judicial Legacy: Completing the Puzzle and Summing Up," *Judicature* 72 (April-May 1989): 318-325. See also Fund for Modern Courts, *The Success of Women and Minorities in Achieving Judicial Office: the Selection Process* (New York: Fund for Modern Courts, 1985); Carl Tobias, "The Gender Gap on the Federal Bench," *Hofstra Law Review* 19 (Fall 1990): 171-184; Terence Moran, "Bush Judge Appointments: White, Male, and Cautious," *Connecticut Law Tribune* February 4, 1991, 2; Carl Tobias, "Closing the Gender Gap on the Federal Bench," *Texas Lawyer*, January 13, 1992, 23; and A. Leon Higginbotham, "Seeking Pluralism in Judicial Systems: The American Experience and the South African Experience," *Duke Law Journal* 42 (March 1993): 1028-1068.

10. Estimate of Bureau of Justice Statistics, Office of Justice Programs, Department of Justice, February 1992; cited in "Number of Law Enforcement Officers Grew By 5.4 Percent from 1987 through 1990, Says Justice Department," U.S. Newswire, February 5, 1992.

11. Carol Kleiman, "Women Employed Opening Doors to Non-Traditional Careers," *Chicago Tribune*, January 7, 1991, 4; and Carol Kleiman, "Women Shouldn't Rule Out Trade Jobs; Technical Fields Offer Good Salary Opportunities," *Orlando Sentinel Tribune*, February 3, 1991. The figures were obtained from the Bureau of Labor Statistics and analyzed by the Women Employed Institute, the research arm of Women Employed, a Chicago-based organization.

12. *Hoyt v. Florida*, 368 U.S. 57 (1961).

13. *Taylor v. Louisiana*, 419 U.S. 522 (1975).

14. See Anne Rankin Mahoney, "Women Jurors: Sexism in Jury Selection," in Crites and Hepperle, *Women, the Courts, and Equality*, 208-223.

15. For a review of some of these studies, see ibid.

16. For a summary of conflicting findings concerning arrests, convictions, and sentencing, see Meda Chesney-Lind, "Female Offenders: Paternalism Reexamined," in Crites and Hepperle, *Women, the Courts and Equality*, 114-139.

17. Cesare Lombrozo, *The Female Offender* (New York: Wisdom Library, 1958; originally published 1899).

18. Otto Pollak, *The Criminality of Women* (Westport, Conn.: Greenwood Press, 1978, reprint; originally published 1950).

19. President's Commission on Law Enforcement and Administration of Justice, *The Female Offender* (Washington, D.C.: Government Printing Office, 1967); Freda Adler, *Sisters in Crime: The Rise of the New Female Criminal* (New York: McGraw-Hill, 1975).

20. Michael J. Hindelang, "Sex Differences in Criminal Activity," *Social Forces* 72 (December 1979): 143-156.

21. The primary source of arrest statistics is *Uniform Crime Reports for the United States*, issued periodically by the Federal Bureau of Investigation. For various analyses of female arrest rates, see Rita James Simon, *Women and Crime* (Lexington, Mass.: Lexington Books, 1975); Adler, *Sisters in Crime*; Clarice Feinman, *Women in the Criminal Justice System* (New York: Praeger, 1980); Meda

Chesney-Lind, "Young Women in the Arms of the Law," in *Women, Crime, and the Criminal Justice System*, ed. Lee H. Bowker (Lexington, Mass.: Lexington Books, 1978): 171-196; Carol Smart, "The New Female Offender: Reality or Myth?", Darell J. Steffenmeier, "Trends in Female Crime: It's Still a Man's World," in *The Criminal Justice System and Women*, ed. Barbara Raffel Price and Natalie Sokoloff (New York: Clark Boardman, 1982): 105-116, 117-129; and Chesney-Lind, "Female Offenders," 114-139.

22. Meda Chesney-Lind, "Chivalry Re-Examined: Women and the Criminal Justice System," in Bowker, *Women, Crime, and the Criminal Justice System*, 197-223; and Feinman, *Women in the Criminal Justice System*, 25.

23. Many view prostitution as but another example of the sexual exploitation of women. But even feminists who sympathize with that view support at least the decriminalization of prostitution. For excerpts from the writings of feminists with varying opinions, see Mary Joe Frug, *Women and the Law* (Westbury, N.Y.: Foundation Press, 1992): 624-681.

24. Stuart S. Nagel and Lenore J. Weitzman, "Women as Litigants," *Hastings Law Journal* 23 (November 1971): 171-198.

25. "Alabama Law Review Summer Project 1975: A Study of Differential Treatment Accorded Female Defendants in Alabama Criminal Courts," *Alabama Law Review* 27 (Summer 1975): 676-746.

26. Simon, *Women and Crime*.

27. Carl E. Pope, *Sentencing of California Felony Offenders* (Washington, D.C.: Criminal Justice Research Center, 1975).

28. Cassia Spohn, Susan Welch, and John Gruhl, "Women Defendants in Courts: The Interaction between Sex and Race in Convicting and Sentencing," *Social Science Quarterly* 66 (March 1985): 178-185.

29. "Drug Offenses Account for Larger Percentage of Jail Inmates," U.S. Newswire, April 24, 1991 (based on "Profile of Jail Inmates," issued by the Bureau of Justice Statistics).

30. For a review of conditions in women's prisons, see Lee H. Bowker, "Females in Corrections," in Bowker, *Women, Crime, and the Criminal Justice System*, 225-259; and Peter Applebome, "U.S. Challenged by Women behind Bars," *New York Times*, November 30, 1992, 10A.

31. President's Commission on Law Enforcement and Administration of Justice, *The Challenge of Crime in a Free Society* (Washington, D.C.: Government Printing Office, 1967), 21. See also Vivian Berger, "Man's Trial, Woman's Tribulation: Rape Cases in the Courtroom," *Columbia Law Review* 77 (January 1977):1-103; Note, "The Rape Corroboration Requirement: Repeal Not Reform," *Yale Law Journal* 81 (June 1972): 1365-1391; U.S. Department of Justice, Bureau of Justice Statistics, "The Crime of Rape Bulletin," March 1985.

32. *Rusk v. Maryland*, 406 A.2d 624 (Ct. Spec. App. Md. 1979), reversed by the Maryland Court of Appeals, 424 A.2d 720 (1981).

33. Pamela Lakes Wood, "The Victim in a Forcible Rape Case: A Feminist View," *American Criminal Law Review* 11 (Winter 1973): 335-354.

34. Leigh Bienen, "Rape III: National Developments in Rape Legislation," *Women's Rights Law Reporter* 6 (Spring 1980): 170-213.

35. For an analysis of jury verdicts in general and the attitudes of jurors toward rape cases in particular, see Harry Kalven, Jr., and Hans Zeisel, *The American Jury* (Chicago: University of Chicago Press, 1971; originally published 1966).

36. The rule is examined in "The Rape Corroboration Requirement," 1365-1391; and Note, "Corroborating Charges of Rape," *Columbia Law Review* 67 (June 1967): 1137-1148.

37. For a review of state laws on rape as of January 1986, see Patricia Searles and Ronald J. Berger, "The Current Status of Rape Reform Legislation: An Examination of State Statutes," *Women's Rights Law Reporter* 10 (Spring 1987): 25-43.

38. On the condom rape case, see Ross E. Milloy, "Furor over Decision Not to Indict in a Rape Case," *New York Times*, October 25, 1992, 30; "Second Jury Charges Man in Condom Rape Case," *New York Times*, October 28, 1992, A15; "Condom-Wearing Rapist Sentenced to 40 Years," *Chicago Tribune*, May 15, 1993, 15; Christy Hoppe, "Rapist Gets 40 Years: Consent Defense in Condom Case Unsuccessful," *Dallas Morning News*, May 15, 1993, 33A.

39. *Michael M. v. Superior Court*, 450 U.S. 461 (1981).

40. U.S. Commission on Civil Rights, *Under the Rule of Thumb: Battered Women and the Administration of Justice*, 1982. See also Laurie Woods, "Litigation on Behalf of Battered Women," *Women's Rights Law Reporter* 5 (Fall 1978): 7-33; "Assault: A Family Affair," *Washington Post*, July 26, 1986, A22.

41. A 1974 study cited by the Civil Rights Commission in *Under the Rule of Thumb* (24), reveals a conviction rate of 8 percent for intrafamily assaults and a rate of 18 percent for intrafamily aggravated assaults, compared with a conviction rate of 32 percent for crimes between strangers. A 1977 study cited by the commission (24) found that 52 percent of the charges in cases in which the parties knew each other were dismissed, whereas 29 percent of the charges in stranger-to-stranger cases were dismissed.

42. For a detailed analysis of the inadequacies of Michigan's laws concerning wife abuse, see Sue E. Eisenberg and Patricia L. Micklow, "The Assaulted Wife: 'Catch 22' Revisited," *Women's Rights Law Reporter* 3 (Spring-Summer 1977): 138-161.

43. Lisa Lerman, "Protection of Battered Women: A Survey of State Legislation," *Women's Rights Law Reporter* 6 (Summer 1980): 271-284. See also U.S. Commission on Civil Rights, *Battered Women: Issues of Public Policy*, 1978; and "Developments in the Law: Legal Responses to Domestic Violence," *Harvard Law Review* 106 (May 1993): 1498-1620.

44. "Arrest the Wife Beaters," *Parade Magazine*, October 16, 1983, 8.

45. Ellen Cohn and Lawrence Sherman, *Police Policy on Domestic Violence, 1986: A National Survey* (Washington, D.C.: Crime Control Institute, March 1987).

46. Woods, "Litigation on Behalf of Battered Women"; updated in *Women's Rights Law Reporter* 7 (Fall 1981): 39-45.

47. Dirk Johnson, "Abused Women Get Leverage in Connecticut," *New York Times*, June 15, 1986, 1.

48. Howard Kurtz, "Battered Women, Reluctant Police," *Washington Post* February 28, 1988, 1.

49. Crystal Nix, "For Police, Domestic Violence Is No Longer Low-Priority," *New*

York Times, December 31, 1986, B1.

50. There are indications that some judges continue to be reluctant to take wife abuse seriously. See, for example, U.S. Commission on Civil Rights, *Under the Rule of Thumb*; and Laura L. Crites, "Wife Abuse: The Judicial Record," in Crites and Hepperle, *Women, the Courts, and Equality*, 35-53.

51. *Roe v. Wade*, 410 U.S. 113 (1973).

52. In the first case that it decided after the landmark 1973 decision, the Supreme Court invalidated a law that, among other things, required spousal and parental consent and prohibited the widely used saline amniocentesis procedure. *Planned Parenthood v. Danforth*, 428 U.S. 52 (1976). The Court upheld the denial of public funds for abortions, in *Maher v. Roe*, 432 U.S. 464 (1977); and in *Harris v. McRae*, 448 U.S. 297 (1980).

53. *Webster v. Reproductive Health Services*, 492 U.S. 490 (1989); and *Planned Parenthood v. Casey*, 112 S. Ct. 2791 (1992).

54. *The 2nd Report of the New Jersey Supreme Court Task Force on Women in the Courts*, June 1986; "Report of the New York Task Force on Women in the Courts," *Fordham Urban Law Journal* 15 (1986-1987); and Unified Court System Office of Court Administration, *Report of the Commission to Implement Recommendations of the New York Task Force on Women in the Courts*, April 1987.

CHRONOLOGY

1873 *Bradwell v. Illinois*: The Supreme Court upholds the constitutionality of the state's refusal to permit women to become lawyers.

1961 *Hoyt v. Florida*: The Supreme Court holds that the state's absolute exemption of women from juries is constitutional.

1969 Passage of Title VII of the Civil Rights Act of 1964 (also known as the Equal Employment Opportunity Act), which prohibits discrimination in employment on the basis of race, color, creed, national origin, and sex.

1972 Passage of Title IX of the Higher Education Act of 1972, which prohibits discrimination on the basis of sex in any educational program or activity that receives federal funds.

1973 *Roe v. Wade*: The Supreme Court holds that the right to an abortion is a fundamental right that cannot be infringed by a state unless it has a compelling interest.

1975 *Stanton v. Stanton*: The Supreme Court invalidates a state law that defines the age of majority differently for males and females.

1975 *Taylor v. Louisiana*: The Supreme Court invalidates the state's absolute exemption of women from juries.

1976 *Planned Parenthood v. Danforth*: The Supreme Court invalidates most of Missouri's abortion restrictions (such as spousal and parental consent requirements and prohibition of the saline amniocentesis abortion technique), though it upholds such provisions as those requiring a woman's informed consent and the keeping of certain records.

1977 *Maher v. Roe*: The Supreme Court upholds the authority of Connecticut to exclude first trimester abortions from Medicaid coverage unless they are medically necessary.

1978 *Harris v. McRae*: The Supreme Court upholds the constitutionality of the Hyde amendment, which prohibits the use of federal Medicaid funds for abortions unless the life of the woman is endangered by the pregnancy or the pregnancy is the result of rape or incest.

1979, 1981 *Rusk v. Maryland*: Maryland's Court of Special Appeals reverses the conviction of a rapist on the grounds that the fact that he "lightly" choked his victim does not constitute force and that the victim thus consented to sexual intercourse. The state appeals that decision, which is overruled by the Maryland Court of Appeals.

1981 *Michael M. v. Superior Court*: The Supreme Court upholds the constitutionality of a California statute that prohibits "an act of sexual intercourse with a female not the wife of the perpetrator, where the female is under the age of 18." It rejects Michael M.'s argument that the gender distinction violates the Equal Protection Clause of the Fourteenth Amendment.

1989 *Webster v. Reproductive Health Services*: The Supreme Court upholds the constitutionality of several Missouri provisions restricting abortion (prohibiting the use of public facilities or employees to perform abortions and requiring physicians to perform viability tests before performing abortions if the woman is in her twentieth week). The case is significant because the Court would seem to be moving away from *Roe*.

1992 *Planned Parenthood v. Casey*: The Supreme Court upholds several Pennsylvania restrictions on abortion (such as parental consent and a twenty-four-hour waiting period) but invalidates a husband notification requirement. Significantly, the Court reaffirms what it sees as the essence of *Roe* (that the right to an abortion is constitutionally protected) but seems to adopt the less stringent "undue burden" standard for judging the constitutionality of state abortion laws.

SUGGESTIONS FOR FURTHER READING

Cedarbaum, Miriam Goldman. "Women and the Federal Bench." *Boston University Law Review* 73 (January 1993): 39-45.

Cook, Beverly B., Leslie F. Goldstein, and Karen O'Connor. *Women in the Judicial Process*. Washington, D.C.: American Political Science Association, 1988.

Deckard, Barbara Sinclair. *The Women's Movement: Political, Socioeconomic, and Psychological Issues*. New York: Harper and Row, 1979.

Estrich, Susan. *Real Rape*. Cambridge, Mass.: Harvard University Press, 1987.

Holtzman, Elizabeth. "Women Lawyers in the Political Arena." *Women's Rights Law Reporter* 14 (Winter 1992): 1-7.

Rhode, Deborah L. *Justice and Gender: Sex Discrimination and the Law*. Cambridge, Mass.: Harvard University Press, 1989.

10

A Revolution in Progress

Women's lives can be changed dramatically by changes in public policy. Title VII of the Civil Rights Act of 1964, Title IX of the Higher Education Amendments of 1972, and the 1973 Supreme Court decision in *Roe v. Wade* created new choices and opportunities for women. Likewise, changes in women's lives can make new demands on public policy. The entry of women into the work force, for example, translates into a need for governmental action in the areas of pay equity, protection against sexual harassment, and the care of children and the elderly. Clearly, Roseanne Connor's world is very different from that of June Cleaver.

More women than ever in American history are running for and winning election to public office; they are calling for changes in the public policy agenda as well as in the public policy process. The research described in Chapter 3, emphasizing the interest of female state legislators in health care policy, suggests that they are more likely than their male counterparts to give priority to women's rights issues and issues that concern children and families. The evidence also suggests that these women officeholders are more likely than their male counterparts to support bringing citizens into the public policy-making process and to be responsive to previously disempowered groups such as the economically disadvantaged.[1]

The study of women and public policy raises a number of important questions. How far can and should the government go in encouraging or facilitating cultural change? Is it the role of government to respond to the needs created by cultural change? A public policy in one area can affect women's status and the indirect consequence may be cultural change. Access to credit, discussed in Chapter 5, can empower women and facilitate their entry into the economic elite. Government can take the lead in facilitating cultural change and improving the status of women, as Con-

193

gress did in passing the Equal Pay Act of 1963 (discussed in Chapter 4) and Title IX of the Higher Education Amendments of 1972 (see Chapter 2). Government can also be slow to react to cultural change, thus creating difficulties in women's lives. The government's failure to take the necessary action in the areas of care for children and for the elderly (Chapter 8) as women increasingly joined the work force is an example of public policy failing to keep pace with cultural change. What is clear from all of the issues raised in this volume is that the concerns of women have expanded the role of government and that government is now seen as having a legitimate role to play in areas of interest to women.

A number of models of the policy-making process have been developed by scholars studying that process in the United States (see Chapter 1); three are useful in helping us to think in more general terms about women and public policy.

The first model suggests that government policy is based on and reflects the preferences and values of a dominant elite whose members hold important positions in the government and in major social institutions, the educational system, business, and the media. They are thus able to shape public policy so that it reflects their values. Any major policy change, then, will require major changes in the membership of the elite that are likely to be more extensive in times of crisis. The economic dislocations of the Great Depression of the 1930s, for example, led to a political realignment and the coming to power of the Democratic party after almost seventy years of Republican rule at the national level. This newly empowered elite created and implemented a set of "New Deal" policies and in doing so ushered in a period of activist government in the United States.[2]

Although it would be a gross exaggeration to claim that women have become *the* political elite in the United States (much less a monolithic, single-minded elite), the more modest claim that women are making inroads is supported by the results of the 1992 elections, and of a special Senate election in Texas in 1993. Women now hold 7 of the 100 Senate seats and 47 of the 435 House seats in the 103d Congress.[3] In addition, President Clinton's original cabinet included an unprecedented number of women—five department heads, including the first female attorney general. This trend of women becoming members of the political elite has been accelerated at the state level. As pointed out in Chapter 1, as a result of the 1992 elections, women hold more than 20 percent of all statewide elected executive offices and 20.4 percent of the seats in state legislatures.[4] The year 1992 has frequently been referred to as the "Year of the Woman" in American politics. Indications are that this was not an idiosyncratic phenomenon and that women will continue to become members of the political elite. The effects on public policy are likely to be pronounced as women bring to public office their sensitivity to issues and different styles of leadership. The impact of the increased movement of women into the political elite will not be felt, however, until more women attain positions of authority in all areas of American culture. As indicated in Chapter 4, women have yet to assume an equal number of executive positions in the business sector; many still hold low-paying, low-level jobs. The consequences of this marginalization of women were examined in the discussion of public policy with regard to health care in Chapter 3. Although women are the principal consumers of health care and large numbers of women are employed in the health care professions, they are concentrated in the less powerful positions and their voices have only recently begun to be heard in the policy-making process.

Women are increasingly moving into the more highly skilled and highly paid professions and are beginning to enter the business and media elites, but their rate of progress is slow. In 1987, fewer than one in eight corporate board members of Fortune 500 companies were women, for example, and companies owned by women generated less than 14 percent of the receipts of American business.[5] Producers of television shows have the power to increase the nation's understanding of what it means to be a woman and to alter significantly the societal construction of gender. Of the 101 producers of twenty of the top-rated television shows of the 1986-1987 season, however, only twenty-one were women. Only six of these shows employed a woman director and women directed only 12 percent of the twenty top-rated shows' episodes in that season. Women did better as writers for these shows; 85 percent of the twenty top-rated shows used women writers at some point during the 1986-1987 season.[6]

Chapter 9 suggests that a large number of women are now ready to assume decision-making positions in the legal system. To the extent that women have achieved influence in the criminal justice system and changed their status in society, there have been improvements in the legal treatment of women, particularly in areas such as rape law.

The second model asserts that public policy is the outcome of conflict between organized groups and reflects the interests of the groups that are dominant in a particular historical era. Thus, if women are not sufficiently organized to make known their policy demands, their interests are not likely to be reflected in the content of public policy.[7] Conversely, if women are well organized, their interests should be reflected in public policy's content. The latter is clearly true in the areas of health care, education, and employment policy. The organized women tend to promote those issues which most affect them, however, and as is often the case in American politics, their interests are those of the middle class.

The evidence discussed in this volume suggests that women's interest groups have been most successful in promoting issues when they demand a share in the system rather than a change in the system. This is consistent with the findings of Joyce Gelb and Marian Lief Palley (see Chapter 1), which show that feminist groups are more likely to succeed when the issues they promote are framed as an attempt to achieve "role equity" rather than "role change." When a policy demand is presented in terms of role equity (as a demand that women be granted the same rights and benefits as men), policy change is more likely to be generally viewed as contributing to fairness. When, however, a demand for alternative policies is perceived as an attempt to change women's societal roles, both policy makers and public opinion tend to be much less supportive of policy change. To the extent that the policy changes sought by women are viewed as a demand for more than incremental change, they tend to be regarded unfavorably by decision-making elites.[8]

Many role equity issues (such as pay equity and credit equity) are based on the idea of gender-neutral public policy; when placed on the agendas of women's interest groups, this principle has been criticized as reflecting a bias. Chapter 6 is an in-depth discussion of gender neutrality as it pertains to insurance.

Gender neutrality can be a standard that works both for and against women (see the discussions in Chapters 3 and 6). In reality, all public policy creates or influences the public perception of gender. The critics of attempts to use gender neutrality as a basic principle in the design and implementation of public policy stress the impact it has had or will have on women who are unwilling or unable to model their life plan on that of a middle-class, white, heterosexual man. The women who benefit from gender-neutral laws are those "who have been able to construct a biography that somewhat approximates the male norm, at least on paper," observes Catharine MacKinnon.[9]

The life plan promised by gender neutrality is that of an autonomous, unencumbered individual. The more a woman differs from this model, the more likely she is to be disadvantaged by gender neutrality. A focus on gender neutrality can disadvantage women in two ways. First, it can eliminate policies that specifically advantage women. For many women, gender neutrality has translated into male advantage in the areas of child custody and alimony and has weakened their case for financial support after divorce.[10] As explained in Chapter 7, a legal right, such as the right of a wife to own property, does not automatically mean that a woman is her husband's economic partner, particularly if she, as a homemaker, receives no wages and her husband is entitled to control the family assets that are purchased with his earnings. Second, a focus on gender neutrality can divert attention from the needs of women unable or unwilling to adopt the life plan of the middle-class, white, heterosexual man. Many women might be better served by an emphasis on adequate housing, health care, and protection against violence than by an emphasis on equal access to education, employment and credit—that is, different, not merely equal, treatment. For women whose lives are shaped by differences in gender, race, and class, gender-neutral policies can be low priorities, if not meaningless symbols.[11]

According to the third model, policy is the result of past policies, with minor (incremental) changes that have been made over time. Policy makers pursue incremental change strategies for a number of reasons, such as limits on time and information and lack of funds necessary to evaluate all the feasible alternatives to the existing policy. Because of these limitations, governmental decision makers have generally accepted the legitimacy of existing policies. Furthermore, the investment of substantial resources in existing policies militates against radical policy change. But since preferences for policy change may not be widely evident and the unintended consequences of policy change may be feared but not easily estimated, incremental change is safer for those who must make the policy decisions. If incremental policy changes prove to be unpopular or have serious unintended consequences, incremental change can more easily be further altered, and is more likely to be rewarded, than more extensive change. Political pragmatism fosters slow, gradual change in policy.[12]

Some conclusions that can be drawn from this consideration of women and public policy suggest that the third model has the most to offer with regard to the crucial area of implementation. Rapid cultural change can necessitate and result in changes in public policy, but the implementation of these policies can also change, as this model would suggest. Equal employment opportunity policy (discussed in Chapter 4) is an example of a public policy that was prevented from keeping pace with cultural change because major changes were made in its implementation and enforcement. Under the Reagan and Bush administrations, implementation became an attempt to limit the impact of equal employment opportunity laws and executive orders. To this end, the resources available to enforce such laws were reduced. Reagan and Bush administration officials disapproved of administrative agencies' use of the disparate effects test; their attitude inhibited the implementation of equal employment opportunity policy. Some regulations were changed and other changes were proposed to Congress, with the same goal—limiting the impact of the laws and executive orders. To inhibit the enforcement of equal employment opportunity laws, litigation activities were initiated, including the filing of amicus curiae briefs. Despite their assertions of support for affirmative action, Reagan administration officials revealed, by their actions, an effective opposition to equal employment opportunity. They attempted to persuade more than fifty state and local government agencies that had previously concluded affirmative action agreements with the federal government to change those agreements, abolishing all goals and timetables for the hiring, training, and promotion of women and minorities.

Affirmative action plans specify goals for the employment of persons in protected categories and timetables for achieving them. Goals are based on the labor market availability of persons in the protected categories (such as women) who have the requisite skills. However, many officials in the Reagan and Bush administrations who were charged with enforcing equal employment opportunity laws chose to equate goals with quotas, or mandatory requirements to hire a specified number of women or minority race members regardless of their qualifications for the job being filled.[13] The Reagan administration refused to acknowledge that goals are supposed to be interpreted as levels of employment of protected categories of individuals that a firm or government agency seeks to achieve, and that timetables specify the temporal framework within which the firm or agency seeks to fulfill those goals.

Although many Reagan administration officials were opposed to goals, a notable exception was Secretary of Labor William Brock, who made a clear distinction between quotas and goals. He said that quotas imply that if a numerical standard is not met, a company is, by definition, in violation. A goal implies that if a company is making a good-faith effort, and if the effort is of sufficient integrity and efficacy, then the company is not in violation.[14] Some Reagan administration officials continued to insist on equating goals with quotas, however. Although factually incorrect, the equating of goals with quotas was politically astute, for opinion polls show that the public disapproves of using sociodemographic quotas in hiring.

In addition to its basic assertion that the objectives of civil rights programs were seriously flawed, the Reagan administration argued that the management of civil rights law enforcement in previous administrations had been marred by the enforcement agencies' financial mismanagement and their competition for jurisdiction, as well as by confusing and excessive regulations that made compliance difficult.[15]

The Reagan administration's criticisms of the performance of the Office of Federal Contract Compliance Programs under prior administrations included allegations that there was a lack of clarity about what constituted compliance with an affirmative action program,[16] that requirements for plans were both overly prescriptive and insufficiently clear, and that the OFCCP took an overly adversarial approach to the enforcement of equal employment opportunity laws and executive orders. These problems, combined with budget and staff reductions, inhibited the OFCCP's ability to enforce equal employment opportunity policy.

In attempting to limit the enforcement of equal employment opportunity laws, the Reagan administration also tried to revise Executive Order

11246 (which mandates nondiscrimination in employment by federal contractors) and its implementing regulations. Proposed changes included prohibiting contractors from setting goals and timetables of any kind, including those pertaining to recruitment and training; and forbidding the use of statistics concerning the employment and promotion of minorities and women as evidence of employment discrimination. The secretary of labor would have been required to revoke already existing regulations that use goals and timetables as a remedy for the underutilization of a protected class in the employment pool. Top Justice Department officials thus rejected the use of affirmative action plans and disparate effects tests to establish the existence of employment discrimination patterns.[17]

These proposals and actions provoked strong public reaction. Although a few groups, such as the United States Chamber of Commerce and the Associated General Contractors, supported the proposed revision of Executive Order 11246, many large corporations opposed it. The National Association of Manufacturers objected to the back pay requirements that might be imposed under Executive Order 11246, but it supported the use of goals and timetables.[18] Why did major employers oppose the revocation of affirmative action plans that include goals and timetables? These goals and timetables provide a defense against lawsuits alleging discrimination. But if such aspects of affirmative action were made voluntary, corporations might not be protected from the risk of lawsuits charging reverse discrimination in employment.

The Reagan administration in effect argued that rather than emphasizing measures designed to prevent discrimination against minorities and women, the focus should be on seeking remedies in individual cases where discrimination as a consequence of intention to discriminate can be proven. Intent to discriminate can rarely be proven, however, because there is seldom a written statement of such an intention or a witness to a spoken statement. The Reagan administration thus disapproved of both class action suits and pattern and practice investigations as tools for implementing affirmative action.

Clearly, cultural change affects the membership of the nation's elites, as well as the composition of interest groups and their agendas; it also contributes to the success or failure of policy implementation. Cultural changes will continue to have an impact on public policy, but it is difficult to predict which specific areas will be affected. As the population of the United States ages, the problems of the elderly will come to dominate the public policy agenda—particularly issues of concern to elderly women, such as pensions and retirement annuities, discussed in Chapters 5 and 7.

Other areas of concern to women have arisen as a result of advances in science and technology. The United States does not have a uniform national policy on the termination of life support, an issue not limited to but of particular importance to elderly Americans, the majority of whom are female. Nor is there a consistent policy on reproductive technology. Policy silences in these areas mean that Americans must struggle with questions such as whether it is proper for a state to link welfare eligibility to a woman's consent to Norplant implants, or to refuse the elderly access to physician-assisted suicide.

Gender is now frequently a significant consideration in the making of public policy. This is particularly evident in the area of health care. Gender was not a salient factor in the formulation of the federal government's two major health care programs, Medicare and Medicaid. Now many health care issues are examined for their specific and perhaps differential impact on women.

Some areas of public policy, however, have yet to be "gendered." Transportation is a case in point. In 1956, Congress enacted major legislation granting the states federal aid for highways that essentially set the patterns for where people would live and work. Congress gave little, if any, consideration to this act's effect on evolving gender roles. The construction of highways and the subsequent distancing of workers from their homes contributed greatly to the burdens of working parents and the isolation of mothers who were not employed outside the home.

As government becomes more active in shaping the definition of what it means to be a woman in today's society, it is important that public policy reflect the experiences of women as well as those of men. To that end, women must continue to make their many voices heard in all areas of political and cultural life. Culture is not monolithic, and neither are women. They have certain needs as women, however; that is, although these needs may be modified by differences in age, race, and sexual identity, they are fundamentally linked to gender.

NOTES

1. For a discussion of women's interest in these and other issues, see Center for the American Woman and Politics, *The Impact of Women in Public Office: Findings at a Glance* (New Brunswick, N.J.: CAWP, National Information Bank on Women in Public Office, Eagleton Institute of Politics, Rutgers University, 1991), 4, 7.

2. For a discussion of political realignment and policy changes, see James Sundquist, *Dynamics of the Party System,* rev. ed. (Washington, D.C.: Brookings Institution, 1981).

3. Eleanor Holmes Norton is the nonvoting delegate from the District of Columbia. She brings to forty-eight the number of women actually serving in the House.

4. All data from Center for the American Woman and Politics, *1992 Post-Election*

Wrap-Up (New Brunswick, N.J.: CAWP, National Information Bank on Women in Public Office, Eagleton Institute of Politics, Rutgers University, 1993).

5. Paula Ries and Anne J. Stone, eds., *The American Woman, 1992-93: A Status Report* (New York: Norton, 1992), 348-349.

6. Sally Steenland, "Behind the Scenes: Women in Television," in *The American Woman, 1990-1991: A Status Report*, ed. Sara E. Rix (New York: Norton, 1990), 232-233.

7. David Truman, *The Governmental Process* (New York: Knopf, 1951); Earl Latham, "The Group Basis of Politics," in *Political Behavior*, ed. Heinz Eulau, Samuel J. Eldersveld, and Morris Janowitz (New York: Free Press, 1956); Jeffrey Berry, *The Interest Group Society* (Boston: Little, Brown, 1984).

8. Joyce Gelb and Marian Lief Palley, *Women and Public Policies* (Princeton, N.J.: Princeton University Press, 1987), chap. 1.

9. Catharine A. MacKinnon, *Feminism Unmodified: Discourses on Life and Law* (Cambridge, Mass.: Harvard University Press, 1987), 37.

10. See, for example, Nancy D. Polikoff, "Gender and Child-Custody Determinations: Exploding the Myths," in *Families, Politics, and Public Policy: A Feminist Dialogue on Women and the State*, ed. Irene Diamond (New York: Longman, 1983), 192; Nan D. Hunter, "Women and Child Support," in Diamond, *Families, Politics, and Public Policy*, 204; and Catharine MacKinnon, *Feminism Unmodified*, 35.

11. For a historical discussion of efforts to formulate public policy that synthesizes equality and difference, see Wendy Sarvasy, "Beyond the Difference versus Equality Policy Debate: Postsuffrage Feminism, Citizenship, and the Quest for a Feminist Welfare State," *Signs* 17, no. 2 (Winter 1992): 329-362.

12. For an in-depth discussion of these points, see Thomas Dye, *Understanding Public Policy*, 7th ed. (Englewood Cliffs, N.J.: Prentice-Hall, 1992).

13. See the comments of former attorney general Edwin Meese, reported in Merrill Hartson, "Meese Assails Racial-Quota Backers," *Washington Post*, September 18, 1985, A8. See also "Civil Rights Activities," *Special Analysis J, Civil Rights Activities, Budget of the United States Government, Fiscal Year 1984*, Executive Office of the President, Office of Management and Budget (1983), J-17.

14. Howard Kurtz, "Affirmative Action Policy Gains a Reprieve," *Washington Post*, October 25, 1985, A1, A19.

15. "Civil Rights Activities," J-2.

16. Ibid., J-22, J-23.

17. Anne B. Fisher, "Businessmen Like to Hire by the Numbers," *Fortune*, September 16, 1985, 27.

18. Ibid., 28.

SUGGESTIONS FOR FURTHER READING

Duke, Lois Lovelace, ed. *Women in Politics: Outsiders or Insiders?* Englewood Cliffs, N.J.: Prentice-Hall, 1993.

Fowlkes, Diane L. *White Political Women: Paths from Privilege to Empowerment.* Knoxville: University of Tennessee Press, 1992.

Goldfarb, Jeffrey C. *The Cynical Society: The Culture of Politics and the Politics of Culture in American Life.* Chicago: University of Chicago Press, 1991.

Merelman, Richard M. *Making Something of Ourselves: Our Culture and Politics in the United States.* Berkeley: University of California Press, 1984.

Phillips, Anne. *Engendering Democracy.* University Park: Pennsylvania State University Press, 1991.

Roelofs, H. Mark. *The Poverty of American Politics: A Theoretical Interpretation.* Philadelphia: Temple University Press, 1992.

Traube, Elizabeth G. *Dreaming Identities: Class, Gender, and Generation in 1980s Hollywood Movies.* Boulder, Colo.: Westview Press, 1992.

Index

Abortion, 46-49, 184-186
  Clinton administration policy, 48
  gag rule, 48
Abuse, wife, 183-184
ACLU. *See* American Civil Liberties
  Union
Act for Better Child Care, 168
Adams, Abigail, 1, 2, 172
Adams, John, 172
AFDC. *See* Aid to Families with Depen-
  dent Children
Affirmative action, 70, 198
Aid to Families with Dependent Chil-
  dren (AFDC), 141, 176
AIDS, 49-50
*Akron v. Akron Center for Reproductive
  Health*, 48, 54
Alabama, legal surnames in, 146
Alimony, award and payment of, 138-
  140
AMA. *See* American Medical Associa-
  tion
American Academy of Actuaries, 115
American Civil Liberties Union
  (ACLU), 163
*American Federation of State, County,
  and Municipal Employees v. Washing-
  ton State*, 76
American Medical Association (AMA),
  41, 49

American Telephone and Telegraph
  (AT&T), 66
Anderson, Jim, 124
Anderson, Margaret, 124
Annuities, 106
Aristotle, 111
Arizona Governing Committee v. Norris,
  108, 116-117, 121
Arizona property law, 127
Artiss v. Artiss, 147
Asian Health Project, 43
Associated General Contractors, 199
Association of American Colleges, 29
Association of Junior Leagues, 150
Athletics, intercollegiate, 28-30
AT&T. *See* American Telephone and
  Telegraph
Auerbach, Judith, 152

Baird, Zöe, 148, 164
Benefits. *See* Retirement benefits
Better Child Care Act, 160
Big Dan's rape case, 182
Birth control, 46-49
Black, Hugo, 127
Boston Women's Health Book Collec-
  tive, 49
Bradley, Joseph, 172
Bradwell, Myra, 171
Bradwell v. Illinois, 171, 172, 191

Brazelton, T. Berry, 156
Brock, William, 198
Bush, George, 72, 160, 164, 173, 185
  equal employment opportunity policy, 69, 76-77, 197-198

Califano v. Goldfarb, 146
California
  gender-based insurance ratings, 109, 121
  no-fault divorce law, 134-135
  property law, 127, 136, 138, 142-143, 146
California Federal Savings and Loan Association et al. v. Guerra, 163-164, 168
California Supreme Court, 146
Carter, Jimmy, 121
  judicial nominees and appointees, 173
Catholic church, 47
Census Bureau, 140
Chamber of Commerce, U.S., 163, 199
Chapman v. Phoenix National Bank, 146
Child care, 148-168
  chronology, 167-168
  cultural context, 151-153
  Enlightenment perspective, 158
  historical background, 157-160
  importance of, 153-157
  Nannygate, 148, 164
  need for public awareness about, 164-165
  perspectives on, 152-153, 158
  tax credits for, 168
  types available to working parents, 154-155
Child custody, 140-142
Child support, 140-142
Child Support Enforcement Act, 141
Children, needs of, 150-151
Chodorow, Nancy, 152
Civil Rights Act of 1964, 121. *See also* Title VII, Title IX
  Higher Education Amendments, 36, 69
Civil Rights Act of 1991, 72, 82
Civil Rights Commission, 27

Civil Rights Restoration Act, 32, 36, 70, 82
Cleaver, June. *See* "Leave It to Beaver"
Clinton, Bill, 48, 49, 67, 164, 169, 174
  abortion policy, 48
  debt to women, 164
  pro-choice platform, 186
Clinton, Hillary Rodham, 1, 2
Cohabitation and property, 142-144
Commission on the Status of Women, 6, 62, 172
Community property law, 127-128, 137
Comparable worth concept, 74-76
Comprehensive Development Act, 159
Comstock, Anthony, 47
Comstock Act, 47
Condore v. Prince George's General Hospital, 146-147
Congress, seats held by women, 194
Congressional Caucus for Women's Issues, 43
Congressional Joint Economic Committee, 100
Connecticut wife abuse law, 184
Connor, Roseanne. *See* "Roseanne"
Constitution, U.S.
  equal rights amendment (ERA), 6, 7, 121, 122
  Fourteenth Amendment, 130
  Nineteenth Amendment, 9
  post-Civil War amendments, 5
  women's suffrage amendment, 6
Consumer Credit Protection Act, 87, 101
Contraception, 46-49
Contract compliance, 68
Convictions, 177-178
Corrections officers, women, 174-175
Coverture, common law doctrine of, 143
Credit discrimination, 83-91
  chronology, 100-101
  practices, 84
  unresolved problems, 89
Credit equity, 196
Crime victims, women, 179-184
Criminal justice system, 169-192
  chronology, 191-192

convictions and sentencing, 177-178
jails and prisons, 178-179
women as criminals, 175-179
Criminal law, 131-132, 169, 170
Culler, Kristen W., 18
Culture
attitudes toward health and health
care, 39-40
defining, 1-5
and health care policy, 39-43
and public policy, 8-13

Davis, Nancy, 124
Day care centers, 155. *See also* Child care
Declaration of Rights, 5
Declaration of Sentiments, 125
Democratic party platform, 47
Department of Education, Office of Civil
Rights, 31
Department of Health, Education, and
Welfare (HEW), 27, 28, 29
Department of Justice. *See also* Supreme
Court
appointments, 173
Office of Civil Rights, 11
Department of Labor
Employment Standards Administra-
tion Wage and Hours Division, 63
Office of Federal Contract Compli-
ance Programs (OFCCP), 68
Women's Bureau, 62, 81
Discrimination
credit, 83-91, 100-101
employment, 57-58, 71-72
sexual harassment, 70-71
against women in higher education,
23-25
Disparate effects test, 71-72
Disparate treatment test, 71
Divorce, 124-147
attitudes toward, 126
laws and public policies governing,
134-144
no-fault, 134-135
Divorce policy, 134-144
Doe v. Bolton, 48, 54

Domicile, of married woman, 128-129,
146
Downsizing, 95

Earnings sharing plans, 133
Economic Opportunity Act of 1965, 159
Education. *See* Higher education
Education, Department of. *See* Depart-
ment of Education
Educational policy, 18-37
adjudication, 31-32
chronology, 36
in cultural and historical context, 19-
21
future, 32-34
process, 25-26
EEOC. *See* Equal Employment Opportunity Commission
Eisenstadt v. Baird, 47, 54
Elderly women, 94
Elections of 1992, 3
Emily's List, 3
Employee benefits. *See also* Retirement
benefits
family leave, 67, 82, 148, 153-157, 160-
165, 168
sick pay, 161
Employee Retirement Income Security
Act (ERISA), 95-96, 101
Employment. *See also* Women's employment
downsizing, 95
effects of equal opportunity policy on,
72-74
glass ceiling, 169
patterns of, 58-60
Employment discrimination
criteria for proof, 71-72
Supreme Court decisions, 72
theories of cause and change, 57-58
Employment policy, 60-68
Employment Standards Administration
Wage and Hours Division, 63
Equal Credit Opportunity Act, 85, 101
amendments, 101
enforcement of, 85-87, 90-91

impact of, 88-89
revisions, 87-88
Equal educational opportunity policy,
26, 30, 31
Equal Employment Opportunity Act.
See Title VII
Equal Employment Opportunity Commission (EEOC), 63, 65-66, 161
Equal employment opportunity policy,
56-82, 197-198
during Bush administration, 69, 76-
77, 197-198
chronology, 81-82
development of, 61-62
effects on women's employment, 72-
74
federal legislation, 62-63
implementation of, 68-70
outlook for women, 76-77
during Reagan administration, 11, 69,
76-77, 197-199
Equal pay
comparable worth concept, 74-76
legislation, 62-63
Equal Pay Act of 1963, 3-4, 62, 81, 121
effects on women's employment, 72-
74
1972 amendment, 25
Equal Protection Clause, 129
Equal rights amendment (ERA), 6, 7,
121, 122
Equal rights policy, implementation of
assessing, 89-91
conditions for, 89-90
Equal treatment feminists, 163-164
Equal work, 69
Equity
credit, 196
economic, 83-101
pay, 196
role, 9
ERA. *See* Equal rights amendment
ERISA. *See* Employee Retirement Income Security Act
Executive Order 8802, 61, 81

Executive Order 11246, 67, 72-74, 77, 82,
198-199
Executive Order 11375, 67, 72-74, 82
Executive Order 11478, 72-74
Executive orders, 67-68

Fair Labor Standards Act, 62
Fairness requirements, 110-113
Family, definition of, 126
Family and Medical Leave Act, 67, 82,
148, 168
Family law, 124-147
chronology, 146-147
Family leave
historical background, 157, 160-164
importance of, 153-157
need for public awareness about, 164-
165
Family values, 150
"Father Knows Best," 124
Federal Bureau of Investigations (FBI),
176
Federal legislation. *See also* Legislation
equal pay, 62-63
on gender-based insurance ratings,
109-110
Federal regulations, on gender-based
insurance ratings, 107-109
Federal Reserve Board, 85, 88
Regulation B, 86
Federal retirement benefits, 138
The Feminine Mystique (Friedan), 6, 172
Feminists, 163-164
Fernandez, John P., 157, 158
Financial support
for children, 140-142
marriage obligations, 130-131
Financing, health care, 43-46
*Firefighters Local Union No. 1784 v.
Stotts*, 70
Forbush V. Wallace, 146
Ford, Gerald, judicial appointees, 173
Fraser, Nancy, 5
Freedom of Choice Act, 186
Friedan, Betty, *The Feminine Mystique*, 6,
172

Frontiero v. Richardson, 121

Gag rule, 48
Garland, Lillian, 163
Gelb, Joyce, 9, 196
Gender consciousness, 2
Gender discrimination. *See also* Sexual
   harassment
   criteria for proof, 71-72
Gender neutrality, 196-197
Gender-based insurance ratings
   proposed federal legislation on, 109-
      110
   public policy implications, 110-118
Gender-based legislation
   Supreme Court decisions, 130
Gender-neutral insurance, 45-46
   costs of, 113-116
   effects, 117-118
General Electric v. Gilbert, 161, 167-168
Ginsburg, Ruth Bader, 174
Glass ceiling, 169
Green v. Commissioner, 146
Griggs v. Duke Power Company, 72
Griswold v. Connecticut, 47, 54
Grove City College v. Bell, 31-32, 36, 69-
   70, 82

Hale, Matthew, 132
Harris v. Forklift Systems, Inc., 71
Harris v. McRae, 48, 54
*Hartford Accident and Indemnity Co. v.
   Insurance Commissioner,* 109
Hawaii, cohabitation and property law,
   143, 147
Health care. *See also* Women's health issues
   attitudes toward, 39-40
   financing, 43-46
   as women's issue, 40-42
Health care policy, 38-55, 200
   chronology, 54
   culture and, 39-43
   on public policy agenda, 42-43
   silences, 49-51

Health, Education, and Welfare (HEW),
   Department of. *See* Department of
   Health, Education, and Welfare
Hewitt, Virginia, 143
Hewitt v. Hewitt, 146
Higher education. *See also* Education
   discrimination against women in, 23-
      25
   status of women in, 21*t,* 21-23
Higher Education Act. *See* Higher Edu-
   cation Amendments
Higher Education Amendments, 36, 69
   Title IX, 3-4, 25-32, 36, 41, 54, 172, 191
Hill, Anita, 70
Hill v. Estate of Westbrook, 146
House Select Committee on Small Busi-
   ness, 87
Housing, 91-93
   accessibility of, 91-92
   adequacy of, 91
   affordability of, 91
   availability of, 91
   Section 8, 92-93
Housing policy, 92
Hoyt v. Florida, 121, 174, 191
H.R. 5050, 88
Hyde, Henry, 48
Hyde Amendment, 48, 54

Idaho property law, 127
Illinois
   cohabitation and property law, 143,
      146
   legal surnames, 129-130
Illinois Supreme Court, 146
Income, retirement, 93-98
Individual retirement accounts (IRAs),
   96-97
Ingram, Helen, 5
Insurance, 102-123
   chronology, 121-122
   coverage, 45
   gender-neutral, 45-46, 113-116, 117-
      118
   misconceptions, 103-105
   old-age and survivors, 94

Insurance law, 103
Insurance ratings, 45
    basics, 103-105
    fairness requirements, 110-113
    gender-based, 105-118
    status quo ironies, 116-118
Intent to discriminate test, 71
Intercollegiate athletics, 28-30
Interest groups, women's, 195-196
Internal Revenue Service (IRS), 122, 141
IRAs. *See* Individual retirement accounts

Jails, 178-179
Jerry, Robert H., II, 102-123
Johnson, Lyndon B., 121
    Executive Order 11246, 67, 82
    Executive Order 11375, 82
    judicial appointees, 173
Judges, women, 171-174
Jurors, women, 174-175
Justice, criminal system, 169-192
Justice, Department of. *See* Department
    of Justice

Kamerman, Sheila B., 150-151
Kamper, Julie, 38
"Kate and Allie," 124
Kennedy, John F., 6, 121
Keogh plans, 96
Kimball, Spencer, 103
Kowalski, Sharon, 126
Kozlowski, Irma, 143
Kozlowski, Thaddeus, 143
Kozlowski v. Kozlowski, 143, 146

Labor, Department of. *See* Department
    of Labor
Lanham Act, 158-159, 167
Law. *See also* Legislation; *specific laws*
    criminal, 131-132, 169, 170
    divorce, 134-144
    family, 124-147
    function of, 170-171
    marital, 126-134
    property, 127-128

rape, 180, 181, 192
    tax, 170
Lawyers, women, 171-174
League of Women Voters, 163
"Leave It to Beaver," 4, 153-154, 164
Legal surnames, 129-130, 146
Legislation. *See also specific laws*
    equal pay, 62-63
    gender-based, 130
    on gender-based insurance ratings,
        109-110
Leonard, Jonathan, 77
Lichtman, Judith, 162-163
Life expectancy, 112
Life insurance, 106
*Los Angeles Department of Water and
    Power v. Manhart,* 107-108
Louisiana property law, 127
Lynn, Lawrence, 158

M., Michael, 183, 192
MacKinnon, Catharine, 196
Manhart, Marie, 108
*Manhart v. City of Los Angeles Depart-
    ment of Water and Power,* 108, 116-117,
    121
Marital exception rule for rape, 132
Marital property law, 127-128
Marriage, 124-147
    attitudes toward, 126
    laws and public policies governing,
        126-134
    property division in, 135-138
    rights associated with, 126
    same-sex, 126
    support obligations, 130-131
Married women
    domicile requirements, 128-129, 146
    legal surnames of, 129-130
    rights of, 143
Married Women's Acts, 127
Married Women's Property Acts, 135
Martin, Lynn, 73
Martin Marietta Corporation, 65-66
Marvin, Lee, 142-143
Marvin, Michelle Triola, 142-143

Marvin v. Marvin, 142-143, 146
Maryland
  gender-based insurance ratings, 122
  legal surnames, 130, 146
  rape law, 180, 192
  support obligations, 131
Maryland Supreme Court, *Condore v. Prince George's General Hospital*, 146-147
Massachusetts
  Big Dan's rape case, 182
  domicile requirements, 129, 146
  rape reform law, 182
Maternity leave, 163
McCarrick, Earlean, 124-147, 169-192
McCarty v. McCarty, 147
Media
  television sitcoms, 4-5, 124-125, 153-154, 164
  women in, 195
Medicaid, 42, 43-44, 46, 54
Medicare, 42, 43-44, 46, 54
Michael M. v. Superior Court, 183, 192
Minnesota, pay equity in, 75
Montana
  gender-based insurance ratings regulations, 122
Moral Majority, 47, 159
Mothers, working, 156
Muller v. Oregon, 60, 81, 160, 167

Nannygate, 148, 164
NARAL. *See* National Abortion Rights Action League
Nashville Gas v. Satty, 161, 168
National Abortion Rights Action League, 47
National Association of Manufacturers, 199
National Black Women's Health Project, 43
National Breast Cancer Coalition, 43
National Commission on Consumer Credit, 84, 100
National Council of Jewish Women, 150
National Institutes of Health (NIH), 43

National Latina Health Organization, 43
National Organization for Women (NOW), 7, 42, 45, 48-49, 163
National SEED (Seeking Educational Equity and Diversity) Project on Inclusive Curriculum, 33
National Women's Health Network, 42
National Women's Political Caucus, 3, 47, 163
Native American Women's Health Education Resource Center, 43
Neutrality, gender, 196-197
Nevada property law, 127
New Jersey, support obligations in, 131, 146
New Jersey Supreme Court, 143, 146
New Mexico property law, 127
New York
  legal surnames, 129, 146
  pay equity, 75
NIH. *See* National Institutes of Health
Nixon, Richard, 159
  judicial appointees, 173
Noddings, Nel, 33
No-fault divorce, 135
North Carolina
  gender-based insurance ratings regulations, 121
North Haven v. Bell, 31, 36
NOW. *See* National Organization for Women

O'Connor, Sandra Day, 171
OFCCP. *See* Office of Federal Contract Compliance Programs
Office of Civil Rights (Education), 31
Office of Civil Rights (Justice), 11
Office of Education, Advisory Council on Women's Educational Programs, 26
Office of Federal Contract Compliance Programs (OFCCP), 68, 198
Office of Research on Women's Health, 43
Office of the Comptroller of the Currency, 89
Old-age and survivors insurance, 94

Older Women's League, 134
Our Bodies, Ourselves. See Boston Women's Health Book Collective
"Ozzie and Harriet," 164

P. L. 88-38. *See* Equal Pay Act of 1963
P. L. 88-352. *See* Civil Rights Act of 1964
Palley, Marian Lief, 9, 196
Pay equity, 196
   comparable worth concept, 74-76
   legislation, 62-63
Pennsylvania State Supreme Court, 109, 122
   insurance decisions, 122
Pension Benefit Guarantee Corporation, 96
Pension plans, 96-97
People ex rel. Rago v. Lipsky, 146
Phillips, Ida, 65-66
Phillips v. Martin Marietta, 65-66
Planned Parenthood of Southeastern Pennsylvania v. Casey, 48, 54, 185, 192
Planned Parenthood v. Danforth, 191
Policy-making process, 8-11. *See also* Public policy; *specific policies*
   models, 11-12, 194-197
Poverty, 93-98, 141
Pregnancy Discrimination Act, 3-4, 67, 82, 121, 161-162, 168
Pregnant women, public policy regarding, 161-162
Prisons, 178-179
Project Head Start, 159
Property
   cohabitation and, 142-144
   division of, 135-138
Property law, marital, 127-128
Prosecutors, women, 171-174
Prostitution, 177
Public Health Services Act, 26, 36, 41, 54
Public Law 88-38. *See* Equal Pay Act of 1963
Public Law 88-352. *See* Civil Rights Act of 1964
Public policy, 1. *See also specific policies*
   concerns of women's movement, 7

contemporary women's health issues and, 43-49
   cultural change and, 8-13
   history of, 5-8
   process, 8-12
   silences, 12-13
   women and, 1-17
Public policy agenda, women's health issues on, 42-43

Randolph, A. Philip, 61
Rape, 179-183
   Big Dan's case, 182
   laws, 180, 192
   marital exception rule, 132
   shield laws, 181
   statutory, 182-183
Reagan, Ronald, 31, 124, 173, 185
   equal educational opportunity policy, 26, 30, 31
   equal employment opportunity policy, 11, 69, 70, 76-77, 197-199
Reed v. Reed, 121
Regulation B, 86
Reno, Janet, 169-170, 174
Reproduction, issues concerning, 46-49
Reproductive technology, policy silences, 199-200
Republican party platform, 47
Retirement benefits, 93-98
   earnings sharing plans, 133
   federal, 138
   pension plans, 96-97
   Social Security, 94, 97-98, 132-134
Revised Order No. 4, 68
Rights
   of married women, 143
   of victims, 181
Rights, Declaration of, 5
Roe v. Wade, 3-4, 47-48, 54, 185, 191
Role change, 9
Role equity, 9
Roosevelt, Franklin D., 61
"Roseanne," 4-5
RU-486, 49
Rusk v. Maryland, 192

Rust v. Sullivan, 48, 54

Sanger, Margaret, 47
Schneider, Anne, 5
Schroeder, Patricia, 164
Section 8, 92-93
Seneca Falls Convention, 5, 125
Sentencing, 177-178
Separate property law, 127-128, 137
SEPs. *See* Simplified employee plans
Sexual assault, 181
Sexual harassment, 70-71
Shalala, Donna, 23
Sheppard-Towner Act, 42-43, 54
Shultz v. Wheaton Glass Company, 69
Sick pay, 161
Sillery v. Fagan and Fagan, 146
Simplified employee plans (SEPs), 96
Skocpol, Theda, 46
Smith, Howard, 64
Social Security Act, 42, 134
Social Security benefits, 94, 97-98, 132-134
Stanton v. Stanton, 191
States
  community property law, 127-128, 137
  gender-based insurance ratings regulations, 109
  separate property law, 127-128, 137
Statutory rape, 182-183
Stevenson, Adlai, 124
Stuart v. Board of Supervisors of Elections for Howard County, 146
Suffrage, 6
Supreme Court
  Akron v. Akron Center for Reproductive Health, 48, 54
  appointments, 185
  Arizona Governing Committee v. Norris, 108, 116-117, 121
  Bradwell v. Illinois, 171, 172, 191
  Califano v. Goldfarb, 146
  California Federal Savings and Loan Association et al. v. Guerra, 163-164, 168

Doe v. Bolton, 48, 54
Eisenstadt v. Baird, 47, 54
employment discrimination decisions, 61, 72
federal retirement benefits decisions, 138
Firefighters Local Union No. 1784 v. Stotts, 70
Forbush v. Wallace, 146
Frontiero v. Richardson, 121
gender-based legislation decisions, 130
General Electric v. Gilbert, 161, 167-168
Griggs v. Duke Power Company, 72
Griswold v. Connecticut, 47, 54
Grove City College v. Bell, 31, 36, 69-70, 82
Harris v. Forklift Systems, Inc., 71
Harris v. McRae, 48, 54, 191
Hoyt v. Florida, 121, 174, 191
Los Angeles Department of Water and Power v. Manhart, 107-108
Maher v. Roe, 191
Manhart v. City of Los Angeles Department of Water and Power, 108, 116-117, 121
marriage and criminal law decisions, 132
McCarty v. McCarty, 147
Michael M. v. Superior Court, 192
Muller v. Oregon, 60, 81, 160, 167
Nashville Gas v. Satty, 161, 168
North Haven v. Bell, 31, 36
Phillips v. Martin Marietta, 65
Planned Parenthood of Southeastern Pennsylvania v. Casey, 48, 54, 185, 192
Planned Parenthood v. Danforth, 191
rape decisions, 183
Reed v. Reed, 121
Roe v. Wade, 3-4, 47-48, 54, 185, 191
Rust v. Sullivan, 48, 54
Shultz v. Wheaton Glass Company, 69
Stanton v. Stanton, 191
Taylor v. Louisiana, 174-175, 191

Title VII decisions, 107-109, 116
Trammel v. United States, 146
United States v. Yazell, 146
Ward's Cove Packing Co. v. Antonio, 72
Webster v. Reproductive Health Services, 48, 54, 185, 192
Weinberger v. Wiesenfeld, 146
Surnames, legal, 129-130, 146
Survivors insurance, 94

Tax credits, 168
Tax laws, 170
Taylor v. Louisiana, 174-175, 191
Teachers Insurance and Annuity Association, 96
Technology policy, 199-200
Television sitcoms, 4-5, 124-125, 153-154, 164
Texas
property law, 127
rape decisions, 182
Thomas, Clarence, 70
Thompson, Karen, 126
Title VII, 6-7, 25-26, 61, 64-67, 70, 81, 82, 162, 191
comparable worth concept, 74-76
effects on women's employment, 72-74
1978 amendments, 66-67
Supreme Court decisions, 107-109, 116
Title IX, 3-4, 25, 41, 54, 172, 191
Grove City College challenge, 31-32, 36, 69-70, 82
implementation of, 26-30
Trammel v. United States, 146
Transportation policy, 200

Uniform Crime Reports for the United States, 176
United States v. Yazell, 146

Victims
rights of, 181
women as, 179-184
Violence against Women Act, 182

Vocational Education Act, 26, 36

Ward's Cove Packing Co. v. Antonio, 72
Washington State
pay equity, 75-76
property law, 127
Washington, D.C., rape law, 180
Watson, Rita E., 163
WEAL. *See* Women's Equity Action League
Webster v. Reproductive Health Services, 48, 54, 185, 192
Weinberger v. Wiesenfeld, 146
White House Conference on the Care of Dependent Children, 158, 167
White House Conference on Standards of Child Welfare, 158, 167
Wife battering, 183-184
Woman, Year of the, 3, 194
Women. *See also* Married women; Pregnant women
choices of major area of study, 21-22
as crime victims, 179-184
in criminal justice system, 171-175
as criminals, 175-179
discrimination against. *See* Discrimination
elderly, 94
employment of. *See* Women's employment
health issues. *See* Women's health issues
in higher education, 21-23
legal status, 125-126, 127
legal surnames, 129-130, 146
needs of, 150-151
special treatment of, 163-164
working mothers, 156
Women's Campaign Fund, 3
Women's Educational Equity Act of 1974, 25-26, 36
Women's employment
effects of equal opportunity policy on, 72-74
glass ceiling, 73
patterns, 58-60

Women's Equity Action League
  (WEAL), 28, 42, 45
Women's health issues
  contemporary, 43-49
  on public policy agenda, 42-43
Women's movement
  history of, 5-8
  policy concerns, 7
Wood, Kimba, 148, 164

Work, equal, 69
Working mothers, 156
Works Progress Administration, 158-
  159
Wyman, Jane, 124

Year of the Woman, 3, 194

Zigler, Edward F., 163